Rewedded Bliss

Rewedded Bliss

Love, Alimony, Incest, Ex-Spouses, and Other Domestic Blessings

DAVIDYNE MAYLEAS

BASIC BOOKS, INC., PUBLISHERS

NEW YORK

Library of Congress Cataloging in Publication Data

Mayleas, Davidyne.
  Rewedded bliss.

  1. Divorce—United States. 2. Remarriage—United
States. I. Title.
HQ834.M35   301.42'8   77-74575
ISBN: 0-465-06983-5

To all of us—my husband, Bill,

our daughter, our ex-wife,

and myself without whose

antics this book would never

have been conceived . . .

ACKNOWLEDGMENTS

I OWE SO MUCH to so many. To among others, I owe thanks to all those remarkable remarried couples with children who have shared with me their experiences, their dilemmas, their frights, and their laughter, experiences so similar to mine that I am embarrassed to recognize how "un-unique" I actually am. And in the same breath I thank God for my being so un-unique. It does not lighten the responsibility, but it does make it less lonely. I am glad that my problems have not been simply a function of my own simple mindedness. My own selfishness. My failure of insight and courage. No, my bewilderment was indigenous to my breed. I have friends. My kind of failure is widespread among fine and decent couples, whose good will toward each other and their bio- and/or poly-children I respect, and I see as far outstripping my own capabilities. If they too have similar problems, then perhaps it is not my shortcomings that make my field so hard to cultivate, but perhaps it is hard for everyone. Because we are all like pioneers in a strange country—experiments of nature, the testings of a brand new cultural phenomenon—as such some of us will survive and some will not. The old guidelines for family and love no longer work. That is exactly why I wrote this book—to try to establish new guidelines.

Also, the thinking in this book has drawn regularly upon many in-vivo researchers in psychology and anthropology. It is their firsthand contact with the varieties of human emotion, family structure, and custom that prepared me to recognize the kind of deep change that we are ourselves experiencing in the United States family style in this, the last third of the 20th century. I would particularly like to thank Sigmund Freud, Margaret Mead, and Harry Stack Sullivan for having been alive and well in the first half of the twentieth century so that their original and fruitful insights were available to me for survival, to say nothing of what is owed to them by millions of others.

CONTENTS

PART III

The Joy of Incest

PART IV

All about the New Manners, Modes, and Customs

PART I

The Synergistic
Family

1

The Synergistic Family

> Synergism: The action of separate substances that in combination produce an effect greater than that of any component taken alone.
> *Funk & Wagnall's Standard College Dictionary*

MY GRANDDAUGHTER, at the moment unborn, may live well into her nineties, if not beyond, and be married at least twice, maybe three, perhaps four times. Her divorces will be no-fault divorces. It is also likely that she will be the complacent biologic mother of two or three children by various fathers and the affectionate social mother of another brood via her several husbands and their ex-wives. Her family ties, biological and social, will be more extensive than mine and possibly more amiable. She will probably have decent, even loving relations with all her wide family connections. I also believe that for her generation, her mating and marital habits will not seem unusual or "unstable." If anything, given her blood lines, she will probably represent the "Establishment," being a fully paid-up member in good standing of the typical American family of the twenty-first century—what we must call, because no other term is so accurate, the Synergistic Family.

I am sure that there are many who will find this glimpse of my granddaughter's life tantalizing: the prospect of two, three, or even four different spouses, a kind of joyously legalized hedonism. I am equally sure that there are others who will see her life as proof of the decline of the West. When that many divorces are considered as American as apple pie, decadence has arrived: "In God We Trust," like "Senatus publicas quintas romanus," is no more.

Actually, how you respond to my fantasy about my granddaughter is only a measure of how you accept or reject the Western civilization dream of monogamy.

Up until forty years ago, the national, patriotic, family pattern of the United States as sanctioned by state and church was monogamous. The ideal family unit consisted of one property owning and accumulating man, married to one woman, with or without property, sharing a home and providing for the care and feeding of this woman and their biologic brood. The man and his wife were also presumed to be married for the first time and sexually faithful; and the marriage was for life. Deviations from this ideal were not greeted with shouts of enthusiasm.

But new realities are upon us. Many family arrangements in America are at odds with the myth. First marriages do not last a lifetime. Some do not last a week. Sexual fidelity is under constant challenge. And to add insult to injury, the percentage of first marriages is now running a poor second to the percentage of remarriages. The statistics these days make a cynical comment on the American way of monogamy.

True to our tradition boy meets girl, boy gets girl: lots of boys lots of girls. But with each passing year, our tradition grows less hallowed. Millions of boys and girls out there in monogamy land are simply not waiting for death to let them part. In 1975 the number of divorces granted in the United States passed the one million mark for the first time in our history. In just seven years—since 1968—the rate of divorce had doubled. Pioneers as always, the United States has the highest divorce rate of any country reporting to the United Nations. Divorce lawyers have become as American as apple pie.

That the American marital casualty rate is high is inevitable. Monogamy may be the most difficult marriage form that the human race ever invented. It is also the one that for Americans contains the most inner contradictions.

The Declaration of Independence has promised every man, woman, and child of us the right to "life, liberty and the pursuit of happiness." But if we are to pursue this bluebird of happiness, we must be free to choose and choose again for our greater and greater happiness. To choose the work we do and choose another work when that seems more promising; to choose where we live and then move our home when we wish to; to try different foods, new fads, exotic clothes; to choose the God we pray to and to exchange that God for another, if we choose to. With so much choice, why then should marriage be an exception? We must be free to choose our own mates—and not only once, but as often as necessary.

Given our history, it is completely consistent—in fact, it is hoped for and expected—that each ideal boy should pursue his ideal girl, that they should meet, "fall in love," and then be free—unrestrained by friends, family or society—to choose each other as mates.

After that, of course, they will engage together in the harmonious pursuit of more happiness.

The romantic notion of "love at first sight," before two people even know each other's sleeping and toilet habits, is an American madness. Boy meets girl, on a bus, on a ski slope, at the check-out counter in the supermarket, and the choice of his fate for life can take place. Caution is canceled out by sexual

chemistry. Disregarding all warning signals that suggest clash-
ing tastes in food, music, movies, books, friends, and dissimilar
levels of intelligence, education, ambition, the loving couple
blithely head for the altar. There they will contract a state in
which they are emotionally, as well as legally, presumably
bound for life.

Tactfully, few ask if the man can hold a job or make a living—or if he can't, can she, and is she willing to support both
of them. Discreetly, few suggest that the girl may have only
moderate skill in home-making or lovemaking. Few mention
that she wants four children while he wants one. That she
loves the country, he the city. That she is sexually conservative.
That he has been known to feel a third person in bed is fun.
With very little knowledge of each other and needing only
the price of the license to sanction their adventure, if "no legal
impediment is shown," the ideal couple marry and expect to
"live happily ever after."

It is hardly a surprise then that the American dream of
monogamy can become the American nightmare. Given the
profusion of cultures and lifestyles, the odds are astronomical
against finding one's ideal opposite number simply on the basis
of a sudden, compelling physical attraction.

The romantic method of free marital choice invites heartache, headache, tension, incompatibility, and hives. But remember our Declaration of Independence. Remember we are
free to choose and choose again. In behalf of happiness of
course. And as Margaret Mead has said, "choice carried to its
final limits means in marriage, as it does at every point in
American life, that no choice is irrevocable."

What has actually happened is that given the added push of
new technologies—better methods of contraception and safe
and legal abortion—Americans have simply begun to live out
in marriage the destiny implicit in the "pursuit of happiness."
Our young and not-so-young lovers have never been historically
predisposed to accept their "lot in life." They want to catch the

brass ring. And when the ideal girl who wanted four children while her husband only wanted one says, "I want a divorce," he says, "Kiddo, you can have it."

It is out of this commitment to happiness through freedom of choice that a phenomenon which is also pecularily American has arisen to rescue our family code with its impossible expectations and contradictions. In 1977, as more and more we come to realize that divorce is possible in any marriage—after four months or forty years—a truly fascinating marital statistic has made its quiet but stunning entrance.

It reads this way: "The remarriage rate has been rising steadily since the sixties, while the rate of first marriages has been as steadily declining." If we allow for the difference in the statistical base, there is a higher percentage of remarriages than first marriages. In fact, four out of every five divorces in the United States end in remarriage.

What's more, these remarriages include about 6.6 million children under 18, who were born before their parents entered their current marriages. In addition it is estimated, that since 1972, over 1 million children per year have parents who have been involved in divorce proceedings. These children help compose the approximately 11 million children waiting in the wings for their Momma or Papa—currently divorced, separated, widowed—to remarry. Or if single, to marry. That adds up to about 25 percent of the children of America living with or about to live in a Synergistic Family: the family made up of one or more previously existing families.

What is happening, in other words, is that a new and surprisingly orderly transition is taking place from one major mode of family style to another. The monogamous family, for thousands of years the religious and romantic ideal of Western civilization, is quietly being replaced by the synergistic family. Rather than being the exception, the synergistic family is on its way to becoming the American norm, the premier family style of the twentieth century. It is the American way of squaring the pursuit of happiness with the Judeo-Christian ethic of marriage.

What, you may ask, *is* this so-called synergistic family? Isn't it, after all, just the old monogamous family revised? No, it definitely is not. I realize this may sound irreverent to you, even frightening. Our respect for the rational is only exceeded by our awe of the supernatural, and the sanctity of monogamy is derived from God himself. In the Old Testament, the Book of Genesis, Second Chapter, Verse 22 reads: "Yaweh built the rib he had taken from the man into a woman and brought her to the man. The man exclaimed! 'This is at last bone from my bone, flesh from my flesh. This is to be called woman because this was taken from man.' That is why man leaves his father and mother and joins himself to his wife and they become one body. . . ."

Obviously, remarriage after one or both partners are divorced from a previous spouse meets none of the criteria for monogamy suggested by Genesis.

It is not a first marriage. Vows have been broken. If you think this is a minor update, you deceive yourself. There are millions of people living through endless years of marital misery because that minor update is not an option they have. The Catholic Church has not moved one iota off its dead-center definition of monogamy—one marriage, one man, one woman till death do you part. Not one second sooner.

And with good reason. For if it is not a first marriage, but a divorce and remarriage, then it runs contrary to the teachings of both the Old and New Testament. Consider only Mark 10 Verse 42: "Some pharisees approached him and asked, 'Is it against the law for a man to divorce his wife?' They were testing him. He answered them. 'What did Moses say?' 'Moses allowed us' they said, 'to draw up a writ of dismissal and so to divorce.' Then Jesus said to them. 'It was because you were so unteachable that he wrote this commandment for you. But from the beginning of creation God made them male and female.

This is why a man must leave father and mother and the two become one body. They are no longer two but one body. So then what God hath united man must not divide.'

"Back in the house the disciples questioned him again about this and he said to them. 'The man who divorces his wife and marries another is guilty of adultery against her. And if a woman divorces her husband and marries another, she is guilty of adultery too.' "

With the American proclivity for divorce and remarriage, this whole concept of sexual exclusivity drops by the wayside. Yet our self-delusions die hard. It is no easy matter to give up the beliefs of our forefathers, to admit that this new synergistic union lacks the religious overtones of monogamy: an abiding, lifelong, sexual commitment to one person. One person only. Hundreds of generations of millions of human beings have committed their lives to the Judeo-Christian philosophy of monogamy. How can we do otherwise?

But unless we do otherwise we deceive ourselves dangerously about the nature of our new families. And in deceiving ourselves, we seriously threaten the chances for our family's survival. Let us then examine the synergistic family for what it actually is, not what we pretend it to be.

The synergistic family is a family formed after divorce and remarriage, where one or both partners already have children and one parent is not the biologic parent of the other's children. Yes, there is one wife and one husband at the core of the synergistic family, and an ex-wife and an ex-husband in what seems a secondary relationship. But how secondary is it? Here I believe, is the deliberately overlooked, primary, genetic distinction between the monogamous family and the synergistic family. It is one thing to regard an ex-wife or an ex-husband as being of secondary significance to the new family. It is quite another to unconsciously ignore the fact that, as biologic parents of children, they are *never ex-mothers or ex-fathers.*

Inevitably then, the synergistic family has more than one

mother and father rotating around the family orbit and in-
fluencing family decisions. The only kind of remarriage that is
reminiscent of monogamous marriage is one where there are no
children belonging to either spouse.

The synergistic family is also not the step family. The step
family was always a pseudo-monogamous family, drawing its
personality and reputation from the fact that it existed in a
world where it was an aberration, where monogamy was the
standard. Until only very recently, even in non-Catholic, Judeo-
Christian countries, divorce has been the exception rather than
the rule. Remarriage has followed the same tradition as in
Catholic countries—it was aceptable only after the death of a
spouse. As a result, the step family was a counterfeit or, to be
more exact, a vaguely sinister abnormality carrying with it the
taint of death. For centuries, as implied in the Cinderella myth,
the step family was the family with children, formed almost
always by a widow or widower. Under the circumstances, the
word "step" itself carried with it an ancient, ominous innuendo,
suggesting to both stepparent and -child that at the heart of
their relationship is irreparable loss.

*Again, the key to understanding the nature of the synergistic
family is the recognition this is the family with children created
by remarriage after divorce, not after death.* This fact must be
fully grasped. No attempt to understand the essential adaptive
differences between the synergistic family and the step family
is possible otherwise. The latter form of remarriage, the step
family, grew out of the conventions of our total society that
inisisted that death be the only reason for remarriage. The
synergistic family, quite to the contrary, has evolved out of the
increasing emphasis individuals in the society have put on their
right to be happy in marriage, and to choose to change partners.

Incidentally, this is not to say that there are no widows or
widowers among the synergistic families. There are. But as the
prime cause of remarriage has shifted from death to divorce, it

is the psychology of the majority—the divorced—which colors the attitudes and trends of the new remarrying population.

One of these unnerving trends is a rather too ready acceptance of failure, an almost fatalistic tendency on the part of some remarriers to redivorce. A wealthy divorce lawyer has remarked forebodingly, "The first divorce is always the hardest." Statistics show that among people who have divorced once, the median duration of marriage before the first divorce was 6.5 years; if both had been divorced once before, the duration before (the next) divorce was 3.5 years; and if both had been divorced twice, the duration of (re)marriage before the next divorce was only 1.7 years.

To be fair to all concerned, when the synergistic family fails, it fails for some of the same reasons that disrupt the monogamous family: human error. Mismatings do happen. You do not have to be a psychological misfit to make more than one marital mistake.

Redivorce may also come because of personality changes. In the synergistic family, just as in the monogamous family, there is no guarantee that both partners will grow through the years in the same or reciprocal directions. With neither malice nor incitement, they may grow apart; one or both may feel the desire for a change of partner.

These separating influences depend on the luck and intelligence of the draw. This book is not concerned with them. My purpose here is to focus on the failures that are needless, the failures of the synergistic family to adapt successfully because of what I see as a mistaken identification with the monogamous family. It is the refusal to recognize our differences from, rather than our similarities to, the monogamous family that most often leads to confusion, frustration, and even redivorce.

These mistakes become apparent in the particular way a synergistic family copes with the financial, psychosexual, and social problems it encounters. In these contexts, the hand-me-down guidelines of the monogamous family are worse than useless. They make mischief. They lack the dimension of time.

That's the heart of it. The single, most incisive, and most often overlooked characteristic of the synergistic family that distinguishes it from other family styles is that it is a time blend composed of itself and families that were; the ghosts of Christmases past mingle with the experiences of Christmas present.

You could say the same holds for the step family. As far as it goes, this is true. What makes the synergistic family unique is that though it embodies within its now the customs, psychology, emotional ties, and memories of families that once existed, its uniqueness evolves from the fact that these families *still exist* in a new form. In another neighborhood. In another town. In another country. At the end of the telephone line. Looking perhaps a little worse for wear. Or looking better than ever. But either way, these source families are very much alive and influential.

This is the dilemma: the existence of the past within the present. This time blend factor causes most of the financial, psychosexual, and social confusions that the synergistic family must juggle. To take an obvious example: How often do you find a synergistic family that is not weighted with the carrying charges and the financial obligations of a prior family that still exists today? Almost never.

This book, however, is intended to do more than point to the perils. It is also meant to suggest answers, not final answers, by any means, but at least reasonable approximations that, by providing useful insights—like a mirror in which we see ourselves—will help us come to terms with our changed condition.

To this end, I want to put forth what might be considered a radical theory of adaptation. For the adaptation to be successful, it requires only a deepening understanding of our lives in transition and of the new challenges we face, created by ourselves and by the accelerated thrust of more and more families like ourselves.

If you yourself are not at this moment the mother or father of a non-biological child, you certainly have friends or neighbors or tennis partners or bridge buddies who are. Furthermore, someday, willy-nilly, like it or not, you may be one, too. Our life is like that these days. It's time we accepted the fact that the traditional American family, like the oversized automobile, is vanishing. And because it is vanishing, we are deeply in need of new techniques and new ways of dealing with each other as members of an extended synergistic family in which we may be the first, second, third, even fourth husband or wife.

We must also recognize that it is necessary, practical, even urgent that we begin to find ways of creating for the young children of our synergistic family—socially defined as immature until they are eighteen—the sense of safety and continuity that will help them to grow into fully functioning, self-accepting members of their own sex and of society.

That then is what this book is about, the new, large as life American way of family—the synergistic family: how to live with it, love it, get the most out of it, be proud of it, and prosper from the pleasure and the adventure of being on the frontier of social change, as husband and wife, as mother and father pioneering our version of what is, in truth, a very ancient and practical family style.

2

What Is a Family?

THERE IS a soundless season in human history that we suspect lasted for millions of years. No laughter, no singing, no arguments—no voices are heard at all. We have no written records. It is the early spring of the human race, the time of the Garden of Eden. This garden, we are coming to realize, was no brilliant biblical fiction, an acre of vacationland created by the Almighty for the privileged pleasure of Adam and Eve, that super-starred couple.

No, this garden was in fact a real place. In those narrow stretches in and around tropical forests there existed a nonexclusive, busy playland inhabited by a variety of animal species, including the tens of thousands of those oddball primates later to be known as Homo sapiens.

From what we can tell as the new data from anthropology is sifted, life for our earliest, apish ancestor was not a constant struggle for survival. Quite the contrary. It was a summer festival, one in which our wandering, fruit-picking grandfather lived in peace and plenty, primarily on plant foods but occasionally trapping small game. At almost no expense of time and effort he obtained a satisfactory diet, and with leisure to spare.

It gives one pause. And perhaps a brief twinge of envy to

realize that our ancient relative had the time of his life. Perhaps a shorter life, though one cannot even be sure of that, but certainly a merry one. He had the freedom and the wherewithall to do exactly as he pleased—he was undoubtedly the world's first hippie. Free of want, free of care, he had no responsibility to job, to wife, to a family. Though he copulated, he never married; though he fathered children, he never raised them. As far as we know, his only responsibility was to enjoy himself. No wonder we have a race memory of a place called Eden.

Nor was this a one-sided kind of sexual freedom. The ladies of that forest ensemble of long ago also had the time and the wherewithal to be as footloose, as fancy free as the male of the species. Though a female dallied with many swains, she had no husband. Though she bore children, she had no need to care for them. In that Eden of plenty, nature was an excellent mother's helper. A hungry child did not have to sob for "Mama." It reached across a branch and picked a mango.

The idea of family, with all its obligations of kuche and kinder, with all its responsibilities of private property, had no reason to exist. When there is enough food for everyone, what difference does it make which peach you eat? In a climate that required no body covering, no shelter, it was unnecessary to think about owning fur skins or a cave with central heating. And what was the difference which female belonged to which male, or vice versa, when there were no shortages of either males or females, no taboos against choice, and no reason to claim one another *exclusively*?

Until Eden ended. What exactly happened we don't know. We do know that the environment began to work against that forest aristocracy. Climate shifts probably reduced their forest feeding grounds. The Ice Age, plodding but purposeful, was making its appearance on the face of the earth, bringing with it a worldwide frostbite and the freezing of plants and animals. Or, as another theory recently suggests, a dry season over wide continental areas could also have caused the disappearance of edible plants.

Whatever it was, challenging climate conditions and perhaps population pressures among the tree natives, some factor or combination of factors that could not be steadfastly ignored, forced our earliest, apish ancestor—because who would leave Paradise without being forced—to switch uncertainly to hunting as a means of getting snacks and dinner.

Environmental conditions persuaded him to reprogram his appetite for subtle and varied tropical fruits and vegetables to such open savannah diets as grasses, roots, and grains. And in time, to begin in earnest the trapping of small game. What we see is a vegetarian in the process of corruption, being transformed, not by choice but by the old game of sink or swim, into man the hunter. It was the only route to survival when an Eden of plenty changed into an economy of scarcity.

Of course, the hunting era, like all other profound changes in human evolution, was not an overnight success. It arrived slowly at the lumbering pace of millenniums. And through the entire Stone Age the forces of natural selection were working on the hunters. Those who did not need ear muffs, snow shoes, and parkas to physically withstand the climate conditions, they survived. Those who needed insulated underwear, they didn't. Those hunting bands that included executive types with the brains, the know-how to think through beforehand the job of the hunt, to improve whatever crude languages or tools they had, those hunting bands also survived. The others didn't do so well.

This new activity of group hunting also created another first for human history in its social impact on the once self-centered fruit picker. From the beginning hunting involved a need for clubbiness, neighborliness, listening, and being listened to—in short, cooperation. Cooperation increased efficiency. One man alone was not large enough or fast enough, and in the beginning not able enough as a killer, to deal with any but small-fry game

—fawns, a lizard, a hare. Three or four hunters cooperating together was another story. They could track down the big-game meal of the day—a zebra or an antelope. That amounted to a banquet.

It was in this hunting stage that another momentous shift took place in pre-history society—the sexual division of labor. Female hominoids were not as strong or as fast as the males. They were less capable as hunters. When they were pregnant they were even less efficient; as nursing mothers with infants they were a total loss. Especially since human infants required a longer period of mothering than the offspring of other primates, one could hardly expect a wailing baby to be a bouncing joy while the hunter waited in the long grasses for the unsuspecting prey.

Once the hunters realized this discouraging truth, it took no genius to decide it was more practical to leave Mama and the kiddies home. If, however, male-male ties were growing stronger as a result of the hunting experience, it now became necessary for male-female ties to become more intense. For in the hunting years, Mama was totally dependent on the male for food, for defense, and for helping with the care and raising of Junior. Abandoned by the male, mother and child would never survive. And undoubtedly many did not. Abandoned by the male, the species would ultimately have slipped through the cracks of nature. If the human race were to survive, some male had to be induced to take care of some female or females and bring home his share of the hunt.

It was down the avenue of biologic change that nature found a way of binding the wayward male to the nesting female. The female of the human species is the only female in which the mechanism for sexual heat has disappeared. The human female can be sexually receptive throughout the month. And males being what males always have been, this geometrically increased sexual receptivity of the female also multiplied the lady's chances of binding a male to herself and her offspring.

Plus acquainting him with her economic value: as a source of sexual pleasure, a rudimentary housekeeper, and the giver of offspring who would later hunt cooperatively.

Looking back, we have to deeply admire the effectiveness of nature's trap. It worked like a charm. In no time—in evolutionary terms a few million years is not time—the hunting man became the family man. That he brought home to his family the spoils of the hunt is apparent from recent discoveries of very ancient hominoid base camps. Millions of years ago a restructuring of social patterns had begun.

The evolution of the human species that began perhaps 5 million years ago with that freelancing, frivolous fruit picker was completed with the responsible, home-loving Stone Age hunting man. In fact, we today are so like our Stone Age ancestors that the best skeletal relics scientists have of primitive man could be considered modern man. And it is since the Stone Age man that some version of the human family has existed, in which males take on a fathering role and assist females in the rearing of the young. The disappearance of Eden, the economics of scarcity, made the family a crucial social invention. It arrived not a moment too soon for the survival of the species.

Of course, human beings have had at their disposal all the forms of family we could desire. For the family pattern was not biologically given by the genes, as it is, say with eusocial bees. Such a bee does not have to be taught family life in the hive, how to care for the young, or assist parents. A honeybee can be depended on to divide labor and behave cooperatively for two very good reasons: first because its complex familial system is based on the actual biological structure of its body, and second because even if one colony member could learn something new, it cannot communicate it to another member. As yet. "Social" bees, ants, wasps and even more highly developed bird flocks and wolf packs are all biologically chained together by the same repetitive family patterns. It is the province of science fiction to keep us informed on what might possibly happen if those chains come undone.

But man is not chained. Man's familial behavior is always inventive. Though we are only recently and only imperfectly evolved out of our primate stage, though we are animals still, we are animals who have been blessed and burdened with options. Highly intelligent and incredibly adaptable, what we have—by some fluke of nature—is not the authority of instinct to govern us but the option to choose the family styles we feel are most conducive to survival.

And it is just because survival comes first that the family is not necessarily monogamous as in Western civilization, polygynous as with Arab and Negro groups in Africa, polyandrous as in the Marquesas Islands of Polynesia. The numerous forms and customs of the human family are merely the differing solutions, some efficient, some improvident, of the common economic problem of breeding and raising the young so that the family may perpetuate itself.

Even a casual scanning of anthropological studies of human families will astonish us with how variable these institutions can be. In some societies parents collect a dowry for girls to make them desirable wives. In other clans they worry over how to find wives for their boys. In one tribe a man could have many wives. In another a woman might be married off to her son. In a third she would be with her dead husband; in a fourth she was the property owner and her husband worked for the clan. In some cultures the virginity of the bride was crucial. In others it was irrelevant. Sometimes divorce was a religious threat and impossible. Sometimes it was available just for asking. Women's reproductive powers have struck some people as being a source of magical or religious power. In other cultures women make every effort to avoid the child-bearing function. In still other communities males imitate the birth pangs of women in order to obtain supernatural power. From the smallest detail of child-rearing to the largest matter pertaining to property rights, family styles and thinking are often totally contradictory.

And though we know all this, and have known it for ages, we still have difficulty in accepting the variety around us, the differences that exist today and those that are clearly evident in history and in anthropological studies.

It is also with this diversity of family patterns in mind that I want in this book to look at the current and coming American life styles and how we can adapt or fail to adapt to the change. As I have briefly indicated, using a variety of standard anthropological material as source reference at one time or another in our human history, we have managed to organize ourselves into almost every conceivable kind of family arrangement. There have been endless variations.

But, if as is generally believed, the clan is the oldest social institution in the world, then families formed by plural marriages may be the second oldest. People have been remarrying since Adam and Eve began to begat. In Dilmun of 2600 B.C., that fated city where Ziusidra—Noah to you and me—and his wife settled down after the Flood to raise vegetables and mankind, the cuneiform tablets make a discreet admission. The Ark may probably have been the only place on earth—once there was dry earth—where family planning had been unequivocally two by two. Once folks disembarked, marriage, remarriage, concubinage, polygamy, etc., came back into fashion. And synergistic children were once more as common as fleas on the fabled Golden Ass.

King Solomon, that legendary biblical sexual athlete, is reputed to have had 700 wives. That's 700 mothers or 700 polyparents, depending on who was spanking whose child. Kahan, the ancient women's lib type, had 400 husbands. Being a queen, there were no shortages of wet nurses to help her. August the Strong of Saxony had 365 wives. A truly libidinous number but still not in the same league as Solomon. But impressive as these legends are, nothing quite compares with Oriental stamina. In

China in the 7th century A.D., the glorious Emperor Li Yuan, founder of the T'ang Dynasty, had 3,000 concubines at the time of the final census.

What then can one say? How can one fly in the face of tradition? Who has the right to begrudge Mrs. Beverly Nina Avery of Los Angeles her paltry measure of sixteen husbands? Or Artie Shaw his mere nine wives? Or George Balanchine his five? While Bertrand Russell, epistemologist and defender of free love, was forced to make do with just four. Clearly, modern efforts at marital bliss pale beside the long-ago, big-time marriers.

Even in recently ancient Western cultures—Greek, Roman, Hebrew—where monogamy had become more "the thing" than it was with Solomon or Kahan or August or Li Yuan or Barbara Hutton (seven), Brigham Young (twenty-seven), De Wolf Hopper (six), William O. Douglas (four), Calamity Jane (twelve), Claudius Tiberius (four)—even then every man worth his salt had a wife, a herd of goats, and certainly at least two choice concubines. Ipso facto, synergistic families.

Of course, I myself, probably like you, was raised to believe in the monogamous family—one man, one woman, one marriage, complete with children, in sickness and in health, in joy and in sorrow, from this day forward till death do us part. That was a family. My mother and father had a family; I expected the same. When I was growing up, Betty Friedan was still married to her one man. The oral contraceptive was a gleam in the eye of some obscure chemist. A nice girl did not inform her psychiatrist that her husband and/or lover did not "satisfy" her.

When I went to college, because people interested me more than math or art history or government, one of my majors was anthropology. In anthropology I learned that there were human beings who had family arrangements that were startling. So startling that it never occurred to me that these human beings were much like myself. To me, they were primitives. Unevolved. Uneducated. Because they were primitive, they didn't know any better and I felt it wrong to judge them. When they became civilized as we were, they "would see the error of their ways" and they would pull themselves together, straighten out, and adopt our family style: one man, one woman, one marriage, etc.

Take the Todas of southern India. Here the major plot was to keep the property in the family. The son's family. But suppose you had four sons? Well, their neat trick for avoiding nasty disputes with lots of in-laws, cousins, and nephews over who inherited which pots, which beads, the hut, and so on, was quite simple. All the boys in the family married the same girl. That way there were no unnecessary in-laws, nephews, nieces. The idea gave me a few public blushes and a couple of private orgiastic dreams. But to my rational mind it was a perfect example of "the savage mentality." It wouldn't "do" in Chicago or St. Louis, where people ate with knives and forks and even second cousins had a hard time marrying.

Different from the Todas, but still primitive and peculiar to me, were the Trobianders. After all, I'd grown up in a world where fathers paid the rent, the food bills, dental bills, and for the movies. Not so Bagido'u, a typical Trobiand father, an energetic, good-looking chap with a wife, Kadamwasila, and two sons as evidence of connubial bliss. But did Bagido'u— this father, this pillar of society—provide for his little brood the way my father provided for his? He did not. When it came down to the hard business of living, of breadwinning, Bagido'u's earnings belonged to his sister, Bodulela, and her children by some other village Romeo. His entire personal prestige depended not on whether he took care of his own wife and his sons but on how well he provided for his sister and her children. Fortunately, Bagido'u's wife had her own brother, Mitakatu, to supply her with yams for breakfast, lunch, and dinner, or she and her children would have been charity cases. I must admit that, being myself a daughter with no handy brothers, I did not think much of the Trobiander family arrangements.

But the Samoans were the most confusing because they seemed the most "civilized" and were therefore the most contradictory. The Samoans practiced monogamy as I knew it—one man for one woman in one marriage with a family—but after that one-for-one similarity, the resemblance to what I knew ended. The girls were virgins at marriage, or they were not. It didn't matter unless they were royalty. The married couples were faithful, or they weren't. It didn't matter unless they were royalty. If divorce did occur, it was a simple, informal matter. People said the relationship had "passed away." As Margaret Mead has written:

> Romantic love as it occurs in our civilization, inextricably bound up with ideas of monogamy, exclusiveness, jealously and undeviating fidelity does not occur in Samoa. . . . Marriage is regarded as a social and economic arrangement, in which relative wealth, rank, and skill of husband and wife, all must be taken into consideration. There are many marriages in which both individuals are faithful. But this must be attributed to ease of sexual adjustment . . . and to the ascendancy of other interests . . . social organization for the men, children for the women . . . rather than a passionate fixation upon the partner in marriage . . . (so) Adultery does not necessarily mean a broken marriage . . . the amount of fuss which is made is dependent upon the relative rank of the offender and the offended, or the personal jealousy which is only occasionally aroused. . . . Many adulteries occur between a young marriage-shy bachelor and a married woman . . . none of which threatens the continuity of established relationships . . .

Ambivalent Puritan that I was, I grudgingly admired their relaxed promiscuity, their lack of guilt, while the amateur anthropologist in me had to respect their gracious, orderly society, with its absence of interpersonal agonies. For instance, imagine Lotu, a pretty teen-age girl who is passionately devoted to Alo, a bachelor. She meets him regularly under the palms, ignoring the opportunity for other lovers. You might think them a star-fated pair. They're not. When the time comes for Lotu to marry Tata, her family's choice, the romantic rendezvous ends. No tears, no twinges, not a backward glance for Alo, as Lotu romps off into the sunset with her husband. Of course, after Lotu bears Tata three children, and gets her full rating in the motherhood club, back she goes to join again in the moonlight fun and games under the palm trees, meeting perhaps Alo, or Tui, or Fitu—by chance she might even come across Tata, her husband. For Tata will hardly be sitting home suffering pangs of jealousy; if necessary, Tata can happily find his own female amusement in the same way that Lotu finds hers. The important fact between them was not their sexual fidelity, but that Tata was able at politicing and Lotu good enough in the fields. So their sexual escapades did not interrupt the pleasant flow of their married life. They were a family.

Even now I remember my confusion with the Samoans. How come they were so serene and behaved so immorally? It was hard for me to imagine myself not being jealous of my husband's lover. But then it was impossible for me to imagine being one of four wives—the Moslems I knew were permitted four—or having three husbands as a Toda woman might—sexy though it seemed, I didn't think I had the strength.

Polygyny, as practiced by the Arab and Black groups in Africa—one wealthy chief could have 3,333 wives—was simply lack of evolution and education, I thought. Polyandry, as with the Todas and Polynesians, was the same thing reversed. As for the Shi-ah Moslems, who wandered the desert without women and contracted marriage for as short a time as a day— yes, one day—at friendly camps, could that be marriage? They thought so. But I didn't. The Shi-ah Moslems had their idea of marriage and I had mine. In my idea a human family was based on a marriage that was monogamous for life and unswervingly faithful, as the American ideal and my mother insisted. Fathers came home every night to one home, one wife, one family. Even traveling fathers came home on weekends. Anything else was primitive and inferior.

What I failed to understand then was that men and women will improvise and institutionalize any form of marriage and family that will satisfy their needs for intimacy, sex, and the survival of the species. The Shi-ah Moslems would never have practiced our version of monogamy, not because they were primitive but because monogamy would never work for men who are absent from their permanent homes for months, wandering the desert on long seasonal travels without women.

The Shi-ah, the Todas, the Bantus, the Samoans, and dozens of other tribes were not wrong, and we are not wrong. It was simply that the national, patriotic, stars and stripes American family system of monogamy was not and is not the quaintessence of civilization. It was not and is not the natural and necessary, final, civilized solution to the need for all people to live together and experience intimacy. And today, as the new returns have come in from our professional culture watchers—marriage counselors, family guidance workers, psychologists, sociologists, anthropologists, the law makers, the news media, and of course the Census Bureau—obviously the traditional, typical American family—one man, one woman, one marriage—is itself no longer that typical of American life.

The View from the Altar Today

Ever since that cool, nervous summer morning when I first wore virginal white, to match if not my virginity then at least my respect for the Establishment, and my groom-to-be wore one nervous blue sock and one nervous black one, the American marital idea has undergone a severe jolt to its charisma. Just a surface glance at the kaleidoscopic family patterns around us show how far we've come from the American dream of monogamy.

This morning as every morning my daughter Sandy took her oral contraceptive pill. While still at college, Sandy lives in an LTA ("living-together-arrangement" as its currently called) with a young man, Jerry, whom she is fond of but hardly panting to marry. Nor is Sandy a "fallen angel." She is just another scrubbed-face statistic in an impressive trend among women living in the same kind of matter–of–fact style. Hers is the new no-nonsense attitude toward sex and marriage that has replaced the "good girl" creed that you must "save yourself for your husband." Legal that is. Novels like *The Scarlet Letter,* soap operas like *Stella Dallas,* to say nothing of milestone events like that royal dispute over whether or not Elizabeth Tudor was Henry's "legitimate" daughter, are all parts of our sexual past when the state of a woman's virtue was considered sacred and a subject for grand opera. When the loss of her virginity on the non-marital bed was a "fate worse than death," her intelligence, her character, her beauty, often even her rank and wealth could not compensate her for that loss in the eyes of society. But we've come a pace from those "fate worse than death" days. And calendars don't turn back. Today there is a matter-of-fact sexuality among the singles, for a night, a week, a month. Or, as in Sandy's case, there is LTAness. Even more, there is trial motherhood, sometimes accidentally, sometimes not. The rate of births out of wedlock has tripled between 1940 and 1968, while the rate for legitimate births declined during the same period. Nor do all these unhusbanded mothers tearfully give up their babies for adoption. Many do not. They do the unheard of—they decide to raise the children themselves. Where women once married to have children, now some are choosing to have children and think later about marriage. This can't be called monogamy.

And consider the Knowleses and the Carsons—if you were raised, like me, to assume that a heterosexual marriage included only one husband and one wife—who are another, to be sure somewhat uncommon symptom of ongoing change. With four children between them, these two couples have for five years shared a charming, spacious country home which neither family alone could afford. They also share food and car expenses, child care and love. Four people forming one conjugal unit: "We Joan and Betty take thee Robert and Allan . . ." is an example of the new married families of couples and communes.

Again, in this new, evolving, family tradition there is emerging another, even stranger and more special, marital tableau. "Do you John take Peter . . . ?" or, "Do you Ann take Dorothy . . . ?" Where once the American family was defined as one man and one woman, now besides being more than one man and one woman, it is also two men or two women. Homosexual marriages with religious ceremonies are in the newspapers more and more. Plus the fact that there is constant homosexual agitation for recognition, "to permit any form of sexual relationship between consenting adults."

So it is that our history, combining with the current social and technological innovations, has given us a new and diversified landscape of family life. The combination of contraception that makes birth control more reliable and safe and legal abortion, now allows us endless opportunities for sexual freedom. Swinging singles are one version, swinging marrieds playing musical beds are another. And yet, when men and women come together today with any idea of permanence, they live predominantly as couples putting some restrictions on their sexuality. They do not live as three men and two women. Or five women and six men. Or any other variation of the myriad forms now available to them. The bulk of the population live as one man and one woman—a couple. And when they divorce, they remarry as couples—one man and one woman. Even contraception, legal abortion, and the Women's Lib movement has not slowed down the rate of one man and one woman remarrying.

We cannot, nor would we, turn back time to the years when divorce was much more difficult. For the very reasons that made divorce necessary would still remain with us. But so will the need to remarry in pairs. For we Americans are still deeply dependent on the idea of monogamy. Even on that peculiar present-day monogamy that borders on polygamy.

If we concentrate on the mainstream of American life, and allow for but do not overexaggerate the importance of the exotica of the little colonies of communes or the newly arrived strangenesses of homosexual marriage, then major themes begin to emerge. It becomes apparent in Western civilization that though the monogamous and step families were the standards of the past, statistically the synergistic family is becoming the family of the present and the future.

Inevitably, then, as each year passes and we synergistic parents and children grow more numerous, the need for more tribal know-how increases geometrically. How shall we act with each other, think about each other, love each other? What do we do when ———, if ———, in case ———? The questions are endless.

There is a precedent. Glance over your shoulder and you will see that some of our questions have been around for generations in the step family. With the critical difference being that though the questions are the same, the answers the step family gives often cannot apply to our situation. In the synergistic family all questions raised and answers given must take into account that new dimension, that multiplier of complexity: the fact that all parents are alive, and ready to be counted.

Still we can learn from history. Freud has shown how much we can discover about our present from recognizing our past. It is in this connection that the step family can give us insight; it is for this reason that Cinderella, world-famous stepdaughter, is a fascinating teen-ager. What can she tell us about our own children that might be unexpectedly useful? What is it about her story that strikes so deeply into our "collective unconscious"? Is it perhaps that her story tells us something kinky and worrisome about ourselves? But what?

Let us then examine her with more care and perspicacity than we did when we first met her in childhood. Who knows—we may find some ancient wisdom, some vital magic to help us unravel our own synergistic family dilemmas. For instance, it is a telling comment on long-time attitudes toward non-biological parents that Cinderella, world-famous stepchild, should have an equally famous stepmother who always remains anonymous. She is simply known as "stepmother," and the words have a ring of distaste—of fear.

3

The Cinderella Sisterhood

CINDERELLA is the title of the best-known folktale in history. For almost a thousand years the world has been populated by legends of one kind or another concerning that widely traveled young lady. Though her precise birthplace and birthday are unknown, it is generally believed that the first Cinderella had slant eyes and black hair and was fathered by T'van Ch'eng-sheh, a storyteller of the previously mentioned and unabashedly licentious T'ang Dynasty of China. Since then we have had Cinderellas in saris in the folklore of India; Cinderellas in beads in the Zuni culture, farm girls who were befriended by turkeys.

In Europe alone there are more than 500 variations on the Cinderella theme. In German she is called Aschenputtel and Aschembrodl. In French she has been known as Cendrillon. In Italian she is Cenerentola. And in all of these stories, in Kaffish, Finnish, Celtic, Portuguese, Cinderella is a poor, unwashed, unloved, unwed little ash girl who is missing out completely on the moonlight and roses of life. Until one enchanted evening, wonder of wonders, with the magical aid of her dead mother, or her dead mother transformed into a helpful domestic animal —a cow, a goat, a turkey, etc.—Cinderella is able to wash and perfume and at last dress up in baubles and beads and golden slippers. And romp off to the great dance or festival or church bazaar or what have you. There at the festivities, lo and behold who should she meet but Prince Charming. That fated young man, true to all girlhood dreams, falls madly in love with our ash girl heroine. But Cinderella's mother is no giddy Cinderella. She knows that love is fine and dandy but marriage is what makes a princess. She understands that Cinderella must not make things too easy, even for a Prince Charming. With a fine sense of tactics she insists that her daughter return home speedily and wait quietly in the kitchen for the Prince to send out a searching party. But to guarantee that the right Cinderella is found, she advises the girl to leave a clue—either her right or left slipper, whichever is most comfortable. Since Cinderella knows mothers know best, off she goes, plunking her slipper down in full view on the top castle step. In due course, thanks to the logic of fairytales, the Prince does find her and she passes the slipper test or ring test or whatever test. Then the Prince knows that this is his girl, and they marry and live happily ever after.

All this is the pre-French Cinderella.

It took the French—geniuses at love, fashion, wine, revolution, élan vital, and also bikinis—to give America and Europe the Cinderella story we know best. It was Charles Perrault, the seventeenth-century French poet, who in his *Tales of Mother Goose* decided to refurbish Cinderella more elegantly. He it was who endowed her with a beautiful fairy godmother instead of simple barnyard helpers. It is in Perrault's version that we find a Cinderella so incredibly good that she does her best to help her stepsisters and stepmother look beautiful for the ball. Though she knows full well she will have to stay home and mop the kitchen floor. Of course, the minute the crowd leaves, Cinderella gives up her heroic pose and weeps buckets. Then presto! Her fairy godmother appears. With a wave of the wand she gives Cinderella magnificent clothes, her pumpkin coach, her mouse horses, and so on. The use of the witching hour at midnight is another Perrault idea. As is the glass slipper. In the original Chinese the slipper was golden. However, as in most Cinderella legends, hers is the only foot that will fit the slipper —glass or gold. When the Prince finds her, and the slipper fits, the story has its standard happy ending. It is interesting to note that it was pre-modern Chinese society that bound the feet of aristocratic female babies to keep them from growing large and unseemly. So the Cinderella legend clearly bears the stamp of its Chinese ancestry, in those countries where only Cinderella's foot is small and delicate enough to pass the slipper test.

In the Perrault tale Cinderella generously forgives her step-sisters and stepmother for all the mopping and scrubbing and sweeping she had to do. There are numerous other endings in which the outcome is not half so pleasant for her relatives. But Perrault was a French gentleman.

Though there are Cinderella legends everywhere in the world, it is fascinating that these stories are most prevalent and most frightening in the folktales of Europe and the British Isles. Perhaps a look at the high cost of property and the low cost of life in the Middle Ages of Europe will give us some insight into the Cinderella Syndrome. Towns were small and so were houses. Rooms were cold in winter, hot in summer. Beds were crowded with too many bodies; tables were crowded with too many mouths. Most of the people never had enough to eat. Many of the people often starved. In the country, windows looked out on a few cultivated fields. Here and there a new castle was being built which could provide some jobs for village locals. But no factories smoked on these hillsides, no noon whistles ever blew. For most people work was scarce, money was scarcer, and property owning was the blessing of the lucky few. In fact, as late as the eighteenth century, one well-fed moralist could write, "In order for society to be happy, it becomes necessary that great numbers of people be wretched as well as poor."

And great numbers *were* wretched and poor. And out of their wretchedness and their poverty, monogamy for the masses rose like a phoenix from the ashes of concubinage, polygamy, and other more permissive forms of marriage. As more than one sociologist has wryly noted, the monogamous family style seems to be considered god-given and sacred in societies where there is a scarcity of food and property.

So from the fifth century A.D. onward in Europe—in France, Italy, Germany, England—marriage was not a union of spirits —two hearts being as one—but a union of properties. Shakespeare put it succinctly in *Henry V,* when the king proposed to Kathrine, princess of France. "Is it possible I should love my enemy?" asks the somewhat romantic Kathrine. And Henry, with sound English common sense, replies, "No, it is not possible you should love the enemy of France, for I love France so well that I will not part with a village of it. I will have it all mine. And Kate, when France is mine and I am yours, then yours is France and you are mine." The acquisition, protection, and transmission of properties to bloodline heirs was the concern of both the high and low born. Under these circumstances, even divorce was almost impossible. In England it took an act of Parliament; in France a dispensation from the Pope; in Italy poison was best.

But what with plagues, famine, disease, sacking, looting, and everyday warfare, though couples could seldom divorce, there was no shortage of widows and widowers. And remarriage was the standard cure. When Cinderella's mother died of some strange fish poisoning, Cinderella's father, of course, had to marry again. Someone was needed to see that the sheep and geese were fed, the cloth woven, the linens laundered, and the beds made. Fortunately, he married a moderately well-off widow whose husband had died in the Hundred Years' War. Unfortunately, the widow had two daughters of her own. However, with the aid of his new wife's means, Cinderella's father could buy more land and build a bigger house. For buying land, building houses, and stuffing the houses with rugs and tables and plates full of food were the just rewards of a well-spent life. Property was the proper aim of mankind. Inheritance was next.

To her stepmother, Cinderella was the specter of bloodline inheritance, since title to property usually passed from father to bloodline child. Even putting inheritance aside, as long as there was a Cinderella, any dowry for Cinderella's stepsisters would have to be divided three ways. Clearly, a dowry divided two ways would be larger and attract more affluent husbands than a dowry divided three ways with a Cinderella.

As if inheritance worries and dowry dilemmas were not enough to banish Cinderella to the broom closet, one can rely on the forces of psychology to explain why she is urged to wash and scrub and mop and nothing else.

By this time, thanks to Sigmund Freud, it must be generally agreed that the ordinary relations between ordinary mothers and fathers with their own biological sons and daughters are scarcely simple as ABC. Like it or not, Mother's Day and Father's Day aside, these connections are fraught with contrary emotions. Of course there is love between parents and children and tender emotions and concern about Band-Aids® on bruised knees and braces for crooked teeth and home-made Valentines for Mom. But love is by no means all there is. Freud has taught us that there are less angelic emotions running riot in the family—emotions of jealousy, hate, competitiveness, resentment, hostility. The list is unpleasantly long. Consequently, phrases like "ambivalence" or "father fixation" or "Oedipus complex" have become as much a part of our national heritage as Yellowstone National Park. Those members of the American population who somehow missed direct exposure to psychiatry have still gotten their rightful share via books and plays and movies and television. Also comic books. We all know now about boys who have mother complexes and girls who would rather marry their fathers. If all this is true of ordinary, upright, biological, Christmas-caroling families, you can imagine how doubly true it is of the step family.

As one psychiatrist put it, "Those feelings or tendencies which normally exist between a child and its blood parent are more intense and open between child and step-parent." As a mother by remarriage myself, when I think about that remark, I must admit I feel a weakness in my knees.

For instance, consider our classic Cinderella. She did have a mother. She did not spring full blown from her father's ear like Athena did from Zeus's ear. Of course, Athena was a goddess, and Cinderella is a simple folktale. But the most ancient versions of her story make reference to her mother's spirit in some animal form. That means her mother was once alive. Let us then tentatively conjecture what their relationship was like. Remember, Cinderella was an "only" child, and as psychiatric studies have shown, "only" children may relate to their parents in ways that can be more intense than the parent-child relationships in larger families. There are more secret passages in their kinship where love and hate can interchange costumes, often enough to become confusing. At any rate, between Cinderella and her mother there was love, and there were a number of other feelings. When Cinderella's mother brushed her daughter's hair, gave her mulled wine to sip or bright ribbons to wear to church, then life was a cycle of song. But then there were times when it wasn't. Those were the times when her mother put her foot down and insisted that Cinderella mend her stockings, feed the chickens, clean the goat pen, and make lunch. At which point Cinderella might have thrown a tantrum and sobbed that she wasn't her mother's servant and quite properly her mother spanked her hard with the flat of her palm, saying something to the effect that "Cinderella wasn't a servant but she had better be an obedient daughter." Wisely, Cinderella's father avoided taking sides and kept saying, "My, my." When the ruckus was over, life was a cycle of song again.

The fact is that fusses and squabbles between a "natural" mother and her daughter are expected, and are expected to blow over. The negative feelings of jealousy or hostility are inhibited by the opposite emotions of tenderness, affection, and gratitude. When Cinderella's mother died, Cinderella wept her eyes red, then recovered and to all intents and purposes became the lady of the house and the apple of her father's eye. Sometimes she would even put on her mother's Sunday dresses, which of course were three sizes too large, and parade around the house feeling very important. Things went on swimmingly for a year until her father decided to remarry. This display of callousness shocked Cinderella. For one thing, he had not even asked her opinion. For another, she considered the lady in question most inferior to her real mother. Finally, it was bad enough that he was being unfaithful to the memory of her dear, departed, wonderful mother. But worse, he was being unfaithful to Cinderella. Unconsciously, she felt a sharp sense of rejection by her father. Unconsciously, she was jealous as all get out of her stepmother. These feelings of jealousy and hostility that she had been able to repress when her "natural" mother was alive were much harder to hold in check with this new, strange lady who was decidedly "common."

Cinderella's hostility was bound to invite reciprocal feelings in her stepmother. Plus the fact that this lady, lacking the real bond of parenthood, with its incentive to more tender, tolerant feelings, saw Cinderella as a spoiled brat who was also a threat to her security and that of her daughters. Her own daughters might be equally spoiled and frivolous, but then we all know blood is thicker than water. Cinderella was not blood. Inevitably, her stepmother felt less obligated to repress her own tendencies to scold and spank and punish. She may not even have been a really cruel woman, but Cinderella was a psychological problem to her, and so she managed with the aid of a few sensible rationalizations—another Freudian invention—to be genuinely unkind and neglectful toward the young girl.

If Cinderella's father had been divorced instead of widowed, the family chaos might possibly have been even worse. Cinderella's feelings, both good and bad, toward both her parents would have been intensified by seeing them unhappy, seeing them struggle toward divorce. Unconsciously, she would have taken sides, even though loyalty and fear might have prevented her from admitting it. But finally, when the divorce was done, her father was remarried, and her stepmother moved in bag and baggage, what could Cinderella do but hate her on the spot. The full force of the feelings of grief and rejection that she felt in connection with her real parents, but which she had strenuously hidden inside her, now could come out in a blast of resentment at this despised intruder.

As just this small investigation of the Cinderella myth shows, it is neither easy nor simple to play the ring-around-the-rosy of stepchild-stepparent. Not only do the traditions of property and inheritance play havoc with the best intentions in the world, but the undertow of our own psyches may turn us from Jekylls into Hydes. And if you think the Cinderella Syndrome is harrowing, there is even another, more sinister step-relationship which, if not as celebrated, still accounts for its own goodly share of plays, stories, myths, and mayhem in the human race. Here it is not unrestrained hate but uncurbed love that brings the house down on one's head. Here, the powerful incest taboo, which prohibits biologic mothers and fathers from having sexual relations with their children, becomes in the stepparent-stepchild relationship ominously aroused. Especially is this true when the stepparent is of the opposite sex to that of the child. The love of a stepson for a stepmother, or vice versa, has been observed regularly in history and literature. Elizabeth of Valois, the young and beautiful second wife of Philip II of Spain, was beleaguered by the unwanted attentions of her stepson, Don

Carlos. Hippolytus, son of King Theusus of Greece, came to a sticky end because his stepmother, Phaedra, had an un-motherly yen for him. As for the passionate Salome, unlike Cin-derella, she never lived long enough to meet a Prince Charm-ing because her stepfather, King Herod, was infatuated and overindulgent. Yes, love between stepparent and stepchild can prove even more explosive than hate.

Given history, mythology, literature, poetry, and our own good sense, we know now that the stepparent-stepchild relation-ship should be marked "fragile, handle with care." It is some-thing like a beehive. Certainly there is wonderful honey to be had, but until the bees get to know you, and you get to know the bees, it is wise to proceed gently, move carefully, and wear gloves and a mask as self-protection. For we have to invent new techniques, new customs and etiquette, new muscles for loving and living with our non-biologic parenthood. Once we do learn to live with it in comfort, we may find our family rela-tionships becoming deeper and richer than we ever imagined possible. When that happens, then the mask and gloves will no longer be necessary.

Let us learn, then, from the Cinderella myth. Learn once and for all that the property-money, love-hate axis is the central line on which the world of the step family turns.

And what is true for the step family is even more true for the synergistic family, because it is a time-blend, because the con-flicting property-money, love-hate aims of family are never silenced by the death of a parent. They are with us every day of our family life. Of course there are other problems, too, but none as profound, as multi-faceted, as subtle, or as crucial.

PART II

Money
Isn't Everything...
Happiness Is
2 Percent

4

Rewedding Rings
Are Not for Free

ORIGINALLY, I thought of contacting the Mafia. They know more about this sort of thing than I do. Didn't the Mafia work on contracts or something like that? I imagined our conversation.

"She'll be easy to recognize. She's tall and dark. Striking. But strong as an ox, so be prepared."

"Madam, this is my business."

"Just break her up a little."

"Arms and legs were you thinking?"

"I'd say so. Incapacitate her, I wouldn't mind if she was unconscious for a few months."

"Hmmm, madam, I fear you do not understand the nature of your problem. If we incapacitate her it will not do anything to ease the alimony situation. Or the child support."

"I told you I don't mind about the child support. After all these years I've gotten used to it. Sandy has to be fed and clothed and educated. What kind of monster do you think I am?"

"Excuse me, the notion of a monster is a movie conception."

"You're too sensitive. Anyway. I'm talking about the additional child support. ADDITIONAL. DO YOU HEAR ME? And she must make $30,000 a year at least. That's what I said, $30,000 a year. She could contribute to our support."

"The laws in this country are totally antiquated."

"I should think that one woman with no dependents—since we pay for Sandy lock, stock, and barrel—could live on $30,000 a year. Plus she has an expense account. Plus what we pay her in additional support. Which is ridiculous when you consider how much she makes! But my husband won't fight it!"

"No gentleman would!"

"Whose side are you on anyway?" I could feel my temper rising.

"I never claimed to be a gentleman, madam."

"Anyway, she makes $30,000 a year and now she wants us to continue child support despite the fact that we are paying for Sandy's college and she is also living at college. Do you know we haven't had a real vacation in years?"

"Never been to Vegas?"

"Don't be silly. We can't afford to gamble. And at this rate we're not going to have a vacation for another four years."

"A bad scene. She's not a classy type." He shook his head.

"She's a wretch. She never spent the child support money on Sandy anyway. She gave her $10.00 a week allowance. At fifteen, $10.00 allowance. She spent most of the money on herself. She has more clothes than Loehmann's."

"My wife spends a lot of nights there. Uses my driver to take her. It's a nuisance."

"Sandy's college is costing thousands and thousands of dollars. And she's boarding at school. Do you know what that costs?"

"What can you do? It's these affluent kids. Do you think my boy would go to Columbia? He would not. He has to go to UCLA. Costs me an arm and a leg to pay for his suntan."

"Exactly. Now, how can we continue to pay her child support? We have all those college bills. When my husband objected—he really should have socked her, but that would be assault and battery and anyway it's not his style—when he objected and said he couldn't afford to continue her child support, do you know what she said?" I was so angry I could hardly breathe.

"What did she say?"

"She said, 'You can afford it. Davidyne earns money doesn't she? She's a writer.' How do you like that! Who does she think I am? Alex Comfort? And if I were Alex Comfort, does she expect me to pay her child support? She's not my ex-wife."

"Lady! You're screaming."

"I know I'm screaming."

"What about the neighbors? They'll think it's me."

"Don't worry. These old buildings have thick walls."

"Madam, I feel it is my duty to point out to you most emphatically that if we incapacitate her—and of course we can do that easily—it will not ameliorate the child support situation. Blue Cross and Blue Shield and Major Medical will pay her medical bills. . . ."

"She's totally covered under a government medical plan."

"That's what I mean. If necessary, they'll give her a heart transplant. She'll be as good as new. Better than new. Meanwhile she'll still be receiving alimony and child support. However, might I make a suggestion?"

"I see what you mean." I really did.

"I know it costs a little more, but it's worth it. You'll make it up in two years on all the payments you'll save."

"I know. I've thought about that. But murder is so drastic."

"With your kind of problem anything less is wasting your money."

"I suppose you're right."

"There's no point fooling you, madam. We like our customers to be satisfied. That way we keep them. You are married.

You may need us again. I'm just telling you what I would do if I was in your place. Neat. Civilized. It will look like an accident. Think it over. You got my telephone number."

I knew my fantasy killer was right. But how could I have her murdered? I could. But then there was the problem of getting in touch with the Mafia. They don't advertise. And I didn't know anyone who knew anyone, though I must say that I suspected many people I knew might know someone if it was put to them properly.

But how do you bring up the subject at a cocktail party? Or alongside the club pool as you sip gin and tonic.

"By the way, honey, I hear you play golf with Dirty Louie?"

It's a shame that the Mafia has behaved so poorly that respectable people are embarrassed to admit knowing them. Let alone do business with them. I remember reading a story by Izak Dinesen called "The Roads Around Pisa." An Italian count simply went out and hired a young bravo to do some nasty work for him, and it was all very *comme il faut,* and the count never gave it a second thought.

That was the way things were done among aristocrats. With finesse. *Politesse.* But not today. The Mafia has a bad name. They renege. They turn on their employers. They cannot be trusted.

No, I could not contact the Mafia even if I knew how to contact them. I could not even contact the CIA. They'd say it was a domestic problem, and these days that's out for them. Of course, if I could get her to go to Paris. . . .

My feelings on occasion about my husband's ex-wife are fairly typical of the attitude of a fair sampling of other current wives toward ex-wives. What is revealing about these feelings is that the resentment and the indignation most often triggered by an ex-wife are not because of sexual demands they make on our husbands—no way. It is the money pinch that raises our backs.

Now that I think about it, seldom have I heard of a current wife being concerned that her husband would climb back into bed with his ex. But money and an ex-wife, that's something else. Money is the touchstone of family survival. The umbilical cord that feeds and nourishes. What one family gets, the other doesn't. Its a continuous push and pull. This tug-of-war is all quite in keeping with the urgings of nature since families first began. We are no different from our ancestors. Historically, the organizing theme in the maze of family systems has always been the rules each society established to govern not sexuality but the economics of maintaining the family, accumulating property, and guaranteeing its proper inheritance. The adaptive success of each society has depended on the sheer hard-boiled practicality of the family arrangements that are chosen.

With then, a respectful nod to the sanctity of property in nature's scheme, consider this question: How downright practical, how survival-oriented is our newly emerging synergistic family? Would you say it's in excellent shape? Good condition? Fair? Poor?

From my own soundings it seems that though many of us are making a fair go of it, few are the ones who are doing it with a gut understanding of its necessities and, therefore, a lack of resentment of its inevitable drawbacks and sometimes hardships. The bitter pill, the disappointment that is often so hard to swallow, is that this is not a first marriage. This is no longer monogamy.

I know I certainly had my delusions, my idea being that my remarriage would be exactly like my first marriage—except incredibly better. The word "monogamous" did not occur in my thinking. Nonetheless, my thinking was decidedly monogamous. It went something like this: He and me facing the world together. And should we have children, it would be he and me and they facing. . . .

The truth never entered my mind—that it would be he and me, and she number one and she number two facing the world together. She number one being his daughter, Sandy. She number two being his ex-wife.

None of this penetrated. I clung to my self-delusion. Me and he facing the world. It really never dawned on me that, like it or not, this remarriage of mine had created an entirely new family form. From a financial standpoint, our family structure was much less like that of my mother and father—100 percent pure monogamy—and much more that of an East African Bantu chieftain. Of course, on a smaller scale.

My synergistic family bore a striking resemblance to those families organized around one husband and many wives and children. In short, polygamy. Or to be more exact, economic polygamy. It would ease all our guilts, it would make our remarriages potentially more successful, if we began by accepting this new financial reality.

If we make the assumption, as does the Census Bureau, that after a divorce more often than not the wife keeps the children —the semi-official figure is about ten women to one man raising children—it means that quite a few million ex-husbands are paying alimony and/or child support, or both. These are costs I now have had intimate acquaintance with.

In point of fact the Research Center at the University of Michigan guesstimates that almost 50 percent of all previously married men pay a number of thousands of dollars yearly toward the support of their ex-families. In the matter of financial responsibilities, what we see are divorced husbands —not divorced wives—supporting their ex-families. Should one of these divorced husbands decide to remarry, a synergistic family comes into being—a family that is economically polygamous.

(Incidentally, this brings up another unnerving point which I will deal with in a later chapter. When you contribute to the support of a family, for better or for worse, you then remain pretty intimately involved with that family. So it is no wonder if my hair rises when I think about the love-hate interactions implicit in this new non-sexual polygamy.)

The Seventh Veil

It is quite unfortunate that within the established precincts of monogamy a frank auditing of each other's net worth prior to marriage, or an offer to exchange income tax returns, is regarded as crude and unfeeling. The taboo against any such indecent exposure is stronger than a court injunction. It has the force of an Eleventh Commandment.

The same goes for our psychological attitudes toward money. Money, like sex, is one of the most highly charged items in our monogamous culture, and personal money hang-ups can have an almost religious sanctity. Very few indeed are the people who can look at money as money—a medium of exchange—but not as a symbol of godhead, an evidence of love, a proof of one's value, an argument that one is right, insurance the sun will rise, a reason for feeling superior, inferior, or getting drunk, a guarantee of going to heaven, or better still of being immortal. As well as a reason for murder or matrimony.

This lack of open interchange on money matters is a dangerous enough restraint in first marriages where a frank discussion of lifestyle expectations beforehand might even reduce the divorce rate. Be that as it may, remarriers also tend to avoid the money dialogue. And for us this avoidance amounts to setting the stage for another divorce.

Financial Compatibility

I would be willing to wager—and you can name the stakes— that these days there are millions more couples who can solve their sexual compatibility—with or without a little help from books, psychiatrists, consciousness-raising groups, as well as the friendly neighborhood sexual therapist—then there are those who have made any effort to determine if they are financially compatible.

The mildest of intimacies, let alone remarriage prospects, can call forth an animated analysis of sexual requirements—what coital positions are the most enriching as well as what fetishes are the most ingenious releases of rhapsody. There is also much concerned theorizing over the newly accepted clitoral orgasm as compared with the vaginal classic. But not a word is said about money.

Yet remarriage can quickly lead to redivorce when financial compatibility is lacking. There are so many expectations that can turn out to be trap doors, so many lifestyle expenses that when threatened become explosive. And there is always the continuing psychological and financial pressure of adjusting to our economic polygamy.

That's why an open exchange of financial data, both factual and psychological, is as vital as the pre-marital Wasserman. Bank accounts, income tax deductions, how much money a man or woman makes or owes, has in cash, collateral, child support, alimony, has inherited or borrowed, or has otherwise come by via poker, horses, or bingo, should at best be spelled out before a remarriage takes place. Or, at a poor second best, as shortly after as possible.

What should also be exchanged is each other's psychological attitudes toward money as apparent in how and on what money is spent first. Does a woman have to live on a particular tree-lined street to feel at peace with herself? Does a man have to have a new car every two years to be able to hold his head up?

And then there are the trickiest questions of all. The financial questions that relate to our economic polygamy. Allan D. wants to send his son, Tom, to tennis camp. Jean D. wants to redo the living room and her daughter Nancy's bedroom. But her child support payments won't cover the cost of Nancy's room.

How is she going to feel about Tom's tennis camp when she sees Nancy's worn bureau and the desk she's outgrown? What's going to "give," and "who"?

It's a learning experience for everyone.

I remember the Sunday I proposed to my husband, Sandy's father. It was a fine, clear May afternoon and we were getting dressed to go somewhere. For the last few weeks the idea had been growing on me that we knew each other well enough, cared enough, and had been living together on weekends long enough. It was time to get on with our lives. So I said to him, "I have something to say."

Immediately he picked it up. This is an old round robin game that we like to play, and it can go on and on and on if you let it, repeating itself in a circular fashion like "Row, row, row your boat. . . ." He said, "What? You have something to say?"

I said, "Yes, I have something to say. I am going away."

"What? You are going away?"

"Yes, I am going away. But before I go I have something to say." Then I broke the circle by adding to the standard line "Yes, I have something to say" my own notion. "I think we should get married."

"Oh," he said. And then, without breaking a beat, went on. "What? You think we should get married?"

"Yes," I said. "I think we should get married."

"Well," he said. "I have something to say."

"What? You have something to say?"

"Yes, I have something to say. I am going away."

"What? You are going away?" I was suddenly uneasy.

"Yes, I am going away. On my honeymoon. Want to come?"

When I proposed to my husband and he accepted my proposal on that fine May afternoon, it never occurred to me that I was also proposing to his daughter, Sandy. But, of course, I was. You cannot marry a man with a child and not marry his child, too. As a man cannot marry a woman with children and not marry the children, too. Of course, none of this ever occurred to me then. Nor did it occur to me, who'd never raised children, that children cost money. Not once did I stop to think that children eat hamburgers and potato chips and wear skirts and jeans and need dentistry and movie money. Not once. I had to learn the hard way.

It wasn't that it was all kept a deep dark secret. No, it was all spelled out very carefully for me. My husband-to-be said quite firmly, "Sandy takes a good percentage of my income. You know, dental bills, school bills, camp."

"Of course," I said tenderly. "She's my responsibility too now."

I hadn't heard a thing.

The first year we were married she went to camp and we played at being weekend guests a lot of the summer. It's not a part I like, but we hadn't thought it through. All we knew was that if she went to camp, we could only afford to rent a summer house for a month, not for a full season. This stroke of prescience put us a little ahead of the debtor game. At least we could see the alligators in the financial swamp. Many people can't.

Though there are no hard figures on the rate of failure of the synergistic family due to financial pressure, it is easy to make an educated guess that, given the overall increase in family financial troubles, remarriages will rarely escape cliff hanging money squeezes.

If anything, financial pressure may be responsible for a sizeable percentage of the family's redivorce disasters. For example, as of December 1976, one in 20 holders of single family mortgage loans were delinquent.* During 1976 the American Collectors' Association, which represents almost half of all the collection agencies in the country received nearly 44 million accounts to be collected. In 1974 there were 168,654

---

* This survey includes over 7.2 million mortgage loans on single family mortgages and represents one out of every four of the mortgage loans in the country.

personal bankruptcies. As of 1976, the rate of increase of personal bankruptcies was up 22 percent from 1974.

These figures tell us that both the monogamous family and the synergistic family are having desperate moments keeping up with the rising cost of married life. And of the two marital styles, it is certainly the synergistic family that is traveling the hardest road. How could it be otherwise, given our economic polygamy?

The Consumer Credit Counseling Service, whose business is to keep families in business and out of financial holes, has estimated that less than 5 percent of American families live on budgets and know anything about money management. There is almost no planning done and no records kept. The money just trickles away.

The typical procedure is that husbands and wives try to make their incomes stretch as far as possible toward meeting past bills, paying for food, housing, recreation, clothes. When the money runs out and if something comes up that is truly necessary, the family will borrow if they can and run up another debt. The courts are full of families who spent without thinking, whose expectations exceeded their incomes.

If you are now or plan to become a member of a synergistic family, for the sake of its survival you and your partner must thoroughly explore the following four topics to see if you are financially compatible.

1. You Must Know Each Other's Income and Net Worth

Take-home pay ———— (Weekly, monthly, bi-weekly, semi-monthly)
Other Income ————

Source of Other Income ————————

A typical annual report on your personal net worth might look
something like this:

Assets:
   Cash   ————————————
   Checking Account   ————————————
   Savings Account   ————————————
Investments
   Value of house, condominium, co-op   ————————————
   Home furnishings   ————————————
   Automobile   ————————————
   Cash value of life insurance   ————————————
   Pension holdings   ————————————
   Stocks and Bonds   ————————————

Total Assets ————————
Liabilities:
   Mortgage   ————————————
   Car payments   ————————————
   Other debts   ————————————
   Unpaid bills   ————————————

Total Liabilities ————————
Net Worth (Subtract Liabilities from Assets)   ════════════════

2.   You Must Have a Family Budget

A family budget can save a synergistic family from being
sued, losing property or even going bankrupt. (90% of all
backruptcies in the country are personal not business bankruptcies.) Most people do not have the slightest notion of how
to budget their income and chances are you don't either. For as
of today, neither high schools nor colleges train students in the
basics of personal money management. It was to satisfy this
critical lack that the Consumer Credit Counselors were created.
For years now, they have been advising money-troubled families
on how to balance their dollars more judiciously; so that they

can enjoy life while avoiding financial chaos. To do this the Counselors have compiled a list of what I call 48 Almost Inevitable Expenses that must be taken into account in all budgets. It might help your remarriage if you and your spouse-to-be turned to pages 56 and 57, looked the sample form over, copied it, and then sat down with a pencil and filled it in. It's a good way to break the cultural barrier against financial exchange between husband and wife.

> Write down after each item—*how much you believe you spend in a month and then in a year for that particular item.*
> When you add these columns up you will have an estimate of your monthly and yearly expenses. Since you know what your income is, you can see how your expenses relate to your income.
> Naturally, not all the items will apply to you. Cross out what doesn't apply and add what does. Maybe you don't smoke but do like scotch. In that case replace cigarettes with liquor. If some item dear to your heart, and costly to your wallet was omitted, write it in your "Miscellaneous." Like say "pets"—your royal standard poodle—don't overlook the hair trimmings and the dog food.
> (Consumer Credit Counselors' 48 Almost Inevitable Items)

Once you've filled out the list of these 48 Almost Inevitable Expenses, look it over. Now you are more aware of how you think you and your spouse actually spend your money. But this still gives you only a sketchy idea.

To have a more precise idea, the next move for both you and your now or future spouse should be to keep track through each week of the month of everything you spend, listing it after the proper item. At the end of the month, add up what you spent for each item, enter it into the second page of Inevitable Expenses, and compare it with your original budget estimate. It may give you a jolt. You may not have realized how much you are actually spending for certain items, and how this is straining your resources. But jolted or not, you will now have a concrete idea of what the dollar drain is.

How to Use the Budget Form*

STEP 1   Fill in your monthly cost for all expense items, from
          Household through Miscellaneous. For example, if
          you spend $500 each year on family clothing, write
          $42 as the average cost per month ($500 ÷ 12 =
          $42).

STEP 2   Add the Expense items to determine your total
          "MONTHLY EXPENSES."

STEP 3   List your Gross Monthly Wages and All Other
          Monthly Income. Do not forget social security and
          disability payments, any rental income and con-
          tributions from other family members.

STEP 4   Add the Income items for your "TOTAL
          MONTHLY INCOME."

STEP 5   Turn the page over for the LIST OF DEBTS and
          fill in the required information.

STEP 6   Add the "PRESENT MONTHLY DEBT PAY-
          MENTS" column and fill in this figure on the line la-
          beled "TOTAL MONTHLY DEBT PAYMENTS."

STEP 7   Add the "AMOUNT OWED" column and fill in this
          figure on the line labeled "TOTAL AMOUNT
          OWED."

STEP 8   Transfer "MONTHLY EXPENSES" (STEP 2) and
          "TOTAL MONTHLY DEBT PAYMENTS" (STEP
          6) to the Summary Section.

          Add "MONTHLY EXPENSES" and "TOTAL
          MONTHLY DEBT PAYMENTS." The sum is your
          "TOTAL MONTHLY EXPENSE."

* From the Consumer Credit Counseling Service Budget Form. See pages
56–57 for an example of the form.

STEP 9   Transfer "TOTAL MONTHLY INCOME" (STEP
               4) and "TOTAL MONTHLY EXPENSE" (STEP
               8) to the Summary Section.
               Subtract "TOTAL MONTHLY EXPENSE" from
               "TOTAL MONTHLY INCOME." The *Remaining*
               Balance is the amount of money you have to save
               (if positive) or your monthly deficit (if negative).
               A zero figure means you are breaking even.

A good thing now would be to compare your spending patterns with those of your spouse. Ask yourself and each other some probing questions. How compatible are your spending patterns? Is there an equitable distribution of self-indulgences? Family indulgences? Of self-denials? Family restraints? Do you feel cheated when you see the cold, hard figures? Does he or she feel taken advantage of? Is one of you overdoing it on some item? Or not spending enough?

Given the income you know you have at your disposal, how you spend it should now be open to discussion. One or both of you may have to rethink your lifestyle needs and revise your spending patterns. Could either of you cut down on some expenses for the sake of the other, or for the sake of the family, or on behalf of long-term goals, or—and this is the acid test—for the sake of living within your income? Remember, neither of you can have everything you want, for yourself or for the family.

If you are not yet married, fill out the list in terms of how the two of you expect to spend your combined monies after the wedding. What expenses will you add out of self-interest, or in the interest of your spouse, or the family—i.e., a new refrigerator? Whose money will pay for it and how will it be paid for? What expenses will be subtracted—i.e., double rents or mortgage payments? Do you mind pooling your monies and have you decided yet how to handle your combined incomes? Who is responsible for what? Which one of you will be carrying the

48 Almost Inevitable Budget Items*

EXPENSES

		MONTHLY	YEARLY
HOUSEHOLD	RENT OR MORTGAGE PAYMENT		
	ELECTRIC		
	HEATING		
	WATER		
	TAXES		
	TELEPHONE		
FOOD	FOOD/MILK		
	SNACKS/MEALS AT WORK		
CAR	GAS & OIL		
	REPAIRS, TIRES, ETC.		
	COMMUTATION (TOLLS, BUSES, SUBWAYS, PARKING)		
INSURANCE	HOSPITAL		
	CAR		
	HOUSEHOLD		
	LIFE		
PERSONAL	BARBER & BEAUTY SHOP		
	ALLOWANCES (OTB, LOTTERY, ETC.)		
	TOILETRIES		
	CIGARETTES & TOBACCO		
MEDICAL	DOCTOR		
	DENTIST		
	DRUGS		
CLOTHING	FAMILY		
	CLEANING & LAUNDRY		
GIFTS	BIRTHDAYS		
	CHRISTMAS		
	ALL OTHER		
EDUCATION	TUITION & SCHOOL SUPPLIES		
	BOOKS, PAPERS, MAGAZINES		
DONATIONS	RELIGIOUS INSTITUTIONS		
	ALL OTHER		
ENTERTAINMENT	MOVIES & PLAYS		
	DINNERS OUT		
	PARTIES OUT		
	CLUBS, SPORTS, HOBBIES		
	BEVERAGES (LIQUOR, BEER, SODAS)		
	VACATIONS		
	BABY SITTER		
PAYROLL DEDUCTIONS	DUES — UNION & OTHER		
	SOCIAL SECURITY		
	TOTAL INCOME TAXES (CITY, STATE AND FEDERAL)		
	NUMBER EXEMPTIONS CLAIMED ( )		
	SAVINGS BONDS		
SAVINGS	CREDIT UNION		
	BANK		
	OTHER		
MISCELLANEOUS	ALIMONY OR SUPPORT PAYMENTS		
	HOUSE AND APPLIANCE REPAIRS		

STEP 3   **STEP 2** **EXPENSES** $ | $

INCOME

WAGES	GROSS WAGES		
	OTHER WAGES		
	SPOUSE'S WAGES		
ADDITIONAL INCOME	OTHER INCOME		

STEP 4 **TOTAL INCOME** $ | $

* From the Consumer Credit Counseling Budget Form. Budgets used throughout the book are computed on this basic form.

Lists of Debts*

STEP 5 CREDITOR'S NAME (Bank, Finance Co., Stores, Doctors, Travel Cards, Utilities, etc.)	TYPE OF LOAN	ARE YOUR PAYMENTS UP-TO-DATE?	IF NOT, DATE OF LAST PAYMENT	LIST AMOUNT PAST DUE	PRESENT MONTHLY DEBT PAYMENTS	AMOUNT OWED CREDITOR

STEP 6   **TOTAL MONTHLY DEBT PAYMENTS** $

STEP 7   **TOTAL AMOUNT OWED** $

SUMMARY

STEP 8

Monthly Expense	$
+ Total Monthly Debt Payments	$
TOTAL MONTHLY EXPENSE	$

STEP 9

Total Monthly Income	$
− Total Monthly Expense	$
REMAINING BALANCE	$

* From the Consumer Credit Counseling Budget Form.

heavier financial burden, and is it too heavy? If so, where can you lighten it by lightening expenses? Remember, you now have more than one family to think about. You are not monogamous. You are economically polygamous, and as a member of the synergistic family you are a poly-parent. Recognizing this extended responsibility, you have to choose your priorities, discuss them, make compromises, and focus on what's most important to both you and your spouse in terms of family goals, now and in the future.

A budget, like love, should be a staple item in a family that plans to stay together. Get all the children your biologic ones and those that arrived via economic polygamy, into the budget-making process. Let them do some arithmetic. It will startle them to see how food and roller skates and allergy shots can add up. Where money shortages especially affect your poly-children, ask their advice as to what to do. It will help them to identify with the new family and to realize they have equal standing, that they are not second-class citizens.

What I have outlined here are ground rules for managing monies in a synergistic family. But there are many other books available in libraries and bookstores that deal more extensively and more specifically with financial problems like budgets, borrowings, savings, home ownership, insurance, investing, and so on. Find the books, read them, and learn what you can to keep you and your spouse financially compatible.

3. Accept Your Economic Polygamy and Deal with It

DON'T MAKE THE MISTAKES I MADE

Keep open the channels of financial communication between the family core and any ex-spouses relating to the family financially. In this connection I have some suggestions for bringing about a saner meeting of minds on money matters. Before noting them, however, I'd like to admit that I myself have not been very successful at making these new adaptations, which is undoubtedly why I see the need for them.

If I'd known ten years ago, when my synergistic family came into being, what I know now, we might today have a reasonable business association, if nothing else, with our ex-wife, and fewer legal fees. Because, contrary to what I told my Mafia dream contact, I must admit that I do think of her as our ex-wife. Or perhaps, to be more accurate, as my wife-in-law. Like my mother-in-law. (And as such there are certain obligations.) A relative that I acquired via remarriage, who because of her influence on my poly-child is of deep influence in my life. I only wish I'd seen it all coming sooner.

Our current lack of financial rapport has led us into all kinds of sticky confrontations, experiences that you would be wise to spare yourself by building early in your remarriage lines of communication to your ex-spouses. For example, I remember the time the doorman called up on the house phone and, sounding very pained, said, "There is a woman here with a summons for you, and since we wouldn't let her go upstairs she pasted it on the front door with Scotch tape. The super wants to know if you could come down and take it off?"

"Oh. A summons. Hmmm," I said, meanwhile wondering why I did not faint. "You said a summons, didn't you?" I asked.

"Yes, ma'am. It's on the front door, with Scotch tape."

"Well, well," I said lightly. As though it were a box of flowers. "Well, could you bring it up to me, please?"

"Oh no, ma'am. That's against the law. You have to come down and get it," he said. "That's the law."

"Of course," I said. I then hung up the house phone quietly and calmly went into the bedroom, took off my old beat-up Levi's that I'd been wearing while cleaning out a closet, and

changed into a clean, pressed pair of Levi's. I then took off
my old T-shirt and put on a Calvin Klein turtleneck that I
bought on sale at Bloomie's. If I was going to pick up a summons, I was not going to do it looking like a slob.

When I reached the front door, I said to the doorman, "Hi,
George. I hear we have a summons." You might have thought
I'd said, "George, it looks like rain." Or something sparkling
like that.

"Yes," he said. "I was going to tear it off, but the super said
it was against the law."

"That's all right," I said. I'd always liked George. He had
the kind of chivalry that went with another age of doormen.
"I'll take it. I wonder who it's from."

"I don't know, ma'am," he sighed. "Looks like lawyers, I
think."

"Well, tally ho!" I said smiling and reached for the small
white sheet of paper fluttering in the winter breeze that was
indeed Scotch taped to the door. I pulled it off carefully, glad
to see my hand wasn't shaking, and stood there casually—my
God! I was casual—studying it. I was not going to be panicked
by a little thing like a summons. The kind of thing presidents
get almost every day.

The name on the top of the paper read something like
"Reilly, Weiss & Schmorgasborg." That must be the legal firm.
But what was the summons for? We had nothing to hide. As
far as I knew we had had nothing to do with Watergate. Corporate bribes of foreign officials. Nursing home scandals, smug-
gling arms to the Arabs, Israel, or Angola. Illegal political
contributions, Patricia Hearst. Unexplained deficits in the New
York City budget. My husband is a fanatic about the checkbook
and pays bills by the 10th. We'd done nothing to deserve this—
aaah! At the bottom of the page I saw the name of my wife-in-
law. So that was what it was all about. That child support
ruckus no doubt.

I looked up in relief and caught George staring straight ahead while watching me out of the corner of his left eye. I felt obliged to explain to him that we were involved in a matrimonial action. "It's a summons from my husband's ex-wife," I said. "We're arguing about money. Wouldn't you think she'd just telephone? This is so tacky."

"Oh," sighed George in relief, shaking his head in disgust. "Mr. Reynolds in 15J got one of those last month. She never lets him alone and they were only married a year."

When I got back to our apartment I wondered if George would tell the superintendent what the summons was about. On the chance that he wouldn't, I decided to call the super myself, thank him for keeping the process server downstairs, and explain what had happened. After all, I did not want him to think we were financially irresponsible. After all, the head of the building's board of directors had gone to school with my husband. After all, I had not contacted the Mafia, I'd only dreamed it. And while I was about it, I thought I'd give the incident a little pazazz and tell him I was doing a book on the subject of divorce and that this was part of the research. Which it wasn't.

Economic polygamy requires a mature sense of economic responsibility on everyone's part. Unreal financial demands by an ex-wife can severely cripple the functioning of a new family and, by so doing, reduce the monies available for everyone. Unwarranted miserliness by remarriers can only damage the children of the previous marriage. Adults who share the parenthood of children have to learn to talk to each other, to make trade treaties. Whenever possible it is essential that a good financial rapport be established between the new family and the mother or father of the ex-family. It may sound a bit radical at this early stage of development of poly-parenthood, but one way to gain this rapport is to invite the ex-spouse to sit in on a family budget session and cooperate in examining expenses.

Another thought is to have a quarterly, or a semi-annual financial council on the cost of living for all and how best to meet it.

When people realize you truly want to do your best for their children, to be fair to them, and fair to your new family, sometimes you can reach important compromises and avoid crises.

4.   All about the Psycho-Finances of the Synergistic Family

Questions to ask yourself and answer truthfully, so that you can unearth those explosive emotions that often, like mines, lay buried beneath the surface of your self-image:

1.   Which one of you is the Big Spender?
2.   Which one is the Saver?
3.   Do you squirrel away money in secret caches?
4.   Why?
5.   Does your partner seem to do this?
6.   Why?
7.   Would you rather spend money on yourself, the family, your spouse?
8.   Does your spouse run up household debts without telling you?
9.   Do you run up hidden debts?
10.   Do either of you buy as easily on credit as for cash?
11.   Do you both work?
12.   If you both don't work, do you think your financial problems might be easier if you did?
13.   Do you have joint or separate checking accounts? Savings accounts?
14.   What kind of account do you prefer?
15.   Why?
16.   Do you talk to each other freely about money pressures?
17.   If you don't, why don't you?
18.   When you talk about money, is either of you apt to become angry?
19.   Why?

20. What can you do to solve this anger?
21. Do either of you feel the other is not carrying his or her share of the financial responsibility?
22. Is this a fair appraisal?

Undoubtedly the most unsettling rethinking that the synergistic family must do is to give up economic monogamy with its total emphasis on bloodline commitments. Synergistic parents have to resee themselves and their children. To each parent, biologic children and non-biologic children must have equal value. Financial decisions relating to these children can never be made along blood lines, just for the sake of the blood connection. These decisions must always be made with the health of the total family, the biologic one and the polygamous one, in mind.

The questions that follow are therefore all about polygamous parenthood. When one or both parties in a remarriage have children, there is always the unstated hope on the part of the biological parent that the children and the poly-parent will automatically have warm feelings for each other. And, in financial terms, that the child's welfare will be as important to the poly-parent as to the biological parent. It may be that deep in our psyche we have a race memory of genuinely polygamous families and we know they can work. So why not ours? What do your answers to the following questions tell you about yourself and your talents for poly-parenthood?

1. Do you have children?
2. Does your partner have children?
3. Do you want to have a child between you?
4. Have you done the arithmetic to see if you can afford another child?
5. If money were tight, would your impulse be to scrimp on yourself, your children, his/her children?
6. If money were tight, would you resent its being spent on your partner's children?
7. If there was enough money to go around, how would you feel?

8. If you resent spending monies on his/her children have you told your spouse about your feelings?
9. If not, why not?
10. When you are spending money, who in the family comes first?
11. Who comes last?
12. Do your children know your economic situation?
13. Does your spouse's children know their economic situation?
14. Do your children think you have more money than you have?
15. Does your spouse?
16. Do any of the children contribute to the family income? How?
17. If your husband makes alimony and child support payments to a previous wife, how do you feel about these payments?
18. Does your husband know how you feel?
19. If you are a husband whose wife receives a child support income, how do you feel about how she spends that money?

5

The Financially Incompatible

The Synergistic Seven

Within the synergistic family there are about seven principal marital arrangements. Any other designs are variations of these seven.

1. Mary's biological children live with her; John has no children.
2. Mary has no children; John's biological children live with him.
3. Both Mary and John have their own biological children living with them.
4. Mary's children live with her; John's children live with his ex-wife, or wives.
5. Mary's children live with her ex-husband or husbands; John's children live with him.
6. Mary has no children; John's children live with his ex-wife.
7. Either Mary, John, or both have biological children living with them. Then the couple has another in this remarriage.

None of these arrangements is inherently financially incompatible, though some are more susceptible to these problems than others. Of the seven possible synergistic arrangements, however, probably the most common, and also the one most sensitive to financial pressures, is Type 4. In this situation, Mary's children live with her and John's children live with his ex-wife or wives. There are endless variations on this theme.

What makes this couple so redivorce-prone is the collision of lifestyle expectations with reality. This happens, as I indicated earlier, when despite concrete marital history, the couple will behave as if they were making a first, monogamous marriage with no financial obligations to the past. They do not accept their economic polygamy.

To illustrate this kind of self-deceptive blindness, I will describe in some detail a couple I call the Ostrich and the Guilty Conscience. Consider how they leaped, before they looked.

Another distressing example of Type 4 are the Many Splendid Remarriers—this refers to multi-married men and women with children. In these situations, it is the last-in-line wife who usually suffers the most. A wife I know became the disaster victim of such a remarriage. Though she was totally dependent on a sizable alimony and a small amount of child support for her son, she chose to marry a man who had already been divorced twice and fathered four children. She said as explanation, "He makes me feel alive."

Fine. But the man was not wealthy. He had a reasonable income, but one that was seriously depleted by alimony and child support payments. Since she did not work, what did she think they would live on?

I wonder too what the man was thinking of when he chose to remarry without working out beforehand the financial hazards. Where did the couple expect to find the money to sustain the new family in the wife's former lifestyle? Inevitably, remarriage ended her substantial alimony. Since neither partner stopped to take into account the realities of economic polygamy, they wound up in bankruptcy court.

On the other hand, to make clear that it is not the Type 4 arrangement itself that is financially disaster prone but the psychologies of the remarrying couple, I will look in some detail at a variation on the theme, where the financial problems are purely "in the head" of the second husband. Here, in the case of the affluent Ex, there need not have been any strain. That there was strain was simply a result of the fact that the second husband could not accept the reality that though a husband may be an ex-husband, he is never an ex-father.

There are also synergistic families as in Type 2, where the husband has biological children and the wife has none. This is another hazardous financial arrangement because of the psychic pressures on a woman to have children. If you or your spouse fall into this category, and are thinking of having another child, consider the experience recounted later of a second husband and his "virgin" bride.

Probably the most financially deceptive of the synergistic family styles is Type 6—Mary has no children and John's children live with his ex-wife. This, as I know from hard experience, can be the most maddening of the synergistic family arrangements. Superficially, it so resembles monogamy that you are tempted to believe it is monogamy. Because you do not live on a day-to-day basis with your poly-children, because you see them on weekends, vacations, or in whatever patterns are arrived at with the ex-spouse, you are constantly having to switch gears. Also shift viewpoints. You have to discipline yourself to see this guest as your child, if not blood of your blood, still blood of your love, yours by proxy and by virtue of your economic polygamy.

Type 7 is divorce prone because of a peculiar romantic susceptibility. Despite the fact that the husband or the wife or both have come to this remarriage complete with prior children, this enterprising couple will blithely decide to have another baby. All well and good. Providing they have money to burn. If not, along with the standard economic problems of remarriage, the care and feeding and raising of a new baby is a luxury that can lead to redivorce.

The arrangements least subject to financial stress are Type 1, Type 3, and Type 5. This does not mean they are immune to money pressures, simply that the percentages are with them because of the family structure. Take Type 1. Even if John pays alimony to an ex-wife, the financial pressure is not comparable to what it would be if he had children. Type 5 is a very rare, fairly recent innovation. Usually it occurs because at one point Mary 5 decided she did not want to play mother, and went back to work. Remarriage to Mary 5 does not mean motherhood, and the problems of this kind of family are more likely to be emotional than financial. Type 3 tends to be the most realistic remarriers in the synergistic group. When such a family gets into financial straits—as, for example, if they choose to have another child and can't afford it—it is more because they are born bad money managers, and not because they have not faced their economic polygamy. Living every day, each of them, as poly-parents, it would be very hard indeed for either husband or wife to pretend that theirs is a monogamous first marriage and discount the needs of their extended brood.

Incidentally, I would like to point out that among the group of middle, upper middle and upper class marriages that I am exploring, almost always the financial problem is more psychological than real. It is not a matter of hard core food and shelter survival that is at stake because of misconceptions about marriage. Rather, it is dear-to-the-heart lifestyles that are in jeopardy. Still, since for many of us our lifestyles are our identity, the anguish caused by the need for a severe shift because of financial miscalculations is quite real. It is worth noting, and it is worth avoiding when possible. Where on investigation avoidance is not possible, there are only two choices. One is to decide before remarriage that the remarriage is worth the change in lifestyle and to make a conscious adaptation to a lifestyle change. The other choice, of course, is not to make this remarriage.

The Ostrich and the Guilty Conscience

There are, as we all know, ex-husbands who pay out to their ex-families far too little—either alimony and/or child support —and still feel that far to little is far to much. This is an unfortunate circumstance for which an ex-wife can blame only her poor legal counsel. But it is not appropriate to this current discussion. It is the other side of the same coin that I am concerned with here: the ex-husband who gives too much, just to be relieved of the guilt of asking for the divorce in the first place. These men blackmail themselves. The advantage to the first wife—it usually only happens with the first—can be financially considerable. What I think is often overlooked is how it can so strap the ex-husband financially that he becomes resentful of his own children, and of a past that at one time was certainly precious and meaningful to him. This kind of psychological damage is not a gain for either the ex-wife or child who feels the anger, or the man who carried it with him into his future relations with women.

There is also further damage should the ex-husband remarry and be unable to contribute sufficient monies to keep his new family from floundering. That was what happened to Roger Sloan, advertising vice-president earning $60,000 a year. Roger had been married for twenty-three years to Louise Sloan, an energetic, going to plump, good-natured woman who was liked by everyone in the neighborhood who knew the Sloans. Together, Roger and Louise had raised three children ranging in age from twelve to twenty at the time that Roger met Joan Harrison. Joan was not Roger's first affair.

Roger's first affair had started sometime in the seventh year of his marriage. He was making $20,000 a year and living in a pleasant, middle-income suburb of Philadelphia, but his career had hit a snag. He could not seem to get out of media and into account work. It seemed to him a lot of dummies were passing him in the pipeline to the top, and Roger, at 38, was feeling like a has-been.

Around this time he met Edie Sawyer, 28, a copywriter who came to the agency to work on the same food account that Roger serviced. It was chemistry at first sight on both sides. Roger and Edie had everything in common that Roger and Louise did not. Edie loved advertising as much as Roger did; Louise's Lutheran background made her think it was vaguely dishonest. Edie was as ambitious for Roger as she was for herself; Louise thought Roger was making more than she'd ever thought he would. Edie knew all the ins and outs of the power structure and her spy system included every management secretary. She could tell Roger what was happening while it was still only a twitch in the president's nose. Furthermore, Edie was an old school chum of the daughter of the executive vice-president and knew the president's wife on a first name basis. Louise felt uncomfortable with middle management wives and tongue-tied with the spouses of top brass.

Roger and Edie's affair went on for five years, during which Roger became an account supervisor, Edie became a copy supervisor, and there were occasional hellish scenes between them about when was Roger going to get his damn divorce. In their sixth year, Edie, who I can assure you was no born loser, explained to Roger that if she couldn't have him, she was certainly going to have something—and a career was not a bad thing to have. She'd accepted a job with a West Coast agency as its first female vice-president in charge of creative services.

Roger wept. That night he went home and asked Louise for a divorce. Louise developed heart palpitations and had to be rushed to a hospital. That ended any discussion of divorce. You had to admire Louise's resources.

Roger and Edie wrote frequently. Telephoned each other frequently. After a while they stopped writing and telephoning.

The years passed and now Louise paid more attention to her hair, her weight, and to Roger's work. She read a raft of books that broadened her sexual horizons and, following her sister's advice, never mentioned to Roger his fall from grace. However, she did make a practice of calling him at the office on one pretext or another when he had to work late and flirtatiously reminding him what was waiting for him at home. Louise had never been dumb, only lazy. In these years their relationship was better than it had ever been—even in the years before Edie.

It is too bad, but even success palls. Louise took a couple of years to recover from her fright, but when she recovered she put on weight again. She also neglected her sexual studies and forgot to listen with rapt attention when Roger talked about his work.

On Roger's fiftieth birthday he had expected to be executive vice-president. He wasn't. And Louise wasn't that sorry. The bigger house they now lived in and their more stylish friends didn't appeal to her that much. She still preferred gardening manuals and cook books to *Time* magazine, and she only read the newspapers under duress. The day Roger was fifty, Roger met Joan Harrison lunching in a restaurant with her fourteen-year-old son, Grant, Jr. Joan was the ex-wife of an ex-client and a very pretty woman of forty who looked thirty. Joan's ex-husband, Grant, was a self-made millionaire who was more married to his company than to Joan. Even on those weekends when he was at home, he spent three quarters of his time reading financial and marketing reports. When Joan asked for a divorce, he treated it as a business deal. If he gave her sufficient alimony, she'd live well enough to attract some other sucker. Though her child support payments were modest, he agreed they would be modestly increased should she marry.

Joan and Roger had met years ago at a dinner party given by the agency president. They met again at another party Joan gave at her Hill and Dale estate when she and Grant Harrison

Joan Harrison's Lifestyle Budget

EXPENSES

		MONTHLY	YEARLY
HOUSEHOLD	RENT OR MORTGAGE PAYMENT	700	8,400
	ELECTRIC *Included in Rent*		
	HEATING		
	WATER		
	TAXES		
	TELEPHONE	60	720
FOOD	FOOD/MILK	300	3,600
	SNACKS/MEALS AT WORK		
CAR	GAS & OIL		
	REPAIRS, TIRES, ETC.		
	COMMUTATION (TOLLS, BUSES, SUBWAYS, PARKING)		
INSURANCE	HOSPITAL	40	480
	CAR		
	HOUSEHOLD	25	300
	LIFE		
PERSONAL	BARBER & BEAUTY SHOP	100	1,200
	ALLOWANCES ~~(OTB, LOTTERY, ETC.)~~ *Grant, Jr.*	50	600
	TOILETRIES	50	600
	CIGARETTES & TOBACCO		
MEDICAL	DOCTOR	27.50	330
	DENTIST	8.33	100
	DRUGS	8.33	100
CLOTHING	FAMILY	100	1,200
	CLEANING & LAUNDRY	40	480
GIFTS	BIRTHDAYS	8.33	100
	CHRISTMAS	16.67	200
	ALL OTHER	16.67	200
EDUCATION	TUITION & SCHOOL SUPPLIES	250	3000
	BOOKS, PAPERS, MAGAZINES	20	240
DONATIONS	RELIGIOUS INSTITUTIONS		
	ALL OTHER		
ENTERTAINMENT	MOVIES & PLAYS	20	240
	DINNERS OUT *Tanpis*	100	1,200
	PARTIES OUT	100	1,200
	CLUBS, SPORTS, HOBBIES	20.83	250
	BEVERAGES (LIQUOR, BEER, SODAS)	50.00	600
	VACATIONS *Summer House*	333.33	4,000
	~~BABY SITTER~~ *Housekeeper/Cook*	416.67	5,000
PAYROLL DEDUCTIONS	DUES — UNION & OTHER		
	SOCIAL SECURITY		
	TOTAL INCOME TAXES (CITY, STATE AND FEDERAL)	1000	12,000
	NUMBER EXEMPTIONS CLAIMED ( )		
	SAVINGS BONDS		
SAVINGS	CREDIT UNION		
	BANK		
	OTHER		
MISCELLANEOUS	ALIMONY OR SUPPORT PAYMENTS		
	~~HOUSE AND APPLIANCE REPAIRS~~ *Furniture*	41.67	500

STEP 3
STEP 2 **EXPENSES** | $3,903.33 | $46,840

INCOME

WAGES	~~GROSS WAGES~~ *alimony*	3,333.33	40,000
	~~OTHER WAGES~~ *Support*	416.67	5,000
	~~SPOUSE'S WAGES~~		
ADDITIONAL INCOME	OTHER INCOME		

STEP 4 **TOTAL INCOME** | $3,750 | $45,000

(Continued)

Step 5*	No Debt	
Step 6	No Debt	
Step 7	No Debt	
Step 8	Monthly Expense Debt Payments	$3903.33
	Total Monthly Expense	$3903.33
Step 9	Total Monthly Income	$3750
	Total Monthly Expense	$3903.33
	Monthly Deficit	($153.33)†

were still married. Joan and Roger liked each other immediately. There had been something unspoken between them. Now that Joan was an ex-wife and Grant was an ex-client, there seemed no reason to keep the unspoken unspoken. Their affair began the following week after Roger took Joan to lunch and while Grant, Jr. was away at school.

It was a pleasant affair and it made Roger feel young again. He thought he still might have a chance at the executive vice-presidency. Joan was an able and willing partner in bed and an admiring, perceptive listener when he talked. Roger badly needed someone to talk to. And there were no scenes, no screams. Just Joan being warm and appreciative.

If Joan had not started dating a psychiatrist, it is my hunch that Roger would never have changed his position. But she did

* Steps 5, 6, 7, 8, and 9 refer to instructions on "How to Use the Budget form on pages 54 and 55.
† For a woman with a $45,000 income, this kind of deficit could be absorbed by simply taking a shorter vacation one year.

and he did. He made up his mind one afternoon in bed, and that evening he asked Louise for a divorce.

Louise, of course, had palpitations and Roger rushed her to a hospital. When she recovered, he asked her again. This time she wept. She wept steadily for three weeks and regained her figure, which was always good. It made Roger, who still had warm feelings for Louise, feel like a low form of animal life. He wanted to make it up to Louise for leaving her after all their years together, and the best thing he could think of was money. He was half right.

Roger gave Louise, without any sermonizing from her lawyer, $15,000 in child support for the two remaining children and $15,000 in alimony. All in all, what he gave her amounted to half his income. That is $30,000. He did not tell any of this to Joan.

Joan was so ecstatic at the prospect of remarriage to her beloved Roger that she could not think about practical matters, like how much alimony was Roger going to pay Louise. Anyway, Joan believed in alimony. Grant had been very generous with her. I don't think it even occurred to her that once she and Roger were married her alimony would stop. If that thought did happen to cross her mind, I can almost hear her say to herself, "What the hell, now I have Roger." Joan was a natural-born Ostrich who would close her eyes at the sight of anything unpleasant. This naturally extended to unpleasant subjects like bills, money, budgets, and so on. These were things Grant always had attended to, and now she had lawyers and an accountant. (See Joan's lifestyle expenses before she and Roger were married on pages 72 and 73.)

Sometime during the last few days of their honeymoon in Bermuda, Joan asked Roger for money for a whim she'd seen in a shop. Roger suggested she use her own money. He needed his cash to cover cab fares to and from airports. Joan said she had no money. Roger was startled. Didn't she bring money with her? Joan shook her head puzzled. "No." She had no money to bring. What she had in her checking account she'd spent on redoing the master bedroom in her apartment as a welcome home for the two of them. Now she was broke. That was the beginning of the Roger Sloan awakening.

That evening, sitting in the dining room at a candlelit dinner, Roger got his first full picture of Joan's finances. They were nil. Grant's accountant deposited two checks monthly in her bank account. A large one for alimony and a small one for child support.

It came as a blow to his fantasies that Joan's income was largely alimony. Alimony that stopped when she married. Roger had happily fantasized a sizable divorce settlement. Or substantial child support payments. Either way, he had planned on Joan's income to contribute to their happiness.

Now he knew. The truth was—no settlement. The truth was —a pittance of child support. The truth was—alimony that had stopped. How had he been so misled? Angry as much with himself as with Joan, he reviewed what she had told him. Either by conscious calculation or unconscious forethought, she'd given him the impression that her income was more or less permanent. Therefore, he was free to play the Sport with Louise, to donate to her half of his income.

When Roger asked Joan why she had not told him she lived on alimony, she replied with perfect reasonableness that he had not asked her. That was true.

Sitting there in the dining room with the wine glasses glistening, Joan wondered what the fuss was about. Roger certainly made enough money to support them. And the $5,000 a year she received for child support would surely pay for the housekeeper-cook.

Sitting at the table, with his ulcers acting up, Roger thought about how much money he was giving Louise. If he had known then what he knew now, he wondered if he would have asked Louise for a divorce.

On the plane back to the States, Roger explained to Joan

how much money they had to live on and why Mamie, the housekeeper, would have to go. That wasn't all that would have to go.

Grant, Jr. was not going to have an electric guitar if Grant, Sr. wasn't going to pay for it. Because he, Roger, certainly couldn't afford it. This communication did not make Joan happy. She was even more unhappy when Roger pointed out to her in the cab from the airport that Grant, Jr. was going to go to the private school Grant, Sr. preferred to pay for. No matter how wrong Joan thought it was for the boy. Roger could not afford to pay for the artistic, expressive life young Grant enjoyed at the school Joan had paid for out of her alimony.

Adding insult to injury, Roger remarked that Joan would have to watch her charge accounts. Roger knew he would have to watch his tennis membership and his massages. His city club, fortunately, was paid for by the company. And of course they would have to find a new apartment. They did not need six rooms on the twenty-third floor overlooking Philadelphia. What's more, Roger could not afford it.

From that day forward, Roger and Joan regularly lived above their income. Though they rented a smaller apartment, it was only one room smaller. Grant, Jr. had to have a bedroom. And it was still in the same expensive section. Anywhere else was a "slum" to Joan. She wept at the mere suggestion of a change.

Then there was the matter of entertaining. Roger's business ran on entertaining. But without Mamie to cook, Joan could not entertain. She had no idea how to make a three-minute egg, let alone beef Wellington. Every dinner party had to be catered. Otherwise guests were taken to a restaurant. Of course, some of these expenses were clearly business deductions, but some of them were not.

The first time Roger made Joan take back a designer dress she'd bought on sale she did not talk to him for three days. When she did talk, she brought up the subject of Roger's payments to Louise. She never dropped the subject after that.

From the day that Grant, Jr. was transferred to the school of Grant, Sr.'s choice, Roger's sex life with Joan deteriorated. By the time the boy was ready for graduation, Joan had a lover, and Roger, who knew he could not afford another divorce, had a serious ulcer attack.

The failure of Roger and Joan Sloan to pay attention to the mechanics of economic polygamy transformed what had been a pleasant relationship into a shattering series of financial emotional eruptions. If they had known anything about each other's income, each other's expenses and lifestyle expectations, they might never have married each other. Alternatively, they might have recognized in time that there was a serious need for lifestyle compromise, and gone on or not gone on from that point. Though theirs may not have been a marriage made in heaven, it did not have to become a marriage made in hell.

On the pages 78, 79, and 80 you'll see what Roger expected Joan's income to be, and what Joan expected Roger's income to be after remarriage. This couple had never done a budget. But if they had, the one that follows shows how they might have lived if they had combined expenses and if their expectations had been fulfilled. Following this fantasy budget, you will see what their actual income was after remarriage, and what their budget should have been if they had lived within their actual income (but they did not).

Joan Harrison and Roger Sloan's Fantasy Budget

(STEP 1)
EXPENSES

		MONTHLY	YEARLY
HOUSEHOLD	RENT OR MORTGAGE PAYMENT	700	8,400
	ELECTRIC		
	HEATING		
	WATER		
	TAXES		
	TELEPHONE	75	900
FOOD	FOOD/MILK	400	4,800
	SNACKS/MEALS AT WORK	200	2,400
CAR	GAS & OIL	30	360
	REPAIRS, TIRES, ETC.	20	240
	COMMUTATION (TOLLS, BUSES, SUBWAYS, PARKING)	51.67	620
INSURANCE	HOSPITAL	33.33	400
	CAR	29.17	350
	HOUSEHOLD	25	300
	LIFE	166.67	2,000
PERSONAL	BARBER & BEAUTY SHOP	150	1,800
	ALLOWANCES ~~(OTB, LOTTERY, ETC.)~~ *Grant, Jr.*	50	600
	TOILETRIES	75	900
	CIGARETTES & TOBACCO	41.67	500
MEDICAL	DOCTOR	37.50	450
	DENTIST	16.67	200
	DRUGS	16.67	200
CLOTHING	FAMILY	150	1,800
	CLEANING & LAUNDRY	50	600
GIFTS	BIRTHDAYS	41.67	500
	CHRISTMAS	41.67	500
	ALL OTHER	25	300
EDUCATION	TUITION & SCHOOL SUPPLIES	250	3,000
	BOOKS, PAPERS, MAGAZINES *and Equipment*	62.50	750
DONATIONS	RELIGIOUS INSTITUTIONS		
	ALL OTHER	20.83	250
ENTERTAINMENT	MOVIES & PLAYS	33.33	400
	DINNERS OUT	200	2,400
	PARTIES ~~OUT~~ *IN*	125	1,500
	CLUBS, SPORTS, HOBBIES	83.33	1,000
	BEVERAGES (LIQUOR, BEER, SODAS)	62.50	750
	VACATIONS	500	6,000
	BABY SITTER	416.67	5,000
PAYROLL DEDUCTIONS	DUES — UNION & OTHER		
	SOCIAL SECURITY	75	900
	TOTAL INCOME TAXES (CITY, STATE AND FEDERAL)	1,891.67	22,700
	NUMBER EXEMPTIONS CLAIMED ( )		
	SAVINGS BONDS		
SAVINGS	CREDIT UNION		
	BANK		
	OTHER		
MISCELLANEOUS	ALIMONY OR SUPPORT PAYMENTS *Ignored*		
	HOUSE AND APPLIANCE REPAIRS		
	Furniture	83.33	1,000

(STEP 3)   **(STEP 2) EXPENSES** $6,230.83 | $74,770
INCOME

WAGES	~~GROSS~~ WAGES *Roger, Imagined by Joan*	4,166.67	50,000
	~~OTHER WAGES~~		
	SPOUSE'S WAGES *Joan, Imagined by Roger*	2,083.33	25,000
ADDITIONAL INCOME	OTHER INCOME		

(STEP 4) TOTAL INCOME $6,250 | $75,000

Joan Harrison and Roger Sloan's Lifestyle Budget
If They'd Lived Within Their Actual Income

STEP 1

EXPENSES		MONTHLY	YEARLY
HOUSEHOLD	RENT OR MORTGAGE PAYMENT	350	4,000
	ELECTRIC		
	HEATING		
	WATER		
	TAXES		
	TELEPHONE	30	360
FOOD	FOOD/MILK	250	3,000
	SNACKS/MEALS AT WORK	60	720
CAR	GAS & OIL		
	REPAIRS, TIRES, ETC.		
	COMMUTATION (TOLLS, BUSES, SUBWAYS, PARKING)		
INSURANCE	HOSPITAL	33.33	400
	CAR		
	HOUSEHOLD		
	LIFE	83.33	1,000
PERSONAL	BARBER & BEAUTY SHOP	30	360
	ALLOWANCES (OTB, LOTTERY, ETC.) Grant, Jr.	20	240
	TOILETRIES	25	300
	CIGARETTES & TOBACCO		
MEDICAL	DOCTOR	37.50	450
	DENTIST	16.67	200
	DRUGS	4.17	50
CLOTHING	FAMILY	83.33	1,000
	CLEANING & LAUNDRY	20.83	250
GIFTS	BIRTHDAYS	20.83	250
	CHRISTMAS	20.83	250
	ALL OTHER	8.33	100
EDUCATION	TUITION & SCHOOL SUPPLIES		
	BOOKS, PAPERS, MAGAZINES and Equipment	29.17	350
DONATIONS	RELIGIOUS INSTITUTIONS		
	ALL OTHER		
ENTERTAINMENT	MOVIES & PLAYS	16.67	200
	DINNERS OUT	100	1,200
	PARTIES OUT	50	600
	CLUBS, SPORTS, HOBBIES	41.67	500
	BEVERAGES (LIQUOR, BEER, SODAS)	41.67	500
	VACATIONS	208.33	2,500
	BABY SITTER		
PAYROLL DEDUCTIONS	DUES — UNION & OTHER		
	SOCIAL SECURITY	75	900
	TOTAL INCOME TAXES (CITY, STATE AND FEDERAL)	975	14,700
	NUMBER EXEMPTIONS CLAIMED ( )		
	SAVINGS BONDS		
SAVINGS	CREDIT UNION		
	BANK		
	OTHER		
MISCELLANEOUS	ALIMONY OR SUPPORT PAYMENTS Deducted from Income		
	HOUSE AND APPLIANCE REPAIRS		
		41.67	500

STEP 2 **EXPENSES** $2,656.66 $31,880

STEP 3

INCOME			
WAGES	GROSS WAGES Roger	2,500	30,000
	OTHER WAGES		
	SPOUSE'S WAGES Support	416.67	5,000
ADDITIONAL INCOME	OTHER INCOME		

STEP 4 **TOTAL INCOME** $2,916.67 $35,000

Fantasy Budget (Continued)

Step 5	No Debt	
Step 6	No Debt	
Step 7	No Debt	
Step 8	Monthly Expense	$6,230.83
	Monthly Debt Payments	
	Total Monthly Expenses	$6,230.83
Step 9	Total Monthly Income	$6,250.00
	Total Monthly Expense	$6,230.83
	Monthly Surplus	$19.17*

* Even on a fantasy income of $75,000 a year, these two people could still scarcely save a twenty dollar bill.

Real Budget (Continued)

Step 5	$5,000 Bank Loan	$ 167.00
	$2800 Credit Cards	$ 100.00
Step 6	Total Monthly Payments	$ 267.00
Step 7	Total Amount Owed	$7,800
Step 8	Monthly Expense	$2,656.67
	Monthly Debt Payments	267.00
	Total Monthly Expenses	$2,923.67
Step 9	Total Monthly Income	$2,916.67
	Total Monthly Expense	2,923.67
	Monthly Deficit	(7.00)*

* A $7.00 per month deficit is equal to a balanced budget. But these two people were not prepared to live at the reduced scale that living within their means required.

The "Virgin" Bride and/or Groom

Another standard example of how a couple can scuttle their synergistic family is dramatically evident in the "Virgin" Bride or Groom syndrome. Here, either or both partners may choose to think and behave like virgin marriers. They ignore the fact that they live with economic polygamy, that there are other families to whom financial obligations are owed, and that this is definitely not a monogamous, first marriage. So—come hell or high water—these pseudo-virgin remarriers insist on having their own child.

Most often, the urge to give birth will blossom in a childless woman who married a man with children and feels cheated. Less often, but still common, the desire can erupt in a childless man who marries a woman with children and wants one of his "own flesh and blood." Least justifiable in terms of the realities is when the desire for a child overtakes remarriers who already have a considerable brood between them, and not nearly enough income to raise them all properly.

Genuinely virgin brides and grooms behave this way (never giving a second thought to the possible costs) despite the fact that the cost of raising a child is always high. A government study shows that on the average, the cost of raising one child to the age of eighteen, and that means prior to entering college, can range in the United States as high as $64,215. This figure does not reflect the lost opportunity costs or income deprived the family when the mother stays home to care for the child. Obviously even in first marriages, too many children can swamp the family in debt. In a remarriage, another child can be the last straw.

Having another child must never be done without careful financial planning ahead. It is a potent enough threat to a synergistic family when couples remain silent about their lifestyle expectations from remarriage. It is almost certain disaster if they are really financially unprepared and one of their fondest expectations is another child. Take the case of Joel Turner and Gale Slocum.

Joel Turner, 33, lawyer, earned $35,000 a year. Joel's first wife, Fleur, had been a beautiful flower of a girl who could do nothing for herself except write poetry and have children—bang! bang! bang! Because among the many things that Fleur could not do—which included how to boil water, make a bed, change a bulb, drive a car, sew a button on a shirt, get any-place on time—was also remembering to take the pill. So, after five years of marriage, during which three children were born, Fleur decided to have a breakdown. It was all too much.

When she recovered from her breakdown, she continued with her psychoanalysis—five times a week. These visits, plus the part-time mother's helper, was more than Joel could afford, so he went into hock at the bank to cover the costs. One evening, over their usual Swanson TV dinner—Fleur had given up any kind of cooking—she explained that she had made a breakthrough in her treatment. It had all become crystal clear. As a traditional wife and mother she was a washout. Psychologically she wasn't up to it. She was a lyric spirit who could not deal with that kind of responsibility. She must be free to follow where the Muse led her. At the moment, her Muse beckoned from California.

Joel took this in his stride. He braced himself because he knew there was more coming. He asked her what else the Muse had in mind. Clearly, she could not share a marriage bed or play with her children with 3,000 miles between them? It wasn't possible.

Fleur nodded her head. It wasn't possible. But it was a relief that Joel showed so much insight, and he must not worry. Fleur had worked it out for them. In the face of this dire emergency, something had to give. And what would give would be their marriage. Fleur would make the sacrifice. She suggested to Joel that he be thankful she knew her limitations, she was hardly an exemplary mother. It was she who absent-mindedly let the baby's bath flood the house, and it was she who accidently locked Peter in the closet.

Giving Fleur's psychological hang-ups due consideration, she and Dr. Breugel decided that the best all-around solution for everyone concerned was for Joel to give her a divorce. And a morsel of alimony. A little something to keep her going till she found herself. How much of a morsel? Joel wanted to know. Oh, about $350 a month, murmured Fleur, looking pained. Joel looked pained, too, and thought about things. At least it was less than he now paid per month to Dr. Breugel.

Joel told Fleur he'd give her an answer by the weekend. Meanwhile, he had to get back to work at the office. Fleur gave him a feathery kiss, the first kiss in months, and thanked him agitatedly for his kindness, his understanding, his tact. She looked like a child who didn't know why it was spanked. You'd think it was he, not she, who had asked for the divorce.

Driving to the office that night to pick up Gale Slocum and go on to the Sunshine Motel, Joel thought about Fleur and their marriage. The first year was bliss. The bliss started to vaporize when their first child, Peter, was born. With the second child, things really came unglued. The third child led to the break-down. Joel could remember coming home in the evening to unmade beds, dishes in the sink, screaming children, a weeping Fleur—it made him shudder to remember it all. But still . . . still. . . . He couldn't help himself. He was still in love with her. It hurt his pride and something deeper that she no longer wanted any part of him. Any part of their children. He'd known how it was for over a year, but he'd kept on hoping she'd change. What had happened to the loving girl he'd married? What had frightened that funny face? What had he done—or not done? Even as he put his arms around Gale, Fleur's smile drifted before his inner sight.

By the weekend, he knew it was no use. This chapter in his

Joel Turner's Lifestyle Budget

STEP 1
EXPENSES

		MONTHLY	YEARLY
HOUSEHOLD	~~RENT OR~~ MORTGAGE PAYMENT *and Taxes*	400	4,800
	ELECTRIC *House*	100	1,200
	~~HEATING~~		
	WATER *Well*	—	—
	TAXES	—	—
	TELEPHONE	25	300
FOOD	FOOD/MILK	300	3,600
	SNACKS/MEALS AT WORK	30	360
CAR	GAS & OIL		
	REPAIRS, TIRES, ETC.	—	—
	COMMUTATION (TOLLS, BUSES, SUBWAYS, PARKING)	43.33	520
INSURANCE	HOSPITAL *Free Blue Cross and Blue Shield.*	8.33	100
	CAR		
	HOUSEHOLD	—	—
	LIFE	25	300
PERSONAL	BARBER & BEAUTY SHOP	20	240
	ALLOWANCES (OTB, LOTTERY, ETC.)		
	TOILETRIES	16.67	200
	CIGARETTES & TOBACCO	—	
MEDICAL	DOCTOR *3 Young Children*	50	600
	DENTIST	20.83	250
	DRUGS	16.67	200
CLOTHING	FAMILY	62.50	750
	CLEANING & LAUNDRY *Home Clothes Washer*	20.83	250
GIFTS	BIRTHDAYS	8.33	100
	CHRISTMAS	8.33	100
	ALL OTHER	8.33	100
EDUCATION	TUITION & SCHOOL SUPPLIES		
	BOOKS, PAPERS, MAGAZINES *and Equipment.*	28.33	340
DONATIONS	RELIGIOUS INSTITUTIONS	8.33	100
	ALL OTHER	—	
ENTERTAINMENT	MOVIES & PLAYS	20	240
	DINNERS OUT	100	1,200
	PARTIES ~~OUT~~	—	—
	CLUBS, SPORTS, HOBBIES	20.83	250
	BEVERAGES (LIQUOR, BEER, SODAS)	33.33	400
	VACATIONS	125	1,500
	~~BABY SITTER~~ *Housekeeper*	500	6,000
PAYROLL DEDUCTIONS	DUES — UNION & OTHER		
	SOCIAL SECURITY	75	900
	TOTAL INCOME TAXES (CITY, STATE AND FEDERAL)	525	6,300
	NUMBER EXEMPTIONS CLAIMED ( )		
	SAVINGS BONDS		
SAVINGS	CREDIT UNION		
	BANK		
	OTHER		
MISCELLANEOUS	ALIMONY OR SUPPORT PAYMENTS	350	4,200
	HOUSE AND APPLIANCE REPAIRS	29.17	350

STEP 3
INCOME

STEP 2 EXPENSES $2,979.17 $35,750

WAGES	GROSS WAGES	2,916.67	35,000
	OTHER WAGES		
	SPOUSE'S WAGES		
ADDITIONAL INCOME	OTHER INCOME		

STEP 4 TOTAL INCOME $2,916.67 $35,000

Fleur were still in one piece. They were introduced at a fund-raising political dinner that Gale had engineered. Politics had the same appeal to Joel as sports have to other men. He enjoyed the rough and tumble as a relief from the computerized reasoning and hard negotiating that characterized his legal work. To Joel, Gale was a contradiction. She looked so small, fragile, helpless; and she was a powerhouse. It proved you never knew about people. Especially women. He estimated that from what she said about her job, she made at least $23,000 a year. Grudgingly, he admitted you had to hand it to her.

Gale Slocum was thirty when she met Joel, and two years older than he. As public relations director for a small insurance company, she made even more money than Joel calculated. Gale's husband, Bob Slocum, was a soft-spoken, sardonic intellectual who had a minor reputation around town as a photographer. At party headquarters he trailed after Gale spouting epigrams and amiability. Gale and Bob had been childhood sweethearts. Now, these many years later, they had an unspoken arrangement. They were good friends who would live and let live, not asking each other embarrassing questions, not about Gale's office relationships or Bob's artistic friends. After a social outing together, they still liked to sit up till dawn dissecting and vilifying the character of everyone present.

The evening Gale first saw Joel, something clicked. Her nerve ends exploded. She liked big, raw-boned men and usually they liked her. Moreover, he resembled Sam Paley, her sponsor in the company, the man who'd seen to it that her talents were recognized long before there was an EEO. She knew Sam would never leave his wife, and when it came down to it, Gale had never wanted him to. He was too old for that. There was a twenty-five-year gap between them. In a few years Sam would be put out to pasture. Gale would then have been the wife of his retirement, not his power years. Sam was an important man, but he was no William O. Douglas. The prospect of Sam's declining years had no appeal for Gale. It kept her fantasies in check. Joel was more to the point of what she was looking for. Smart, ambitious, a driving young lawyer. One way or another he would make it. She had learned the hard way to identify the type. Having paid the bills for years for a charming, talented man who only occasionally earned his keep, there was nothing Gale wanted more than to be the wife of a successful man.

Fleur arrived at the fund-raising dinner just before the end—Fleur being always late—and upset Gale's dreaming. The look on Joel's face when he saw Fleur informed Gale that she was wasting time. It was too bad, too, because she and Joel had understood each other. He was a high I.Q. man and she was a high I.Q. woman. They both had broad-gauge minds and educated opinions on a wide range of subjects. Meanwhile, there was that undercurrent of chemistry between them, adding a subtle dimension to their talk.

When Fleur arrived, the transmission switched off. Like a sudden current break. Not that Joel lost interest in Gale. No, he was interested and he knew he was interested. But Fleur came first. Gale could always face unpleasant facts.

Over the years, as Gale and Joel saw each other again and again at political meetings, she wondered what Fleur's hold was. Yes, Fleur was exceptionally pretty: long dark hair, baby skin, luminous eyes. But Fleur did not live in this world. She was somewhere else. What was a man like Joel, with a future to build—she was convinced he had a big future if he played it right—doing married to a pixie? Someone who lived six inches off the ground? Maybe she was a great whore in bed. Gale thought about it a lot, and that was her only answer. She did not ask Bob for his comments.

It must have been about two years after they met that Joel started coming and going from meetings alone. Fleur never came anymore. Not even in time to go home with Joel the way she used to do. That was Gale's cue. Ever since the first evening, she'd kept her distance politely. There was no sense spending energy unless there was an even chance of winning. Now, in-

Gale and Bob Slocum's Lifestyle Budget

STEP 1
EXPENSES

Category	Item	MONTHLY	YEARLY
HOUSEHOLD	RENT OR MORTGAGE PAYMENT	300	3,600
	ELECTRIC	50	600
	HEATING	75	900
	WATER	20	240
	TAXES	83.33	1,000
	TELEPHONE	50	600
FOOD	FOOD/MILK	150	1,800
	SNACKS/MEALS AT WORK	100	1,200
CAR	GAS & OIL		
	REPAIRS, TIRES, ETC.		
	COMMUTATION (TOLLS, BUSES, SUBWAYS, PARKING)		
INSURANCE	HOSPITAL *Free Blue Cross and Blue Shield*	—	—
	CAR		
	HOUSEHOLD	25	300
	LIFE		
PERSONAL	BARBER & BEAUTY SHOP	60	720
	ALLOWANCES (OTB, LOTTERY, ETC.)		
	TOILETRIES	30	360
	CIGARETTES & TOBACCO	41.67	500
MEDICAL	DOCTOR	25	300
	DENTIST	8.33	100
	DRUGS	4.17	50
CLOTHING	FAMILY	150	1,800
	CLEANING & LAUNDRY	30	360
GIFTS	BIRTHDAYS	20.83	250
	CHRISTMAS	8.33	100
	ALL OTHER	16.67	200
EDUCATION	TUITION & SCHOOL SUPPLIES		
	BOOKS, PAPERS, MAGAZINES *and Equipment (Deductible)*	145.83	1,750
DONATIONS	RELIGIOUS INSTITUTIONS	—	—
	ALL OTHER		
ENTERTAINMENT	MOVIES & PLAYS	41.67	500
	DINNERS OUT *(Deductible)*	150	1,800
	PARTIES ~~OUT~~ *(Deductible)*	200	2,400
	CLUBS, SPORTS, HOBBIES	100	1,200
	BEVERAGES (LIQUOR, BEER, SODAS)	168	2,000
	VACATIONS	416.67	5,000
	BABY SITTER	—	—
PAYROLL DEDUCTIONS	DUES — UNION & OTHER	—	—
	SOCIAL SECURITY	141.67	1,700
	TOTAL INCOME TAXES (CITY, STATE AND FEDERAL)	916.67	11,000
	NUMBER EXEMPTIONS CLAIMED ( )		
	SAVINGS BONDS		
SAVINGS	CREDIT UNION		
	BANK		
	OTHER		
MISCELLANEOUS	ALIMONY OR SUPPORT PAYMENTS		
	HOUSE AND APPLIANCE REPAIRS	166.67	2,000

STEP 3
INCOME

STEP 2 **EXPENSES** $3,694.17 $44,330

Category	Item	MONTHLY	YEARLY
WAGES	GROSS WAGES	2,500	30,000
	~~OTHER WAGES~~		
	SPOUSE'S WAGES	1,333.33	16,000
ADDITIONAL INCOME	OTHER INCOME		

STEP 4 **TOTAL INCOME** $3,833.33 $46,000

(Continued)

Step 5	No Debts	
Step 6	No Debts	
Step 7	No Debts	
Step 8	Monthly Expense	$3,694.17
	Total Monthly Debts	
	Total Monthly Expenses	$3,694.17
Step 9	Total Monthly Income	$3,833.33
	Total Monthly Expenses	$3,694.17
	Monthly Surplus	$ 139.16 *

* In these days of rising costs, for a childless couple with two incomes to save almost $2000 a year is still a neat accomplishment. If Gale and Bob had stayed together they would have built a nice nest egg for investment.

stinctively she sensed a change in the odds. She decided to re-open their dialogue. "Joel, is that your firm handling the Union Glass negotiation?"

When Joel and Gale started seeing each other intimately, Gale was earning $30,000 a year and Bob, her husband, was making $16,000. Gale and Bob had no children. Originally, this happened by choice. They were young. They enjoyed each other's company. They had other things to do. There was time for children. Later, when Gale wanted children, it was too late. The intensity of their sexual relationship had cooled and Bob's kinky sexual tastes surfaced. Gale had never seen herself as becoming a childless woman. The idea conflicted with her self-image. Yet she wryly acknowledged she could hardly insist on her "connubial rights." That wouldn't do. But things change. She felt she was still young enough to look around at her leisure. Meanwhile, their marriage was a pleasant, comfortable convenience for both of them. (Their lifestyle expenses are shown on pages 88 and 89.)

After the divorce between Joel and Fleur became final, Joel and Gale had a sudden, frequent need to explain themselves to each other. The recurrent phrase was, "I understand how you feel, but. . . ." Sometimes during these excursions into self-examination, they would fall into silence. A trap door had opened up under their common meeting ground of rationality, and there was nothing more to say.

For Gale, it all came down to one threatening, unforeseen fact. Joel strenuously opposed her asking Bob for a divorce on his account. He wanted no part of it, and he would make no commitment. He liked Bob Slocum and he did not relish the picture of himself as a homebreaker. Actually, he was quite content with the status quo. He was still too wounded over the loss of Fleur to be ready to trust another commitment. And knowing nothing about the realities of the Slocum marriage, the one, ominous resemblance Gale had to Fleur was her willingness to leave her husband.

There was also a shallowness in his feeling. Joel was not convinced Gale was a woman he'd want for life. There was something about her—he could not put his finger on it, except to tell himself they were a little too much alike. There was no poetry. She would never talk to a bird or a rose bush and be convinced she was understood. If the bush flourished, Gale would assign the reason to soil and sun. As would he. Fleur would have seen other reasons. Fleur was a little mad, but in a way that was all right. It put Joel in touch with a more imaginative, playful reality. It was enough that he was competent and super rational. What would it be like with two rational people living in the same house? Joel wasn't sure he liked the prospect.

Gale felt Joel's cautious withdrawal. Through the maze of self-explanations, she had come to understand Fleur's hold on him. He actually liked that fey temperament. If Gale didn't watch her plays, Joel might just bump into another "crazy."

She took a deep breath and placed her chips on the table. She would ask Bob for a divorce without telling Joel.

Bob had known for a year that something was going on with Gale, and he was reasonably certain Joel was the man. But since Gale hadn't brought it up, Bob didn't either. What had worked in their marriage was that they respected each other's privacy. If the fire between Joel and Gale blew out—fine! If it didn't blow out, Bob would know soon enough. Sufficient unto the day, was his motto. Or why borrow trouble, was another thought. While he waited, he had the summer house to think about and work on, which of course he would insist on having as part of a divorce agreement if Gale happened to ask for a divorce. He also had his reading, his fishing, his photography, and his own friends. He was never unoccupied and seldom alone. So he was hardly dismayed when the subject came up.

Gale and Bob were working on staining and waxing the dining room floor of the summer house when Gale mentioned divorce. Seven hours later, after they had finished restoring the fine, old oak, as they sat sipping wine and admiring their handiwork, they settled the division of property. Everything was neatly tied up, and with no anguish. They would always be close friends. The summer house, as Bob had expected, was now entirely his.

Gale went to Mexico to get her divorce and told Joel she was going to Detroit on business. Gale did travel occasionally for the company, so Joel accepted the lie. Even if he had known the truth, he could not have stopped her.

When she returned, she told Joel she was divorced, and Joel knew that he'd been mouse-trapped. In good faith, he saw no way to avoid asking her to marry him. So he tried to look at the bright side. Think of the added income. Certainly two incomes would be better than one when it came to raising three children. This last fact he neglected to mention to Gale. But frequently before he fell asleep at night, he would drowse pleasantly over the prospect of Gale's income (see pages 92 and 93) and how it would improve the quality of his life.

Gale Slocum Turner felt about Joel a passion she had never

Joel Turner's Dream Lifestyle Budget

STEP 1
EXPENSES

		MONTHLY	YEARLY
HOUSEHOLD	RENT OR MORTGAGE PAYMENT *and Taxes*	400	4,800
	ELECTRIC *House*	100	1,200
	HEATING		
	WATER *Well*		
	TAXES		
	TELEPHONE	50	600
FOOD	FOOD/MILK	400	4,800
	SNACKS/MEALS AT WORK	200	2,400
CAR	GAS & OIL	30	360
	REPAIRS, TIRES, ETC.	50	600
	COMMUTATION (TOLLS, BUSES, SUBWAYS, PARKING)	20	240
INSURANCE	HOSPITAL *Free Blue Cross and Blue Shield*	8.33	100
	CAR	20.83	250
	HOUSEHOLD	16.67	200
	LIFE	41.67	500
PERSONAL	BARBER & BEAUTY SHOP	60	720
	ALLOWANCES (OTB, LOTTERY, ETC.)	20	240
	TOILETRIES	30	360
	CIGARETTES & TOBACCO		
MEDICAL	DOCTOR *3 Children*	62.50	750
	DENTIST	29.17	350
	DRUGS	16.67	200
CLOTHING	FAMILY	150	1,800
	CLEANING & LAUNDRY *Home Clothes Washer*	30	360
GIFTS	BIRTHDAYS	20	240
	CHRISTMAS	30	360
	ALL OTHER	30	360
EDUCATION	TUITION & SCHOOL SUPPLIES		
	BOOKS, PAPERS, MAGAZINES *and Equipment*	61.67	740
DONATIONS	RELIGIOUS INSTITUTIONS	20.83	250
	ALL OTHER	20.83	250
ENTERTAINMENT	MOVIES & PLAYS	83.33	1,000
	DINNERS OUT	200	2,400
	PARTIES ~~OUT~~	200	2,400
	CLUBS, SPORTS, HOBBIES *Political*	125	1,500
	BEVERAGES (LIQUOR, BEER, SODAS)	60	720
	VACATIONS *Summer Home and Camps*	458.33	5,500
	BABY SITTER *and Housekeeper*	500	6,000
PAYROLL DEDUCTIONS	DUES — UNION & OTHER		
	SOCIAL SECURITY	150	1,800
	TOTAL INCOME TAXES (CITY, STATE AND FEDERAL)	1,575	18,900
	NUMBER EXEMPTIONS CLAIMED ( )		
	SAVINGS BONDS		
SAVINGS	CREDIT UNION		
	BANK		
	OTHER		
MISCELLANEOUS	ALIMONY OR SUPPORT PAYMENTS	350	4,200
	HOUSE AND APPLIANCE REPAIRS *and Furniture*	83.33	1,000

STEP 3
STEP 2 EXPENSES $5,709.17 $68,450

INCOME

WAGES	GROSS WAGES	2,916.67	35,000
	~~OTHER WAGES~~		
	SPOUSE'S WAGES	2,500	30,000
ADDITIONAL INCOME	OTHER INCOME		

STEP 4 TOTAL INCOME $5,416.67 $65,000

(Continued)

Step 5	Bank Debt $10,000 (Interest only) Credit Cards and Charge Accounts $3000 (He wanted to clean them up in one year)	$ 100 250
Step 6	Total Monthly Payments in debt and interest	$ 350
Step 7	Total Amount Owed	$13,000
Step 8	Monthly Expense Total Monthly Debt Payments	$ 5,704.17 350.00
	Total Monthly Expenses	$ 6,054.17
Step 9	Total Monthly Income Total Monthly Expenses	$ 5,416.67 6,054.17
	Monthly Deficit	($637.50)*

* A second bank loan would be needed to cover this deficit until Joel's rising income caught up with the rising expenses of his dreams.

felt for Bob. It pleased her to realize this. Perhaps, she thought to herself, it's because I am more mature, more experienced, and more capable of deep feelings. She was glad now that she had not had a child with Bob. It made her marriage to Joel seem more like a first marriage. Now more than anything she wanted Joel's child. So as with the divorce, she decided to become pregnant without telling Joel.

She waited until two weeks after they returned from their honeymoon to tell Joel. When she broke the glad news, Joel was aghast.

"Good Lord! You have to have an abortion," said Joel.

"Oh no, it's too late." Gale was puzzled. "And anyway, I want the baby. I thought you loved children."

Gale and Joel Turner's Actual Budget

STEP 1
EXPENSES

		MONTHLY	YEARLY
HOUSEHOLD	RENT OR MORTGAGE PAYMENT	400	4,800
	ELECTRIC *House*	100	1,200
	~~HEATING~~		
	WATER *Well*		
	TAXES		
	TELEPHONE	35	420
FOOD	FOOD/MILK	350	4,200
	SNACKS/MEALS AT WORK	20	240
CAR	GAS & OIL		
	REPAIRS, TIRES, ETC.		
	COMMUTATION (TOLLS, BUSES, SUBWAYS, PARKING)		
INSURANCE	HOSPITAL *Free Blue Cross and Blue Shield*	8.33	100
	CAR		
	HOUSEHOLD	16.67	200
	LIFE	25	300
PERSONAL	BARBER & BEAUTY SHOP	40	480
	ALLOWANCES (OTB, LOTTERY, ETC.)		
	TOILETRIES	20	240
	CIGARETTES & TOBACCO		
MEDICAL	DOCTOR *3 Children and Pregnant Wife*	83.33	1,000
	DENTIST	16.67	200
	DRUGS	8.33	100
CLOTHING	FAMILY	50	600
	CLEANING & LAUNDRY *Washing machine*	30	360
GIFTS	BIRTHDAYS	12.50	150
	CHRISTMAS	8.33	100
	ALL OTHER	16.67	200
EDUCATION	TUITION & SCHOOL SUPPLIES		
	BOOKS, PAPERS, MAGAZINES *and Equipment*	20	240
DONATIONS	RELIGIOUS INSTITUTIONS		
	ALL OTHER		
ENTERTAINMENT	MOVIES & PLAYS	30	360
	DINNERS OUT	50	600
	PARTIES ~~OUT~~	50	600
	CLUBS, SPORTS, HOBBIES		
	BEVERAGES (LIQUOR, BEER, SODAS)	50	600
	VACATIONS *Camp*	150	1,800
	BABY SITTER *Part Time*	250	3,000
PAYROLL DEDUCTIONS	DUES — UNION & OTHER		
	SOCIAL SECURITY	75	900
	TOTAL INCOME TAXES (CITY, STATE AND FEDERAL)	500	6,000
	NUMBER EXEMPTIONS CLAIMED ( )		
	SAVINGS BONDS		
SAVINGS	CREDIT UNION		
	BANK		
	OTHER		
MISCELLANEOUS	ALIMONY OR SUPPORT PAYMENTS	350	4,200
	HOUSE AND APPLIANCE REPAIRS *and Furniture*	60	720

STEP 3

STEP 2 **EXPENSES** | $2,825.83 | $33,910

INCOME

WAGES	GROSS WAGES		
	OTHER WAGES		
	SPOUSE'S WAGES		
ADDITIONAL INCOME	OTHER INCOME		

STEP 4 **TOTAL INCOME** | $2,916.67 | $35,000

(Continued)

Step 5	Bank Debt—$10,000 (Interest only)	$ 100
	Credit Cards and Charge Accounts—$3000	150
Step 6	Total Monthly Debt Payments	$ 250
Step 7	Total Amount Owed	$13,000
Step 8	Monthly Expense	$ 2,825.83
	Monthly Debt Payments	250.00
	Total Monthly Expenses	$ 3,075.83
Step 9	Total Monthly Income	$ 2,916.67
	Total Monthly Expenses	3,075.83
	Monthly Deficit	($ 159.16)*

*About $160.00 per month can be saved in many ways, so this budget can be considered as being in balance. However, no expenses have been allotted for the children's future schooling. And, as it is, living within this budget was hardly Joel's or Gale's dream life.

"We can't afford another child. You won't be able to work if you have the baby."

"I don't intend to work. I gave my resignation a month ago."

"You what?"

"I quit. I want to stay home and be a real wife to you, and a mother to your children. The way Fleur wasn't."

"You're a grown woman. A working woman. You can balance a checkbook. You know we can't afford another child. As it is, I thought your income would help with the children we already have."

"You said yourself that after taxes your take-home from the partnership is $28,000 and going up. Why wouldn't that cover our expenses?" Gale was as angry as she'd ever been and trying not to show it.

"Because Allan will be ready for preschool next fall. That's

$1,500 a year. Frostie has to be put in nursery school. Another $750 a year. And Mamie, the housekeeper who also takes care of the baby, is not cheap—$6,000 a year. And then there's alimony."

"I can take care of Ariel now."

"And clean the kitchen? And dust and mop the bedroom? And polish furniture?"

"Sure."

"Can you get your job back?"

"I just finished training Rosemary for the promotion they gave her to fill it."

"What a mess," said Joel, sitting down with his head in his hands. (For a look at their actual budget, if they had lived within their income, see pages 94 and 95.)

After the dust settled, Joel accepted the additional economic burden, and buried his resentment in longer hours of work. He took on two outside clients to increase his income. Some evenings he came home at midnight and went straight to sleep exhausted. With a new baby coming, Joel found that he was running to stay in place financially, and that his feelings about Gale were mixed.

In the months that followed, while waiting for the baby, Gale had a lot of time to think about motherhood. At first, she enjoyed the novelty of housekeeping and taking care of her new children. They were lively and loving and young enough to accept her as Mama. Days would pass with them and she'd never think of Fleur.

But age thirty-seven is not the best time to start playing full-time Mama to three young children going like engines all day. Once the novelty wore off, Gale found that, much as she cared for them, they were more of a drain on her energy than any job had ever been. Now even the idea of her own baby was less appealing.

Then, too, Joel was getting to her. They spoke very little about the coming baby; in fact, they didn't talk much at all.

The one pleasant evening they had in months came when Gale told Joel her old office had phoned to ask advice. Joel was delighted. Gale was privately furious. She knew Joel bitterly resented her loading him with another fatherhood role. She knew he deeply wanted her to go back to work. But she could be stubborn, too. She was going to be her idea of a wife—the elegant hostess, the charming mother, the power behind the throne. She was going to stay home with the children, though she hated it. She knew very well Joel could not afford another divorce.

One evening, two months after Jenny was born, Joel telephoned and told Gale he was staying downtown for a political meeting, to have dinner without him. He'd be late. Gale hung up the phone and thought about that. She decided to surprise Joel and join him at the meeting. She telephoned Nancy, their once-in-a-blue-moon babysitter, and then changed into her clingiest pre-Jenny wool dress.

When Gale got to the meeting, she spotted Joel standing at the back of the room. Next to him was a slender, dark-haired girl who was talking a mile a minute. Unobserved, Gale watched Joel's attentive smiling face. It gave her a small chill —he used to listen to her that way. But this was Joel's first political meeting in a year—the look didn't mean a thing.

At first, Joel was startled, then he seemed genuinely pleased to see Gale. He introduced the girl beside him. "Carter, this is my wife Gale." He turned to Gale. "You've heard me mention Carter, our new junior partner?"

Gale nodded, looking carefully at Carter. Joel had mentioned her once, omitting to say she was female.

The next day Gale gave up the war. She called the Child Care Agency and asked them to start putting together applicants for her to interview. What she wanted was a full-time housekeeper who could also deal with very young children. The next six telephone calls were made to friends in the business to tell them she was looking for a job.

That evening when Joel came home at midnight, Gale was waiting up for him. When she told him about her job hunt his tired face lit up. He leaned over and hugged her. Then he studied her.

"How come you changed your mind Gale? About working?"

Gale Slocum Turner, otherwise rational, had become irrational when she married Joel. In her unconscious, she could not face the fact of Fleur, Fleur's children, and Joel's economic polygamy. In Gale's fantasy life, this marriage was to make up for everything she thought she'd missed in her first marriage. This included children. Gale never stopped to think how much money children cost, or that the loss of her earnings plus the addition of one more child would inevitably mean that the Turners would have to exchange their standard of living for a less comfortable one. That's a high price to pay for a fantasy image of being a "Virgin" Bride married to a "Virgin" Groom. It's the kind of financial decision that should be made by two people together, not by one blackmailing the other emotionally.

I am not exactly sure how a man can say to a woman, or a woman to a man, "By the way, I am depending on your stock investments to buy the house . . ." or, "Life will be a lot easier when we have two incomes instead of one . . ." or, "You do understand, don't you, that we cannot afford another child."

I am not sure how to say it; I am only sure it has to be said. These are the kind of things people have to talk about to each other before they get remarried.

The Affluent Ex

While unwillingness to look at the consequences of economic polygamy can cause all manner of down-scale lifestyle shifts, the opposite can also occur. A man or woman can remarry into money and have unexpectedly available a long checklist of new luxuries. There are sensible souls who take to their unforeseen comforts enthusiastically and live happily ever after. There are, oddly enough, as many who don't; and because they don't, they illustrate ironically by the perversity of their responses how psychologically charged money is, and how reluctant we are to live with our economic polygamy. Even when it is to our benefit.

I know a very pretty, mid-thirties woman who remarried, after many years of extreme financial pressure, a wealthy real estate developer. Having never had enough of anything all her prior married life, she now had everything. But rather than enjoying everything, she proceeded after remarriage to make her new husband miserable by her hostile attitude toward any monies spent on his ex-wife and children. Every dollar not spent on her, even though she was hardly deprived, made her violently jealous. She once said to me that she would have cared less if he'd been sexually unfaithful. Clearly, for this woman, marriage was a matter primarily of economic monogamy. Eventually, they were divorced.

A similar situation can occur when a man with a limited income remarries a divorced woman with an affluent ex-husband who, for reasons of his own, stays very much around. Such was the conflict that arose between Emily and Hank Palmer because Hank could not accept Emily's ex-husband's generous economic polygamy.

Though the animal is rare, there are ex-husbands who are generous to a fault. They have reasons. Sometimes these reasons are questionable, sometimes not. It depends on the husband. In the case of Eric Jensen, the reasons were questionable. Through the manipulative use of his monies, Eric managed to effectively dominate the life of his ex-wife, Emily, her second husband, Hank Palmer, and their entire household, including Hank's children as well as Eric's own.

Emily Jensen, originally Emily Anderson, a young woman

from Keokuk, Iowa, moved to Chicago after graduating from the University of Wisconsin. In Chicago she went to work in the computer training program of a bank. Her long, elegant legs attracted the notice of Eric Jensen, a supervisor in the commodities department of the bank. Eric also liked her smile. And later he added competence and warmth to her lists of assets. After a six-month probation period, he decided she would make an excellent mother for his children-to-be. Good stock.

A month after Eric and Emily were married, Eric announced to Emily that he had resigned from the bank, that he was joining a brokerage house as a commodities trader. If it had been me, I'd have been on the ceiling. Anxious. Insomniac. Banks are secure. The commodities desk of a brokerage house can't compare with a bank when it comes to security. Furthermore, I like to be consulted, "in on things." Emily wasn't on the ceiling. She wasn't anxious or insomniac. And she didn't have to be consulted. She trusted Eric's business judgment. Deep down she probably even trusted commodities. After all, she was born in Iowa. She turned out to be right.

As the years passed, Eric showed himself to be a shrewd, nerveless commodities trader. He made a fortune exercising his judgment on what the weather, domestic politics, foreign wars, and labor strikes would do to crop prices. Eric was a comer. He was also a good husband. That's what Emily told herself at night. Didn't he provide her with all the comforts of life? Wasn't he unstintingly affectionate to their two beautiful children? What if they made love less and less and less? Emily was mature enough to know that all marriages have flaws. Nothing is perfect. Emily was mature, tranquil, and accepting. I have a more suspicious nature. This time I would be right.

Eric was a man who had one set of rules for himself and another for you and me and everybody—including Emily. Eric had been regularly unfaithful to Emily since the week they returned from their honeymoon. Not because he was bored or experiencing satyriasis. No, it was just the way he saw things. On the other hand, he expected Emily to be, like Caesar's wife, beyond reproach. That she *was* beyond reproach was a constant source of bemused fascination to him. Of course, it was not her offhand report of her daily doings that convinced him, or his own scrupulous reading of her character. A man more vain might have settled for that kind of chancy data. Eric took nothing at face value. Rather, so rare and remarkable did he consider her behavior that he had it confirmed regularly with semiannual spot checks done by a private detective agency. The agency reports of Emily's impeccable fidelity inbued Eric for years with a curious feeling of awe. As well as a surprised satisfaction with his good sense in choosing her. She did have the best legs he'd ever seen.

She had other virtues, too. He respected her ability to manage a comfortable home, to be a radiant hostess as well as the loving and dirty-faced mother of Peter, 11 and Inge, 9. Perhaps because of his own proclivities, Eric Jensen was a firm believer in Küche, Kirche, and Kinder.

Then security made Eric sloppy. Returning from Los Angeles, instead of unpacking himself, he absentmindedly let Emily unpack his suitcase. Stuffed in under his shirts between the dirty laundry and socks Emily found the answer she had not known she was looking for—an encyclopedic address book of names, vital statistics, and telephone numbers of bedrooms around the country.

It took her only one month of visits to a psychiatrist to recover from the blow to her ego. It took another month to realize she had not loved Eric for years. A third month to decide she wanted a divorce. She suggested this option to Eric, who suggested she was overreacting. He stuck to his story. The address book was the firm's property. Not his. A business tool. Nothing else. Emily didn't understand the way money was made.

When Eric reached his office that morning, he checked his

Emily Jensen's Lifestyle Budget

STEP 1

EXPENSES		MONTHLY	YEARLY
HOUSEHOLD	RENT OR MORTGAGE PAYMENT		
	ELECTRIC	60	720
	HEATING	75	900
	WATER	20	240
	TAXES	120	1,440
	TELEPHONE	75	900
FOOD	FOOD/MILK	360	4,200
	SNACKS/MEALS AT WORK		
CAR	GAS & OIL	40	480
	REPAIRS, TIRES, ETC.	20	240
	COMMUTATION (TOLLS, BUSES, SUBWAYS, PARKING)		
INSURANCE	HOSPITAL *Paid for Blue Cross and Blue Shield*		
	CAR	40	480
	HOUSEHOLD	30	360
	LIFE		
PERSONAL	BARBER & BEAUTY SHOP	100	1,200
	ALLOWANCES (OTB, LOTTERY, ETC.)	30	360
	TOILETRIES	50	600
	CIGARETTES & TOBACCO		
MEDICAL	DOCTOR	41.67	500
	DENTIST	16.67	200
	DRUGS	12.50	150
CLOTHING	FAMILY	200	2,400
	CLEANING & LAUNDRY	50	600
GIFTS	BIRTHDAYS	33.33	400
	CHRISTMAS	20.83	250
	ALL OTHER	20.83	250
EDUCATION	TUITION & SCHOOL SUPPLIES	416.67	5,000
	BOOKS, PAPERS, MAGAZINES	10	120
DONATIONS	RELIGIOUS INSTITUTIONS	16.67	200
	ALL OTHER	16.67	200
ENTERTAINMENT	MOVIES & PLAYS	41.67	500
	DINNERS OUT	200	2,400
	PARTIES OUT	100	1,200
	CLUBS, SPORTS, HOBBIES	100	1,200
	BEVERAGES (LIQUOR, BEER, SODAS)	41.67	500
	VACATIONS	250	3,000
	BABY SITTER *Paid by Ex*		
PAYROLL DEDUCTIONS	DUES — UNION & OTHER		
	SOCIAL SECURITY		
	TOTAL INCOME TAXES (CITY, STATE AND FEDERAL)	416.67	5,000
	NUMBER EXEMPTIONS CLAIMED ( )		
	SAVINGS BONDS		
SAVINGS	CREDIT UNION		
	BANK		
	OTHER		
MISCELLANEOUS	ALIMONY OR SUPPORT PAYMENTS		
	HOUSE AND APPLIANCE REPAIRS *and Furniture*	125	1,500

STEP 2 **EXPENSES** $3,140.83 | $37,690

STEP 3

INCOME			
WAGES	GROSS WAGES *alimony*	2,083.33	25,000
	OTHER WAGES *support*	2,083.34	25,000
	SPOUSE'S WAGES		
ADDITIONAL INCOME	OTHER INCOME		

STEP 4 **TOTAL INCOME** $4,166.67 | $50,000

(Continued)

Step 5	No Debt	
Step 6	No Debt	
Step 7	No Debt	
Step 8	Monthly Expense	$3,140.83
	Monthly Debt Payment	
	Total Monthly Expenses	$3,140.83
Step 9	Total Monthly Income	$4,166.67
	Total Monthly Expense	3,140.83
	Monthly Surplus	$1,025.84 *

* Emily Jensen just couldn't spend the money at her disposal. This was so planned by her ex.

wall safe for contents. When he came home that night, he refused to discuss the subject any further. After that, he covered his tracks like any other trained professional.

Emily Anderson Jensen was not the daughter of Iowa farmers for nothing. She watched the skies and waited. Finally, she confronted him. One twilight Emily opened the door on Eric and Juliana Beck, Inge's new piano teacher, asleep in a hotel bed. Under severe pressure, Eric finally agreed to give Emily the divorce she had asked for three years before. So ended a marriage of mixed blessings.

Eric was a promiscuous man, but he was neither stingy nor naive. He could afford to be generous, so he was. He had his reasons. He gave Emily the mortgage-free house, the furnishings, the Buick station wagon, and $6,000 a year for Maria, the housekeeper. He gave Inge the summer house on Lake Michigan and Peter the sailboat. He gave Emily $25,000 a year in alimony in perpetuity plus $25,000 a year in child support. Eric knew all about money, and he wanted his children never to forget their father. He kept for himself the collection of paintings and sculpture and the country club membership. Three years after the divorce, Emily's lifestyle was much the same as when she and Eric were married. Except, of course, that a few married friends dropped her. And she was even oftener alone in bed than before. (See Emily's lifestyle expenses on pages 102 and 103.)

Two years after the divorce, Emily met Hank Palmer, a physicist earning $20,000 a year whose specialty was designing MOS chips to go into micro-processors. He was not much like Eric, who was short, thin-haired, and looked more like a scientist than did Hank, who was tall and looked like an athlete. Eric was interested in money, politics, and women, in that order. Hank paid some attention to money, more to politics, a lot to his work. But music was his passion. Women fitted in somewhere between symphonies. By his own admission, he was an expert on Mozart and hi-fi and spent a lot of time arguing with other physicists about which of Bach's sons was the greater musician—Carl Philipp Emanuel Bach or Johann Christian Bach. And though at his age he could hear no higher than 13,000 cycles, his hi-fi equipment was made to hit 22,000 cycles of clean sound. For Hank, hi-fi replaced the automobile as a sex symbol.

Actually, it was his ear that led Hank to Emily. He noticed her on the tennis court at a Caribbean resort when the ping of her tennis racket made his head oscillate. It pinged at an A flat instead of a B flat, and when Emily agreed to restring her racket, their future was settled. Hank had taken his son, Doug, to the resort for a Christmas holiday on a special low-price seven-day package deal. The afternoon Hank and Doug arrived on the courts, Emily, Peter, and Inge were playing mixed doubles and talking about going home. They had already had five days in the sun, but Eric's generous money gave them options. Go this evening? Go tomorrow? The next day? It was an open question. When Peter wanted to stay to play tennis

Hank Palmer's Lifestyle Budget

(STEP 1)

EXPENSES		MONTHLY	YEARLY
HOUSEHOLD	RENT OR MORTGAGE PAYMENT	250	3,000
	ELECTRIC	40	480
	HEATING		
	WATER		
	TAXES		
	TELEPHONE	41.66	500
FOOD	FOOD/MILK	125	1,500
	SNACKS/MEALS AT WORK	40	480
CAR	GAS & OIL		
	REPAIRS, TIRES, ETC.		
	COMMUTATION (TOLLS, BUSES, SUBWAYS, PARKING)		
INSURANCE	HOSPITAL *Blue Cross, Blue Shield & Major Med.*		
	CAR		
	HOUSEHOLD		
	LIFE	20.83	250
PERSONAL	BARBER & BEAUTY SHOP	10	120
	ALLOWANCES (OTB, LOTTERY, ETC.)	25	300
	TOILETRIES	5	60
	CIGARETTES & TOBACCO		
MEDICAL	DOCTOR	8.33	100
	DENTIST	4.17	50
	DRUGS	4.17	50
CLOTHING	FAMILY	33.33	400
	CLEANING & LAUNDRY	12.50	150
GIFTS	BIRTHDAYS	4.17	50
	CHRISTMAS	6.25	75
	ALL OTHER		
EDUCATION	TUITION & SCHOOL SUPPLIES		
	BOOKS, PAPERS, MAGAZINES	20.83	250
DONATIONS	RELIGIOUS INSTITUTIONS		
	ALL OTHER		
ENTERTAINMENT	MOVIES & PLAYS	20.83	250
	DINNERS OUT	62.50	750
	PARTIES OUT	25	300
	CLUBS, SPORTS, HOBBIES	83.33	1,000
	BEVERAGES (LIQUOR, BEER, SODAS)	20.83	250
	VACATIONS	83.33	1,000
	BABY SITTER		
PAYROLL DEDUCTIONS	DUES — UNION & OTHER		
	SOCIAL SECURITY	75	900
	TOTAL INCOME TAXES (CITY, STATE AND FEDERAL)	308.33	3,700
	NUMBER EXEMPTIONS CLAIMED ( )		
	SAVINGS BONDS		
SAVINGS	CREDIT UNION		
	BANK		
	OTHER		
MISCELLANEOUS	ALIMONY OR SUPPORT PAYMENTS	300	3,600
	HOUSE AND APPLIANCE REPAIRS		
	(STEP 2) EXPENSES	$1,630.42	$19,565

(STEP 3)

INCOME			
WAGES	GROSS WAGES	1,666.67	20,000
	OTHER WAGES		
	SPOUSE'S WAGES		
ADDITIONAL INCOME	OTHER INCOME		
	(STEP 4) TOTAL INCOME	$1,666.67	$20,000

(Continued)

Step 5	No Debt	
Step 6	No Debt	
Step 7	No Debt	
Step 8	Monthly Expense Monthly Debt Payments	$1,630
	Total Monthly Expense	$1,630.42
Step 9	Total Monthly Income Total Monthly Expense	$1,666.67 1,630.42
	Monthly Surplus	$ 36.25 *

* Hank Palmer, a frugal man, and a mathematician, had no trouble living within his means—limited though they were.

with Doug, Emily agreed. What was another few days to the Jensens? Nothing.

New Year's Day, both families flew back to Chicago comfortably, seated side by side. Emily had discreetly changed the Jensens' first-class flight reservations to tourist. That was the beginning.

When Hank Palmer met Emily Jensen, his lifestyle expenses (see pages 105 and 106) kept him neatly within his earning capacity. He unconsciously watched his nickels and dimes. He had been divorced for five years and annually paid $2,400 in alimony and $1,200 in child support for his son, Douglas, aged fourteen.

From the start Hank worried about Emily's money, about Emily's house—huge by his standards—about Emily's sleep-in housekeeper-cook, about Emily's three closets full of clothes, about Emily's everything. It didn't take 20/20 vision to see that Emily Jensen lived in a style to which he was not accustomed. And the smartest thing for him to do was not to get involved.

Still, when she telephoned him in Dayton, Ohio, and invited him to dinner in Winnetka, Illinois, the second time, he went. Even though it meant driving 250 miles. Or spending $68.00 on flying round trip to and from Chicago. He went a third time, too. And again. And yet again. After all, he was human, wasn't he? A man cannot live by equations alone. In Winnetka there was good food, good wine, and a pretty woman—he was tired of eating alone. Even more unique was the truly exceptional hi-fi set owned by the Jensen family. He never understood how Eric came to buy such an exceptional set when he did not understand sound. Or music. Hank usually brought a collection of his own Mozart records along with him to listen to.

Some winter weekends Hank took all three children ice skating. Then later they barbecued franks and hamburgers in the Jensen fireplace and would sit up to midnight listening to Mozart. Some summer weekends they spent at Inge's cabin on Lake Michigan. Then Hank taught everyone how to water ski and also to scuba dive.

When Hank and Emily had been seeing each other a year, they started to talk about marriage. It seemed the sensible thing to do—or why go on seeing each other? Hank was skittish from the start. How could he afford the Jensens—Emily and her children? Emily pointed out that her children were paid for. Only she was available. Well, where would they live in Dayton? They couldn't move into his house as it was all wrong for the Jensens. Emily agreed with that. She'd seen his house on a weekend. However, she had a suggestion. Couldn't Hank find a job in Chicago? Hank explained that no job he could get would pay for the upkeep of Emily's house, even though Emily owned it outright. There was the part-time gardener. The housekeeper. The heating bills. Emily said they would close off the top floor of the house and only heat it weekends when Doug used one of the guest bedrooms on the third floor. And Maria, the housekeeper, was part of the divorce agreement and paid for by Eric. How could Hank object to Maria? How? Then they talked about selling the house and moving Emily, Peter, and Inge to Dayton. They talked and talked. Days, weeks, months. Face to face, on the telephone, at the dinner table, and in bed. Eventually, that's what they did do— move to Dayton. Hank felt he had won a victory. But the house that they bought was almost as big as the one in Winnetka, and of course the housekeeper went along. The surprise was that Hank was surprised at his reactions. He decided he didn't understand himself. Why was he so angry all the time.

For instance, if Peter and Inge wanted their own separate telephones with separate numbers, was it fair for him to oppose it? It wasn't any skin off his teeth, so why was he so hot and bothered? Or was it reasonable to lose his temper with Emily when she bought something he couldn't afford, like a rug or an aquamarine dinner ring. If she bought it with her own children's money, why was he being a killjoy? Everyone knew that Peter and Inge had more disposable income than Emily and Hank. Who was fooling who? Or why should he mind that Eric gave Peter an XK 150 on his sixteenth birthday? Hank never liked foreign cars. He wouldn't give one to Doug if he could afford it. And when Inge was nice enough to offer the cabin on Lake Michigan to Emily and Hank for a private holi- day, what made Hank say, "Not on your life"? Why? He used to like the cabin. Because Hank privately knew what they all knew—that he was violently jealous of Eric's economic polygamy.

Emily and Hank's lifestyle budget varied from day to day, even minute to minute, depending on who was doing the spending. The result being that their lifestyle was either too rich for Hank's blood, or too bread and water for Emily's taste. So they squabbled constantly over how much or how little they should or should not spend on the house, vacations, clothes, food, cars, presents, children, laundry and on and on and on.

This situation typifies the distorted attitudes people can have toward money and their economic polygamy. Here a surplus instead of a shortage was the time bomb that eventually exploded the marriage. Hank, unfortunately, saw Eric's money as a threat to his maleness, his authority. He saw Eric challenging his role as head of the household.

What Hank failed to accept was that marriage to Emily was not a monogamous marriage. Eric rich or Eric poor would still, if he chose to, share Hank's authority as family head. For Eric was the father of Emily's children. If that fact had been fully accepted, if Hank had recognized in depth that Emily had had a previous marriage, he would have found it easier to live in peace with the affluence brought by economic polygamy. But Hank's jealousy grew worse, not better, until one day he could stand it no more. One Saturday afternoon he found Emily in their bedroom modeling a ski suit she'd bought that morning in preparation for their Christmas holiday. She'd also bought Hank ski boots.

Hank just stood there and shook his head. Finally he said, "Emily how did you pay for that ski suit? And those boots?"

"How? The way I always pay for things. I charge them."

"And how do you pay the charge account?"

"By check. You know that?"

"And what money is in your checking account?"

"Hank—what is this? My alimony and the child support payments are in the account. Eric's lawyer deposits it directly to my bank. You know that."

"Emily, in the future I want you to bank the kids' money in a separate account. And not touch it."

"I don't understand you."

Hank was very angry by now because a part of him thought he was being very foolish.

"Look, your alimony is one thing. It's yours. I think you

ought to save it, but if you want to spend it, you do that. But the child support money should only be spent on the kids. Inge and Peter. Not on you—or me. Or the house. Or ski clothes. Or anything else."

"Eric doesn't care how I spend the money. I'm not depriving the children. He knows that."

"I know you're not depriving them, but you're doing something to me." Hank was getting more and more furious. "You're letting Eric's money run our life. And I don't like it!"

"That's the silliest thing I ever heard." Emily meant what she said.

"Eric's money paid for this house! Furnished a lot of it! Pays for our vacations! Buys you ski clothes and buys me ski boots!" Hank had started to shout. "I feel like a guest in my own house!"

"That's all in your mind," said Emily reasonably. "You're my husband. I love you. Eric is my ex-husband. He has his responsibilities and he meets them."

"He certainly does meet them. Sometimes I think he's in bed with us."

This was the first of a series of confrontations between Emily and Hank on the subject of Eric's money. These discussions increased in length, intensity, and volume. After the fifth one, Hank packed up and moved out. Some months later, after an unsuccessful second try, Emily reluctantly initiated divorce proceedings, asking for no money at all.

If Hank had stopped to quietly consider the situation, he would have seen that there were other alternatives open to him. He might have learned himself how to manage Emily's money more ably. His first efforts should have been to encourage her to save, to prepare for the day when the child support payments would stop. When the rewards of economic polygamy would be sharply reduced. In the meantime, since most of the expenses of his new family were financed by their past, by Eric, Hank could have enjoyed his relative financial freedom, plus the pleasures that Eric's money provided. He could have used the cabin. Admired Emily's ski suit and his own ski boots. And with his own money bought himself the records he'd been wanting. And bought Doug the German camera he'd been wanting. He could also have made some investments of his own and Emily's excess money.

If Hank had done any of this, he would have frustrated Eric's game.

Eric, being a shrewd manipulator, had fully expected his monies to control Emily's second marriage. Hank's reaction was exactly what he'd hoped for. And Emily herself, not realizing what was going on, fell in with Eric's plan against her own best interests. When Hank acted predictably—a cliché come true—Eric won the game.

PART III

The Joy of Incest

Disclaimer

DISCLAIMER (An advertising term describing what the product will not do.)

The section that follows is not concerned with your synergistic family in the following ways:

How much, how little, or how to discipline your offspring.
What are your rights versus their rights.
Adroit ways of communicating that it drives you crazy when they don't make their beds, do overeat, refuse to study, and so on.
A new view of Parent Effectiveness Training.
Evaluation of penis envy or sexual role models.
Et cetera.

There are many good and valuable books on these topics, and they can be found in bookstores or libraries.

What this section is concerned with is the nature of the basic, primary emotional interaction between parents and children in the synergistic family. In other words, it is concerned with first causes; in a sense, with the fundamentals of sex education. Yours, not theirs. It is about incest.

6

The Ultimate "No-No"

MY HUSBAND, who does not have the same kind of warm, familial feelings about Sigmund Freud that I have, is given to remarking when he's heard one too many of my Freudian insights that my psychiatric bills in times gone by could probably have paid the tuition of one entire Johns Hopkins graduating class. That is a bit of an overstatement. Closer to the truth is that my monies did substantially contribute to the summer homes, tennis lessons, alimony payments, Mayan sculpture, island hopping in the Aegean, etc., of the eleven successive psychoanalysts with whom I spent forty-five minutes a day, five days a week, between the ages of nineteen and thirty-one.

It was fortunate for me that I was an advertising copywriter. For in advertising, if you are willing to skip lunches, new clothes, the hairdresser, trips to Paris, and live in a sunny apartment with a great view and no furniture, then your salary ought to be just enough to cover your daily visits to the psychoanalyst. Where, as I recall, I wept a great deal.

And it was the payoff of all those tears through all those years that put me on speaking, if not intimate, terms with incest. Better known to the world as the Oedipus complex. Or, as in my case, the Electra complex, Electra being to girls what Oedipus is to boys.

But call it Electra or call it Oedipus, when it came down to the wire, what I really tuned in on was the jargon, the catchwords; the ins-ville lingo. But the essence, the meat and potatoes of the concept, did not penetrate. Did not so much as make a dent. Though incest was revealed and I understood the revelation, though I had my share of shattering "breakthroughs," in the end it was all show and no go—intellectual lip service. It never occurred to me to believe that the Oedipus and/or Electra complex was real. Once treatment was behind me, a thing of the past, in my heart of hearts I dismissed every insight. How could I, the apple of my father's eye, my mother's pride and joy, be capable of such indecent reveries? It was like seeing a flying saucer by moonlight. In the broad daylight it's hard to believe. Furthermore, practically speaking, my father was old enough to be my father. That was too old to be sexy. Psychiatry had its place, but this was real life.

Now I suspect, I might even say I hope, that you yourself have never given much thought to the practice of incest. In fact, it would not be amiss if you actually shudder a bit and regard the whole subject as a rather rococo activity that happens to make colorful newspaper copy when indulged in by the sexually misguided.

On the other hand, if you have had a little psychiatry yourself or spent a couple of weekends or weeks in sensitivity training or with encounter groups or at Esalin, Arica, est, et al., it is quite possible that you are now on somewhat more familiar terms with this recurring, infantile sexual yen. You may even be able to remember yourself, with some embarrassment and scorn, naturally, as a five-year-old junior sex fiend with lecherous designs on your parent of the opposite sex. But none of this is to be taken seriously. You are an adult now, and as we all know, incest is not an acceptable pastime for adults. It is not even an acceptable fantasy. Though we are one and all interested in sex, in its infinite variety and subtlety, it is hard to envision a best-selling book titled *The Joy of Incest*. As a form of Saturday night entertainment, one has to admit that it won't wash. Even masturbation has more cachet.

So committed are we to the incest taboo that, for most of us most of the time, it is as much second nature as our native tongue. One of the more malevolent obscenities on the streets or in a bar is to suggest to someone that he is obviously a "mother fucker." His blood will boil. His hair will rise. Murder, or at least a clop in the chops, will be the appropriate reflex. For one and all, we have tacitly agreed—consciously, that is—that such behavior is degenerate. The vehement revulsion at even the thought is unquestionably instinctive. If not God-given.

Only the impious disagree. For the public relations campaign on the incest taboo may well be more effective and more universal than any ever mounted for Moses, Jesus, or Allah.

Yet, in thinking about this book, about the emotional stresses indigenous to the synergistic family, an awkward fact stubbornly emerged. The unmentionable reality of our new lifestyle that we have somehow all agreed not to talk about in public, or in private either, is the watering down of the incest taboo. I must say, when the idea first occurred to me I looked the other way. This disquieting insight was more than I bargained for.

But the more I itemized and made lists of family interaction that could use repairs and a new paint job, the more I pursed my lips and shook my head. What I was finding was so many bits and pieces of behavior that were not meshing, that led to dreary quarrels, that could drive one to drink if one drank. What I wasn't finding out was why. Where were the underlying principles, the first causes for the prickliness of the synergistic family? What was this addiction to a looking-for-a fight stance? Why did the prevailing winds carry so many yellings?

It was when I stopped looking at behavior and started looking at motives that I spotted Hamlet's ghost. The sudden and astonishing apparition of the incest taboo staring at me, embittered and pale and refusing to be forgotten. Like most unwelcome revelations, this one left me anxious. How could it be? And even if it could be, who was I to cast the first stone at this hallowed tradition? Why should I be considered a giddy alarmist? If the taboo, as is generally believed, is rooted in biological and/or psychological necessity, it should flourish in whatever family soil it is planted. That was logical. To refresh my memory after long years away from my own anthropological and psychological studies, I decided to have a turn around the field. Had anything changed while I was out getting married, divorced, and remarried?

I looked first at Edward Westermark, the eminent anthropologist who, as I remembered, laid out the rationale for what all decent, god-fearing citizens knew intuitively: that there was an innate aversion to intercourse between folks who were blood kin.

On rereading he stood pat. It was reassuring to have one's personal prejudices given staunch scientific approval. Havelock Ellis went the same route, remarking that due to continual childhood contact, brothers and sisters were apt to find each other sexually boring.

Another spiritually uplifting vision. And yet, and yet, an irreverent question persisted. Which families, precisely, had Mr. Westermark interviewed; which mothers and sons, which fathers and daughters had he observed prudently exhibiting an "innate aversion" to each other? My own experience was otherwise. With embarrassment I recalled my seven-year-old self loudly nagging my daddy to marry me. My second cousin, Adele, felt the same way about my uncle. And while we're on this delicate topic, which brother and sister did Havelock have in mind as being sexually bored with each other? Again, where was I? What kind of roughnecks did I grow up with? The brothers and sisters of my early years seemed to be all too frequently "playing doctor" together.

I found it, then, a distinct relief to remember that a similar crew of licentious kindred had been sighted by Sigmund Freud. For that matter, types comparable to my schoolmates had been vouched for by Sir James Frazier, Marion Slater, J. J. Fleugel, T. H. White, Bronislaw Malinowski, and a batch of other law-abiding, morally reputable anthropologists and psychiatrists who devoted their lives to chronicling, among other behavior, the lustful family antics of kinfolk.

All this brought me back to Sigmund Freud. I decided to reread *Totem and Taboo*. For it was Freud who first raised the question of the sanctity of the incest taboo. I wanted to see how well he stood his ground today. He stands it very well. Nothing has changed. There was no apologetic introduction to the book explaining that new psychological data via perhaps transactional analysis or Harry Stack Sullivan had cut Sigmund's theories down to size. They were meaningful, of course, but. . . . There were no "buts." They were alive and well and intact. The opening chapter, titled "The Horror of Incest," may shake your most cherished feelings about your own "innate aversion." I know it shook mine when I closed my eyes and recalled all those years full of forty-five minute hours on the psychoanalytic couch. Now, with the synergistic family on my hands, I only wish I'd been less cavalier about the lessons I learned in my sessions. Let me give you a Freudian sampling should you have a sneaking hope that we are not all in this together: "Psychoanalysis has taught us that a boy's earliest choice of object for love is incestuous and those objects are forbidden ones—his mother and sister. . . ."

See what I mean. What can be said of course for a boy in relation to Mom and Sis holds for a girl in relation to Dad and Brother. Freud's conclusion for both sexes being that there is no "innate aversion" to incest. If anything, friends and neighbors, there seems to be an innate inclination to same.

In the same vein as Freud, that grand old man of anthropology, Sir James Frazier, pulls not a punch. With cool, British irony, he cuttingly intones that one does not forbid men to keep their hands out of fire. What nature punishes needs no legal restraint. Therefore, we should:

> . . . assume that there is a natural instinct in favor of (incest) and that if the law represses it, it does so because civilized men have come to the conclusion that the satisfaction of these natural instincts is detrimental to society. . . .

That hits the nail. Society calls the shots. Gets it through our psyches with no ifs, ands, or buts that should we venture down the incest road, we will assuredly have our knuckles severly rapped. We may even be tarred and feathered. Or hung until blue. So, with a commendable instinct for self-preservation, we unconsciously make a splendid decision. What we absolutely cannot have, we absolutely do not want. The psychoanalysts call this admirable process "repression." Aesop called it "sour grapes." You call it whatever you wish—it works. More often than not.

But will it work for us? That's the question that would not be begged, once I considered the emotional ties of the synergistic family. How the deuce do we fit into the scheme of the incest taboo? The monogamous family has had thousands of years of tradition and training behind its bred-from-birth horror of incest. And still there is no innate psychological aversion. There are even on occasion disreputable slippages in the policing power of the taboo, and the psychiatrists then have a breakdown to treat. If these shocks can come to the monogamous family in full bloom, what can we of the synergistic family expect?

Trouble! Confusion! Households at sixes and sevens. That's what!

For example, a typical question you might ask yourself is: Will you, the poly-mother of a handsome, young teen-age son, be able to shield yourself—will your poly-son be able to shield himself—against the sexual fantasies you may have about each other? Or, given the paternal pressures, will you the affectionate, poly-father of a budding young thing with Cleopatra eyes be able to do likewise? I hope so. Because you may have to. This is the way the world really is.

If you do have fantasies, it is healthier to know that you do. Now is not the time to pale and turn up your nose. You are not too good for it to happen to you—it has happened to others as good as you.

We, as poly parents, do not have the kind of parent-child relationship that, begun at birth, does limit for the most part the parent's sexual impulses. We do not see ourselves in our poly-children—not our way of thinking, of talking, or our knack with numbers or flowers or a tennis racket.

They in turn do not see themselves in us—in our cheekbones, our temperament, or the nonsense that tickles our funny bone. For us there is no clear title to the "honor thy father and thy mother" commandment. We are literally strangers to each other. As strangers, anything can happen.

This criss-crossing of sexual drives is as old as time. You would not be the first mother—biological, step, or poly—or the first father who felt drawn toward a child. Nor is your son the first son, or your daughter the first daughter, to respond. It is not depraved. Disgusting. Or degenerate. It is ancient. It is human. It must also be kept under control. To do this, we must understand the nature and purpose of this universal sexual ambivalence—the better to deal with our children and our ex-spouses, to say nothing of ourselves and our current spouses.

Thou Shalt Not—!

Primitive people have usually been so edgy about the dangers to family life of a too sociable intrafamily sexuality that in many societies the incest taboo is not limited, as with us, to those with primary blood ties—such as mothers and sons, fathers and daughters, brothers and sisters. Incest for them is defined as sexual union between any individuals related to a "prohibited degree."

What constitutes a "prohibited degree" will vary with the culture. And, in our new society of the synergistic family, it is on our heads to decide what a "prohibited degree" should be.

Naturally, you will say for openers, we should carry over the primary incest taboo of the monogamous family which bans sexual union between close blood relatives. Naturally. After all, this blood ban is the most widely held explanation for the existence of the incest taboo at all. The theory being that very early in the game our primitive ancestors figured out that inbreeding would weaken the human stock and invented the taboo as a means of quality control for improvement of the species. It is an eminently satisfying position. It shows our ancestors in an excellent light. Far-sighted. Responsible. Pillars of society; human beings of distinction, in or out of the jungle. And the theory is pure nonsense.

From what we know of present day savages, with their short, childlike memories and inability to see beyond the immediate consequences of an immediate action, it is not likely that our very remote ancestors were any more far-sighted, that they prudently refrained from incest for fear of weakening the human stock. Or that they lost a night's sleep over the effect on the genes of their distant descendants of an afternoon's peccadillo with a sister, a brother, a mother, a father. Actually, they didn't have a clue as to the workings of genetics. The Mendelian laws were tens of thousands of years in the future. The study of animals was the only way possible for these prehistoric human beings who kept no family albums or histories to have observed the long range effects—good or evil—of generations of inbreeding. And since we know that the taboo is far older than animal husbandry, we must agree with Freud, who has written that it is "almost absurd to attribute to such improvident primitives motives of hygiene and eugenics to which consideration is scarcely paid in our present day civilization."

So a curious process of disbelief sets in. The more one looks at anthropological studies, the shakier becomes the case for the primary incest taboo being an automatic protective device, instilled by nature for eugenic purposes. It probably took millions of years for the human animal to deduce the enjoyable manner by which babies came about—that kneeling under a mystic tree or eating a magical fruit was not what caused pregnancy. I for one, these millions of years later, grew up with a girl who was firmly convinced that kissing a boy could make her pregnant.

My friend aside, we do these days know a bit more about how babies are made. But we are still in the dark as to how to obtain the best possible descendants. The ill effects of inbreeding are by no means that cut and dried. It all depends on the inbreeders, on the nature of the genes that are transmitted. Will it be high IQ or hearing defects?

This leaves us with some rude contradictions. There is no "innate" psychological aversion to incest. Worse, primary incest makes no total threat of biological disaster—babies with horns, morons, albinos. On the contrary, what the taboo actually does, to everyone's dismay, is conjure up as fantastic a mystery as ever there was: the presence of a powerful, worldwide custom, which like May Day and Halloween is "half as old as time." But which, unlike these venerable institutions, seems to have no sensible explanation.

Obviously, now we must alter our attitude. What looked so dependable is not that dependable. Still, the monogamous family has been a rousing success century after century. The feat is all the more extraordinary in the light of our new, unnerving knowledge. We could assuredly do a lot worse than to take to our hearts the moralities and bylaws that have fostered its longevity.

For it is the general consensus of anthropologists and psychiatrists that it is the incest taboo that holds the monogamous family together. The plain statement by the anthropologist Clellan S. Ford proves to be aimed so directly at the core of the matter that, if we follow the line of his reasoning, we shall see precisely what he sees and agree that the taboo has indeed abetted human survival.

> The origin of the prohibition against primary incest is lost in history. . . . (But) whatever the origins . . . (the prohibitions) serve at least two useful functions. First, they tend to cut down on competition within the family unit, on jealousies that might interfere with the functioning of this most important social group. . . . Second, they insure that mating will take place outside the family, thus widening the circle of people who will bond together in a cooperative effort and in the face of danger. . . .

So the mystery may be solved. Ford has presented us with a practical, no-nonsense approach to the whys and wherefores of the incest taboo. Actually, it does not take a Visconti-type imagination to see the jealousies that can arise in families where everyone is competing for the same sexual objects— Mama and Papa. At first it might work. Compromises might be arranged. Copulation schedules, so to speak, would be posted, as in a well run bordello. Mom and Dad on Monday. Mom and Junior on Tuesday. Sis and Junior on Monday. Dad and Sis on Tuesday. And so on. But even with the most business-like traffic schedules, jealousy and hate will arise. Human beings are human.

The Synergistic Imperative

Once we agree that the incest taboo is a wordless social contract between close blood kin to keep hands off each other for the sake of family harmony, and that this agreement has made

possible the survival of the monogamous family, then it becomes apparent that the synergistic family can make do with
nothing less. We must accord our own version of the taboo, the
same, well-nigh religious sanctity it has in the monogamous
family, proving we stand for something. We are not fly-by-
nights. Second rate. We pay our bills. Cast our votes. Face our
music. For it is no snap to be a divorced and remarried poly-
and/or bio-parent. Along with the usual sexual hang-ups that
beset the monogamous family, such as occasional or chronic
infidelity, we of the synergistic family have to hound us our
peculiar susceptibility to incest. In fact, it is routine psychiatric
opinion that ". . . the taboo on incest works less powerfully in
regard to [the child's feelings toward] the new parent [of the
opposite sex] than it did in regard to the old." All we had to
do was ask. And listen. The ominous note in this message is
detectable to any human ear. It is well below the range of
dog whistles.

Yes, we had better make our peace, queue up to pay our
dues. The taboo against incest between those related to a "prohibited degree" becomes the Synergistic Imperative. Our prime
Thou Shalt Not. Only thus do we keep our house in order.

Who are those related to a "prohibited degree"? The answer
seems to me apparent to anyone who has lived or lives within
the bedrooms of the synergistic family.

Following the lead of the monogamous family, we adopt the
primary incest taboo, which prohibits the merest hint of sexual
overtures between bio-mothers and sons, bio-fathers and daughters, bio-brothers and sisters. To this base we add the secondary
incest taboo, which prohibits the same between poly-parents
and children of the opposite sex. Nor does it stop there. We
cover more ground because there are more of us to consider.
Poly-brothers and sisters are also off limits for each other. The
logic is cautionary. Watching the mating dance of the young
can be a highly infectious entertainment. When permitted

within the premises of the synergistic family, it may provoke those in the viewing stands into feelings of jealousy, competitiveness, and dances of their own.

Beyond being a threat to family morality, sexual incidents between a poly-brother and sister can do lasting harm to the boy and girl in the hayloft. With little experience of other young people, of even their own tastes, propinquity can drive them into a self-limiting romance, encouraging them to overlook basically incompatible natures. Then they consecrate the disaster by marrying and living miserably until they too divorce.

Or it can go the other way. A sparks-flying infatuation can end "not with a bang but a whimper." Should one of the pair grow weary before the other, there will be an aggrieved and whimpering son or daughter to divide the loyalties of the family. Exit brotherly love. Exit sisterly love.

Finally, there are ex-husbands and ex-wives to be accounted for. It has been said that "any marriage that has a child is never extinguished." Which is why I take nothing for granted and add these former friends and lovers to the list of those "prohibited." Certainly after remarriage, and even after divorce.

None of these sexual prohibitions should surprise you. You knew most of them yourself. You simply had not put it into words. Now that it is in words, it does not require any great shift in psychology to see the common sense of the primary and secondary incest taboos—the Synergistic Imperatives. And now that these are spelled out, it is not too soon to alert ourselves to another species of trouble implied by the taboos—and by far their most popular derivative. It is incest again—but now with a twist. This time it comes at us not wearing the trappings of sexual desire but disguised as its very opposite. What we find ourselves most often coping with is not a more than motherly or brotherly affection but rather a particular kind of vengeful sexual displacement that I call the "Fuck You Sublimation."

The "Fuck You" Sublimation

I use this phrase to describe a grab bag of familiar, repellant, antisocial behavior that includes temper tantrums, jealous uproars, silent accusations, indecent language, immodest exposure, drunkenness, compulsive eating; also door slamming, failing school grades, physical violence, stealing. And in our happy age, hard drug use. This picturesque behavior is typical of either children or parents (both bio- and poly-) who are trying to avoid sexual intimacy. The only way they can bear to live under the same roof together is to be continuously at odds.

This sublimation is makeshift and thoroughly disagreeable for all concerned, but it does the job. In one family I interviewed, a twelve-year-old boy, infatuated with and angry at his poly-mother for replacing his bio-mother, took to stealing her jewelry and then swallowing it. In another family, a teenage girl, jealous of her mother and her new father, rewarded them with her make-life-hell adventures. She'd stay out till all hours and not telephone home. Or, without asking, she'd sleep overnight at a friend's house, while her parents telephoned everyone in their frantic search for her. When she ran out of cooperative friends "to cover for her," she slept in Grand Central Station. Only the presence of a browsing policeman spared her landing in a more serious scrape.

Though neither of these examples contains an actual "fucking" experience, it is still there by implication. The sexual impulses have been displaced by antisocial behavior, and what is being said is an angry "Fuck you!"

There is a general, somewhat misleading, impression that children who are too young to remember clearly the original family arrangement are less affected by divorce than the older children described here. And indeed, studies have shown that it is the children over the age of eight who seem to feel more threatened, who report stronger feelings of insecurity and un-happiness over the divorce than do younger children. Still, re-marriage with a house full of pre-eights will have its own brand of hazards, and it would not be wise, if such is your household, to take these studies as proof that peace has been declared. Psychiatry has continually demonstrated that we human beings have long, eerie memories for our pre-verbal toddler experi-ences, and accepting this fact, one cannot truly be sure how divorce affects, for good or evil, even a very young child. What we can do is be awake to the signals.

For example, should you divorce and then remarry, it is worthwhile to pause and consider what is being said and why, if your poly- or bio- . . .

Four-year-old daughter decides to finger-paint the living room wall
   instead of her coloring book. . . .
Five-year-old son notes how tasty his real mama's waffles are after
   he's just refused to eat the pancakes you made. . . .
Six-year-old daughter starts having nightmares. . . .
Seven-year-old son decides to starve the gerbil. . . .

It may be a transient and episodic phase. Or it may be an "acting out" of unresolved hurts, hidden jealousies and resent-ments relating to the divorce and remarriage. There are count-less variations of hostile kid behavior that one might view with alarm until one has determined the motive. Sometimes, with-out doubt, it is pure animal energy at work. Or prankishness. Or peevishness. Or self-assertion. Or boredom. Or. . . . And sometimes it is something else. At that, there are so many illicit passions at large in the synergistic family that I have the queasy feeling they may be endemic to the lifestyle. And the best way to deal with these feelings is to admit the possibility of their existence.

For injudicious conduct on the part of parents and children in the synergistic clan is more common than reasonable people care to think. Though we see it all around, in acute or chronic forms, wearing any one of its indignant, offended, quarrelsome faces, we like to ascribe it to upset stomachs. Or nerves. Or a toothache. Or a menstrual period. Or anything but what it frequently is—the hostile sublimation of incestuous impulses.

How, you might ask, could this ever happen in your family? To your near and dear? It can happen because you have high ideals. The thought of incest is too remote. Also obscene. And tasteless. To consider the possibility would upset your private harmony, would tamper with your vision of the world. Endowed with such blindness to fate, such trust in your view of "respectability," you believe you will be safe and happy. That you can walk on water. Then you come home one night and the house smells of brimstone.

No, it is not enough to be yourself the soul of moral rectitude and honorable intentions. You must be alert to the fingertips to what might make a muck between a husband and wife. You should be versed in the strategies that keep incest-derived jealousies down to a bare-bone minimum, that remind mother love that too much can be as bad as too little.

In later chapters I will mark out Preventive Ploys to store in your mind, to keep you on your mettle, looking to the right and to the left, for the sake of family well-being. These ploys are extrapolated from a series of all-too-typical cases. They represent the bitter pill of other peoples' experiences, the consequences of not looking at what was right in front of their noses.

But first things first.

For the yet unmarried, there are ground rules, preventive ploys again, the better to see you into a happy remarriage. Because make no mistake, what you do on the way to the divorce court and the remarriage ceremony can decide the fate of your future family.

7

In This Corner– Pre-Divorce, Pre-Remarriage

YOU ARE GETTING a divorce because you and your spouse no longer live in the same world. Not politically. Sexually. Or nutritionally. Or you've discovered what a bitch she really is. Or what a louse he is. Or he's unfaithful. Or she's a rotten housekeeper. Or. . . . Whatever the reasons you have for wanting a divorce, your children are not going to like it. They may even hate it. How long and how virulently they continue to oppose your divorce–it could last years after you remarry–depends in some measure on how you conduct the pre-divorce months. Hopefully, for everyone's sake, it's months not years that we're talking about.

Since you are getting a divorce to find a better life, you do not expose the seamy side of your marital feud to your children. You do not turn dinner time, or watching TV, or shopping outings into a war game with your children as unofficial observers. You do not groom them to be spies, to tattle on your spouse to you. You do not propagandize them into seeing things your way. Taking your side. You will also, as reasonable, responsible men and women, not use your children as confidants in your excursions into infidelity. If infidelity is what you are into. Should you indulge yourself in any or all of this tacky behavior, you'll have no one to thank but yourself should your children start a family insurrection one bleak day.

The child exposed to the jungle practices of a mean divorce rarely forgets how the knives were thrown and the blood streamed. Descendants of scenes of blame and name calling shortly trade in their love and admiration for a thinly repressed anger. When you remarry, the lid's off that repression. You and your new mate become the standing targets for venomous potshots. The hissing, stamping, catcalling, and tomatoes that seem to fill the air around you were brought on by your own inferior performance.

Let us part then in peace. Perhaps peace will be an amulet against disaster.

Or will it? Ironically, the most mature couples among us, who arrive at the divorce decision in quiet, somber tones, can often bring with them children in shock. Children who feel betrayed, who thought they were living in "happy homes," and so are far more indignant than the young cynics who lived through a marital holocaust.

Which way then do you go? Do mature loving parents, though unhappy spouses, turn their homes into war camps in order to prepare their children for divorce? I think not. When in doubt and given a choice, opt for mature behavior. In the long arc of time, your children will regain their sea legs and do better than children from chronically unhappy homes. It's like having a large bank account to draw on. Having known fat years of love, security, and serenity, these children can now draw on those years in these lean times, to tide them through the divorce upheaval and bring them out right side up.

Just do what you have to do tactfully. Take them by the hand

and disenchant them slowly. Talk to them before you talk to lawyers. Share with them soberly the differences in your outlook, goals, personality, or whatever it is that is making divorce desirable. Try to stick to concretes. To say, "Dad travels so much I feel we're no longer a family" is a more concrete reason than, "Dad and I don't get along the way we used to." Or, "Your mother wants to get her degree in law and I'm against it" is more cogent than, "Your mother and I have grown apart."

The sad reality, of course, is that nothing will really console your children for your wanting to divorce. All you are trying to do is give them something that they can vaguely understand and that will not feed their unsettling, unspoken fear that in this world of shifting emotional ties, they are next in line to be cut loose.

Who Gets Custody of the Parents

Now that you know something about the less blissful side of divorce and remarriage, if you are considering your first divorce, it would be worthwhile to stop, look, and think long and hard about how you solve your custody arrangements. As the bio-mother or -father of sons and/or daughters, what's at stake is the psychological and physical well being of your children in the future. To say nothing of your own prospects for a fuller, richer, new life. It comes down too, what family law calls, "the best interests of the child," or as it is more realistically described, the "least detrimental available alternative for safeguarding the child's growth . . ." This "least detrimental alternative" could mean custody going to the mother, to the father, or to other loving relatives.

Parenting is no longer considered a solely sex oriented function. In a society where a woman was primarily wife and mother, it made sense that she should have custody of the child. But today a woman can be a computer programmer, a lawyer, a veterinarian—she seeks a different identity than women did twenty-five years ago and because of this changed self-image, "the law following the basic attitudes of society . . ." is slowly but surely changing its position on making custody awards inevitably to mothers.

There are other reasons too for the shift. We have come to realize that a child's psychological health is as important as its physical health. And children unlike adults, have no conception of blood-tie relationship until quite late in their growth. What has real meaning for them is the "psychological parent," the one with whom they have or will have "day-to-day interaction, companionship and shared experiences. The role can be filled by a biological parent or any other caring adult . . ."

For example, the grandparents of eight-year old Tony B. were awarded custody of the child because he had lived with them since birth. The court made the award to the grandparents because such a move was considered to be in Tony's best interests.

Then there is the case of Joyce A., a six-year old daughter of Arthur and Barbara Allan. She has two sets of toys, friends and cats because her mother and father share joint custody. Neither parent wanted a relationship where they could only see their daughter on weekends or holidays. And since both have careers, neither could have done as well for Joyce alone, as they can do together but separate.

So what I am suggesting is an enlightened self interest on the part of you, the parents, on behalf of your children. You as adults must have some idea where you are going with your new life. Does the day-to-day presence of your children fit into your vision? Will it fit into your remarriage scheme if remarriage occurs? Think hard and think honestly. For it is no slur on you as a woman or mother, if you worry that you cannot cope successfully with your children after divorce. On the other hand, if you as a father want custody, not to make Brownie points, but because you feel truly qualified, the option of custody is more available to you today than it was in the past. But whatever you decide, decide in favor of reality, not in terms of some fantasy you have of family life, or some self-image that you must live up too.

Remember that ancient, grim, gallows humour story about the great King Solomon's ruling in a custody dispute. According to the tale, King Solomon was asked to decide who should be given custody of a baby that was being claimed by each of two furious women as their own flesh and blood daughter. King Solomon thought about the dispute, questioned each lady tactfully, listened to two completely contrary stories, and turned a deaf ear to the names each lady called the other. When the women finished talking, King Solomon pursed his lips and said "Mmmm." Then he offered what seemed a reasonable solution. He would have one of his soldiers slice the baby in half with his sword. He would then give each mother her half of the infant. After hearing his decision, one woman nodded her head vehemently. It seemed an eminently practical arrangement. The other woman screamed and fainted. It took a thorough dousing with cold water in the face before she recovered her senses. When she did come too she tearfully insisted that the other woman was the true mother, that the king give that woman the whole baby, that she was not the mother, and that she did not want half the baby. Half a baby was not better than no baby. King Solomon nodded his head sagely. It was not for nothing that he was known as the wisest of the wise. He forthwith awarded the baby to the soaking wet mother who had refused her fair share of the infant. It seemed to him she was best suited to raise the whole baby, since she so strongly objected to settling for half.

In other words opt for "the least detrimental alternative" for all of you.

You, Just You, and Baby Makes Two

If you arrive at the divorced state with no particular replacement mate in mind, you will find the terrain lonely and isolated. It is like living way outside of town—miles from the shopping center, the post office, the parties. It's a limbo state and a time of short rations emotionally, so you must watch yourself now with a jaundiced eye.

"If the parent's behavior is unusual, the child's reaction will be unusual. . . ."

"Unusual behavior" is to be understood as too much or too little of the stable emotional necessities that children need to thrive. One minute spoiling a child with an extravaganza of affection and the next minute snubbing it with calculated indifference is a pattern not likely to develop character or an independent mind. In such a climate, an adoring mama's boy or a worshipful daddy's girl is more the norm. Male and female homosexuality, too, often owes its inspiration to a doting, bullying mother or an attentive, domineering father. Yes, intimacy is a difficult art for a single parent living alone with children.

Is There Sex after Divorce?

This is the other end of the stick. The divorced bio-parent is romping around enjoying a free and full sex life. Super. But oil the springs of the bed and muffle the moans. This goes for mamas and papas both. Caution must prevail.

A divorced mother, living in small quarters with a young son, who has a series of lovers spending joyous nights in her bedroom is asking for it. "It" being hell to pay. Her son knows the score. And that son is jealous, is hostile, is resentful, and in the course of human events may become a psychiatric study.

Take Judith R. and her son, Lee. On a sufficient number of mornings, twelve-year-old Lee sat down to breakfast with his mother's gentlemen callers. One morning, smiling broadly, he accidentally poured the pot of coffee on the caller's suit. Ruining it, of course, and giving the man a second degree burn. Lee then went off to school whistling "Dixie." Or something like that. When Judith remarried, Lee prepared for war. In his new home he had a large, sunny bedroom with space to house his chemical set, his sporting equipment, his musical instruments. He had a lawn. He had friends. He liked his school. So what. One midnight he left his room, padded down the hall to the master bedroom, and in the dark proceeded to punch his half awake poly-father in the head with his boxing gloves. The next day Lee's mother put locks on the bedroom door. This inspired Lee to practice his trumpet in the early morning hours. Eventually, he was sent to military school.

Lee's emotional security had been rocked by the procession of changing men in his mother's bedroom. Was he as replaceable as they, as was his father? The question hurt. And beneath the hurt was something more insidious. His own incestuous impulses had awakened. To stop himself thinking forbidden thoughts, he substituted hateful, destructive behavior— a precise example of the "Fuck You!" Sublimation in action. Lee's experience in the years before his mother's remarriage made him a divorce casualty, unable to sustain a relationship with his mother or poly-father.

Ann B. didn't have a son, she had a fourteen-year-old daughter, Geraldine, living with her after her divorce. Ann's life was very active, very sexual. Geraldine's emotional security was not threatened by the knowledge of her mother's lovers. If anything, it warmed her imagination. She started thinking. The idea of sex buzzed in her head. She studied her breasts in the mirror for hours, cocking her hips, the seams of her jeans cleaving like a second skin to her body. When her mother told her she was going to remarry, Geraldine was charmed. Each time her new father-to-be was due to visit she combed her hair for hours. When he arrived, she'd insist on making his drink. She hung on his every word. She stared childish, sultry stares into his eyes. Being a bachelor, with no understanding of very young women, one evening, a little drunk, he made a regrettable remark to Gerry. Ann flared, threw him out of the house, out of her life, and slapped Geraldine hard. Geraldine wept— more for pride than pain. Ann wept, too. She knew intuitively that the incentive for Geraldine's mischief had come from watching her own behavior. She was as much out of temper with herself as with Geraldine.

It also seems true that fathers and daughters, fathers and sons who live cheek by jowl and breathe the same air will, unless they keep their signals straight, find themselves in similar difficulties as mothers and sons, mothers and daughters. There is no sense in haggling or hoping to pass the buck. *The more we divorce, the more we are intimately connected.* In a most perverse way, we are in the custody of our children as much as they are in ours. What we say, what we are, what we do—this, the "involuntary everyday real behavior of the parents"—is what molds a child's destiny. More often than not, the old truism applies: "As the twig is bent. . . ." Need I say more?

With this hazard in mind, I urge you strongly, as a divorced bio-parent living alone with a child or children:

a)   not to instruct them in the vagaries of your pre-remarital sexual adventures;

b)   to create sexual barriers between yourself and your children of the opposite sex. You need not adapt an adversary stance to do this, depriving your children of normal, parental affection. What is called for, actually, are old-fashioned virtues; namely, modesty and reticence. You become modest. You do not walk around nude or semi-nude in front of your children. You do not take nude baths together. You are reticent. You do not over-kiss, over-touch, over-pet. In sum, you do not permit yourself accidentally seductive behavior.

Do I Take Thee?—Mate Choice

As was flagged earlier, remarriages are more divorce prone than first marriages. How come, you may ask. Didn't we learn our lesson the first time around? Seems not. Research shows a tendency for marrying the same mistake twice. Even three times. Or, if by happy chance, we don't fall into that trap, then there is the risk of unforeseen financial potholes dead ahead. Finally, there are the children, ah yes, the children—his, hers, or both—to be cared for, taught, improved upon, and scolded into adulthood. It is your children who can make a remarriage into a redivorce. The opportunities for error are endless.

Take heed then. If you are the bio-mother or -father of sons and/or daughters, what with one thing and another, you've much to consider in the matter of mate choice. Standard questions, such as how appropriate will your betrothed be for the kids in a social, religious, and educational sense, are well worth spending a few sleepless nights pondering. Better sleepless before the wedding than later. Questions of finance I've already raised. But now comes the rack. The real scrunch is when you embrace the monster, when you straight talk with your beloved all about the ins and outs of latent primary and secondary incestuous impulses, concluding of course with suitable references to the "Fuck You!" Sublimation. The clincher questions to ask are: What's going on with your spouse? What's up with the

children? With yourself? Nobody is immune. All portents and
comets must be duly noted. It is no happy omen

if she sighs and is spellbound by your son's stamp collection;
if he blushes and grows tongue-tied reading your daughter's poems;
if his children regularly drop your wine glasses;
if her children think it's fun to let the air out of your tires;
if his daughters and your sons or your sons and her daughters are
    looking sheep eyes at each other. . . .

It is little nuggets of insight like these, known well beforehand so that judgments can be made and measures taken, that
will keep your family from falling from grace.

Take, for example, this report of a young woman's teen-age
experience with her poly-brother. It speaks well for both of
them.

"I first met my brother at the wedding of my mother and his
father. He was sixteen and so dreamy looking, and I was very
gawky and skinny and strange and thirteen. After that we lived
in the same house and became very good and dear friends. When
I was sixteen, he went to college and then I didn't see him very
often except a day or two at Thanksgiving and Christmas and
Easter. But he was my model for a man. Any boy that I met,
if he wasn't like my brother and didn't have a sense of humor and the same values as my brother, then he wasn't a
man and I wasn't interested in him. . . . Then there was
the summer when I finished high school, and I spent the summer
at the Vineyard and shared a house with some people. My
brother and a friend came to visit me, and I was so proud because he was my older brother and he was such a neat guy and
he and his friend were such fun. I showed them around and I
knew he'd love the Vineyard, and he did, and I loved it, too. And
because it was a communal household and we didn't have much
money and there wasn't much space, my brother stayed in my
room, which had one bed. And now I sometimes wonder what
would have happened if I wasn't a virgin at that time. Perhaps
it would have been different. Maybe not. But being a virgin was a
bar. I was afraid of being humiliated in front of him because I
didn't know anything really about sex. I was so young. Eighteen.

But I had had a very protected life. . . . Anyway we spent almost all night lying in bed and laughing and telling stories and just catching up, which was so delightful and still is a very wonderful memory of mine of companionship and love and everything. And in the middle of the night, and he was asleep, I knew he was asleep, and I don't know why I woke up but I did and I could feel his arm around me. And I got very tense because I was young and not very experienced but also because I knew it was my brother and I had such a sense that he was there in my bed. I'm sure there was a certain amount of suppressed sexuality knowing that here was the man I loved so much right there beside me sleeping. But I didn't know what to do. He was touching me—not exactly in a sexual way—but still he was touching me. And I thought about it for a second alone in the dark and then the whole possibility of what might happen flashed through my mind. I wasn't a complete dodo, and I realized that it would be very strange if anything sexual did happen. Our parents were living in the same house and we'd lived together in that house for years, and though we were not blood related we were brother and sister and I couldn't see how it would be if we were living in the same house again. So I woke him up and said, 'You know this will never work. We'll be really sorry about this afterwards.' I don't know how awake he was. He never said anything. He could have been half waking, half asleep, heard me, and known I was right. Because he took away his arm and there was no contact again. But he didn't say anything. I must admit, all these years later, that I've never talked to him about it, because it's still one of those things that I don't really understand."

Being human, young, and healthy, this poly-sister and poly-brother were attracted to each other. Coming from a family where the standard of sexual morality was solid, they got out of the way of a sexual attraction that ran counter to the taboo. As the girl quite correctly foresaw, if she and her poly-brother became lovers, it would cause considerable family upset when they were back again sleeping in the same house.

This is the kind of family you will want yours to be. Full of family affection and also family pride. With luck, you can have such a family. Or you can make your own luck.

Pros and Cons of the Synergistic Family

People looking in from the outside tend to think of the children of divorced parents as being alike, all affected in the same manner by divorce. Not so. These children "do not fall into a class by themselves with certain characteristics that distinguish them from other children." They are not all despairing. Or all happy. Or all good-humored. Or all angry. They are as much a mix as children in general.

Since they show no exceptional crippling, one day one may be able to justify divorce with the argument, "For the sake of the children." There are signs that the children of monogamous but unhappy homes turn out more distressed than do the children of divorce.

But now, just when the idea of divorce is losing its acrid aroma of failure and people are seeing it as less of a threat to their basic values, we have to accept a new perspective. In a way we will have to straddle two views, still believing in the new way but restrained by the facts to keeping in mind the virtues of the old. For despite its confusions, problems, failings, its aches and pains and psychiatric costs, the monogamous family does have a great deal to be said for it—like thousands of years of tradition and general social approval, like the incest taboo tuned up and in good working order to help keep the family in line. The synergistic family has none of these riches. It has inherited all the headaches and complaints of the monogamous family, plus a whole new set of quandaries that I am attempting to map in this book. With these pessimistic facts in mind, I find I have slowly, unwillingly altered my position on divorce. I, who for years have been unequivocally in favor of divorce and remarriage if one's monogamous marriage turned out to be "hellish," am no longer so convinced that a change of mate is always for the best. Not when there are children cooling their heels and hovering. Unless you have the stamina, flexibility, knowledge, and good humor to survive in one piece the rigors of the synergistic family, when you divorce you may be going from one marriage made in hell to another in a hotter hell.

My hope here is that you can learn from other people's accidents. That's why road signs were invented. That's why this book was written.

8

Ex Marks the Spot Where Polygamy Begins

MOST DIVORCED COUPLES stubbornly cling to the tacit, if unrealistic, notion that once a divorce is final all prior emotional ties automatically self-destruct. Nonsense. Bonds once forged in sexuality are not that easy to break, sometimes even where there has been outrageous behavior on one side or the other. The conventional wisdom holds that communication between the divorced will be cool, mature, businesslike, and strictly about the offspring. Sure. How often have I heard a divorced parent say, when referring to an ex-spouse, "If it weren't for the children we'd never speak to each other." Perhaps. But my experience tells me that often as not these remarks are as much an expression of pride as of disdain. How else validate the divorce and legitimize the failure of the former marriage? The ex-mate has to be detestable. Still, one cannot stand on one's dignity while discussing financial matters. Or the children's grades. Or teeth. Or tonsils. Substantive issues. Meanwhile, the continuing contact inevitably tends to surreptitiously remind each ex-partner, in one way or another, via hostile or amicable behavior, of the underlying chemistry that originally brought the pair together. What we see in operation is how economic polygamy promotes psychological polygamy. Out of it comes another kind of remark I've also heard rather often: "We get along much better since we're divorced." Some do, too. And it is this psychological polygamy contributing to the continuous confusion of conflicting loyalties, split affections, and nagging guilts about which spouse or child comes first that plague our synergistic families.

So let us bend the rules. I believe it would be wiser all around if we accepted the fact that though divorce does end marriage it does not necessarily end emotional attachments. Ex-wives and ex-husbands, where there are children to be considered, are for all practical purposes members of our synergistic family—as much as are poly-parents, poly-brothers and poly-sisters, aunts, uncles, and in-laws. What are needed are new ways of perceiving our exes and deriving out of these perceptions more subtle responses that can be fine-tuned for coping with this new species of problem arising out of this new kinship.

With this in mind, I have a suggestion. We might take a lesson from primitive peoples. These peoples, living as they do in closer touch with their hormones, are more aware than we of our sexual impulses, are more open to the undertow of their incestuous desires. Knowing what they know of their own inclinations, it behooves them to walk as though on eggshells among the maze of their family relationships, in whatever form these relationships exist. At all costs, they must not bring the house down on their heads. Since it is tacitly accepted by primitive peoples that to break the incest taboo is to do just that.

Undoubtedly then, to avoid such a disaster, the taboo that is usually restricted to blood kinship has been extended to those with whom there is only the remotest of social connection. This is a highly practical insight. If, as was hypothesized, the primary incest taboo evolved out of a need to maintain the structure of the blood kin family, so that members could live together cooperatively with a minimum of jealousy and hostile feelings, then any extension is clearly a recognition that certain non-blood kin family members provide the kind of sexual temptation that would also bring disaster to the family. The custom of designating certain people as taboo is expressed in "avoidance" practices, something we of the synergistic family might give some thought to in order to handle more successfully our many-faceted non-biological kinships. Along these lines I would like to describe certain customs that we may wish to appropriate for our own uses.

Freud has, for instance, a fascinating theory on the nature of the mother-in-law "avoidance" custom. This practice occurs in many tribes and circumscribes a man's interchange with his mother-in-law. The custom not only gives us a sharp insight into our own mother-in-law problems but also, I believe, provides a parallel to that uneasy balance maintained in the synergistic family between the current husband and wife and the ex-wife or ex-husband.

The practice of mother-in-law avoidance is found among Australian aborigines and also in Melanesia, Polynesia, and among the Negro tribes of Africa.

After marriage in the Solomon Islands, a man may not talk to or even see his mother-in-law. Should they meet, he must pretend not to recognize her and then take a turn around the block and leap off in another direction as quickly as possible.

Among the Eastern Bantu, if a son-in-law by chance meets his mother-in-law, it's her cue to hide in the bush, while he whips up his shield to cover his face.

Among the Basoga, a man and his mother-in-law do not have chatty conversations. Instead, should they have something to say to each other, they rush out of each other's sight and then carry on their dialogue by shouting at each other.

In discussing this kind of strict mother-in-law "avoidance," Freud writes:

A mother's sympathetic identification with her daughter can easily go so far that she herself falls in love with the man her daughter loves. . . . And very often the unkind, sadistic components of her love are directed on to her son-in-law in order that the forbidden affectionate ones may be severely repressed.

A man's relationship to his mother-in-law is complicated by similar impulses, though they have another source. It is regularly found that he chose his mother as the object of his love before passing on to his final choice [of wife] who is modeled after her. . . . The place of his own mother . . . is now taken by his mother-in-law. He has an impulse to fall back upon his original choice though everything in him fights against it. . . . A streak of irritability and malevolence that is apt to be present in this medley of feelings leads us to suspect that she does in fact offer him a temptation to incest.

Taking literary license, I will now rewrite some of these Freudian insights, substituting "ex-wife" for "mother-in-law," "new wife" for "daughter," and "ex-husband" for "son-in-law" where these references appear. I will also restate phrases to match the somewhat changed but, I believe, still analogous psychological relationship.

An ex-wife's hostile identification with the new wife often exists because she is still covertly in love with her ex-husband . . . very often the unkind, sadistic components of her love are directed at her ex-husband in order that the now forbidden, affectionate feelings may be more severely repressed.

An ex-husband's relation to his ex-wife is complicated by similar impulses. . . . He chose his new wife as the object of his love because she is modeled after his former wife. . . . Sometimes he has an impulse to fall back upon his original choice though everything within him fights against it. . . . A streak of irritability and malevolence that is apt to be present in this medley of feelings leads one to suspect that, ex or not, an ex-wife does offer an ex-husband a temptation to secondary-incest.

Now this certainly does not mean that every ex-wife and ex-husband are secretly seething with desire to climb back into bed together. No way. As a matter of fact, in many instances there is such an active hostility between the ex-couple that not only is the possibility of sexual or affectionate contact obliterated but also any kind of interaction between the new synergistic family as a whole and the ex-spouses becomes a nightmare. But why should it be so? If these hostile feelings were more sanely and openly examined, with an unembarrassed acceptance of their sexual implications, the air might be cleared; rational solutions might be found for the multitude of practical and vexing problems that often exist between the current couple and their ex-spouses in relation to the children. Anger, jealousy, and resentment can be seen for what they are —low-grade residual social diseases resulting from distortion of once erotic feelings. The best antidote is to acknowledge our hurts, our lost loves. Once recognized, we may then be better able to prevent our hostilities from warping our judgment and causing us to behave in ways that are contrary to everyone's best interests.

For example, an ex-spouse may give or withhold monies, depending on a whole mélange of feelings that can range from erotic to masochistic to sadistic. And these emotions can have very little to do with his financial capabilities or with the realistic requirements of a given situation. In exactly the same vein, what an ex-wife will require often reveals how little or how much she is still locked into her former marriage. By way of concrete example, let me cite what a 10-speed bicycle can mean in different family structures, depending on the personalities of the ex-husband and ex-wife.

1. Paul S., a lawyer of considerable affluence, flatly refused to buy his son, Jamie, a 10-speed bike when his ex-wife, Pat, suggested that that would be the birthday present the twelve-year-old boy most wanted. Instead, he gave him a football and a baseball glove. At Christmas he refused to buy the boy skis, preferring to give him a baseball bat. Even the plea of Paul's new wife, Norma, made no impression. Paul was determined to give his ex-wife and son only the barest minimum over what

the law prescribed. It was Pat who had wanted the divorce, and Jamie, when asked, had chosen to stay with his mother. Under the circumstances, neither of them was going to get any show of generosity from Paul. Paul did not realize that this kind of vengeful behavior only kept him tied to his past and his pain, alienated his son even more, and bound him to Pat as much as if he were still married to her.

2. At the other end of the stick is Ward B., a middle management business executive. When ex-wife Leslie B. decided that their son, Ted, should have a 10-speed bicycle, Ward promptly went to the bicycle store and bought the best bicycle in the place. All's well that end's well, unless your ex-wife is Leslie. Leslie then decided that Ted needed a microscope to pursue his dawning scientific interests. Ward agreed and bought the microscope. The cost of the microscope prevented Ward from buying new stereo equipment for his own home. A little later in the year Leslie telephoned Ward to suggest that it would be nice if Ward bought Ted a sailboat. The boy loved sailing. About now, Diane, Ward's new wife, became impatient. Even jealous. Though nothing overtly provocative was happening, she intuited that something was going on between Ward and Leslie that had nothing to do with their son, Ted. When she mentioned this to Ward, he became indignant. But as they talked, they both realized that unconscious forces were at work. If Ward and Leslie were still married, he would have thought twice about the microscope. And certainly about the sailboat. One of Ward's continuing pre-divorce quarrels with Leslie was her spendthrift habits. But as a divorced father, he felt a guilty obligation to his son for putting him through the divorce. A still more delicate topic was Ward's unacknowledged need to maintain Leslie's respect, since her usual stance was that he did not make enough money to support his family properly. He was afraid if he did not buy the Sun Fish, Leslie would go to her wealthy father, as she had in the past, and get him to supply the boat. If this should happen, Ward was afraid he

would lose Ted's respect. It was these kinds of painful memories that had persuaded Ward to make expenditures in ways that he would normally have regarded as inappropriate. It took tact and patience on Diane's part to make it possible for Ward to realize that he was subjecting himself to emotional blackmail, and that a lack of firmness of character would lose him Ted's respect more certainly than withholding expensive presents that he could not afford.

3. And then there are the Archers, who are, to my mind, as glaring an example of the use of economic polygamy as a conduit for now illicit emotions as any I've come across. They are an extreme example of what can happen in a synergistic family when the consequences of psychological polygamy are ignored.

Walter Archer was a systems analyst for a large engineering company making $35,000 a year when he and his wife, Betsy, decided to divorce. Essentially, the divorce was Walter's idea. Betsy was a beautiful, passionate woman, and also a temperamental, sloppy hysteric. They fought constantly over nothing. Though Walter was intensely attracted to her, he found that living with her on a day-to-day basis drove him crazy. It almost made him incapable of holding his job. When the decision to divorce was arrived at, he felt both regret and guilt, so he tried to compensate with as beneficial a financial arrangement as possible. He paid her $350 a month child support for their twelve-year-old daughter, Laurie, and $400 a month in alimony.

About two years after his divorce, he remarried Elaine Norwich, a home economist, with two sons, aged eight and ten. Elaine's income included $20,000 a year from her job, plus $500 a month child support for the boys. Walter and Elaine's combined incomes, even with the deductions from Walter's take-home pay for alimony and child support, left them sufficient monies to comfortably cover their needs.

In Elaine, Walter found a warmhearted, loving woman who

provided him for the first time in his married life with the kind of intimacy and understanding of which the passionate but self-centered Betsy was totally incapable. Walter's new marriage and new security filled him unconsciously with a desire to hit back at Betsy, who had, for so many years, given him so much grief. He began to fall behind in his alimony payments. Unaware of the dangerous, unconscious elements at work, Elaine silently approved of her husband's financial delinquency. She herself had never fully accepted the demands of economic polygamy, and she privately viewed Betsy as a lazy, self-indulgent, parasitic woman. She resented her presence in their life. Since Elaine was a long-time career woman, she could not understand Betsy's having no career or her continuing reluctance to find a field. She was young, healthy, pretty. Why shouldn't she work? Elaine had not looked at the economics involved—the kind of full-time job Betsy could find would scarcely pay for the housekeeping help necessary to care for her young daughter. And it would take Betsy years to obtain the training and experience necessary to get a well-paying job.

With the passage of months, Walter remained prompt in his child support payments but fell behind in his alimony payments. At one point, he was three months late. Betsy, who occasionally worked as a temporary typist when Laurie was in school, was in no position to live without her alimony. In the second month of Walter's delinquency, she telephoned the house and got Elaine. Embarrassed, she said it was Laurie's birthday and it would be nice if Walter bought the child a 10-speed bike. Elaine said she would relay the message to Walter. When she did talk to Walter, she said in addition that in her opinion a 10-speed bike was too expensive. Walter agreed. But the next day he bought Laurie a 10-speed bike. However, he did not send Betsy the back alimony payments.

The day the bicycle arrived in Betsy's home she telephoned Walter at the office. She insisted he come to her apartment that evening and bring with him her alimony checks. If he did not, she warned him she would take legal action. Childishly, she added that she would also telephone his boss. Knowing her, Walter knew she meant it. Particularly now that she was on the verge of hysterics.

That evening Walter did show up at Betsy's apartment—but without the alimony checks. Presumably, he'd come to see how Laurie liked the bike he'd bought her. But Laurie was out on a sleepover date at a friend's house. Walter and Betsy argued violently, and in the violence their old pattern reasserted itself. Reacting to the scent of her and the familiar way she looked at him, her eyes tearful and furious, Walter felt his desire for her rising. He leaned forward, gripping her arms to shake her. Betsy responded intuitively, made a small moaning noise, and relaxed against him. Silently, they slid from the couch to the rug. "My love," she murmured against his mouth, and slowly, out of long knowledge of each other's bodies, they intertwined and embraced with a passion as intense as ever they'd known.

Hours later, passion spent, Walter left quietly and quickly like a thief. In the morning the alimony checks arrived by special messenger.

How often this scene was replayed Elaine never later knew, but one day she had to accept the ugly suspicion that something was going on between her husband and his ex-wife that was not in the books. He had been paying the alimony checks promptly. And though she respected his shift to a more ethical position, it was not in keeping with his original vindictiveness. He had also sent some additional checks to Betsy, she observed one Sunday when accidentally thumbing through their joint check book. But she could not bring herself to ask what the checks were for. Finally, he mentioned over cocktails one evening that Betsy had broken up with that man, Mike Miller, the osteopath, she had been dating for a year. Elaine, somewhat bewildered, asked how Walter had heard this choice tidbit. After flim-flamming around, Walter came up with the sincere explanation—oh, very sincere—that Betsy had called him at the office that morning to talk about Laurie's camp bill and had mentioned in passing that she was no longer seeing Mike Miller. Elaine thought about this silently as she sipped her Scotch and water. It was something of a blow. She had privately hoped Betsy would marry the osteopath. It would remove her once and for all from their lives. It had seemed so possible. Laurie had told them all about Mr. Miller on one of her weekend visits. And continued to chatter about him on subsequent visits. Elaine had thought it was going swimmingly. Now suddenly the affair had gone pfft. Why? What had made Betsy change her mind?—because that was the gist of the report. She, not he, had had a change of heart. And yet, that was not what was bothering Elaine. No, there could always be another osteopath. Betsy was sufficiently attractive. What struck her as most peculiar was her interior vision of Betsy and Walter discussing Betsy's love life. How intimate were they?

At her desk in the office, Elaine told herself her suspicions were ridiculous. There were mothers she knew who thought everyone wanted to marry their son. She wondered if she had fallen into that class of second wife who thinks that an ex-wife has only one thing in mind—getting her ex-husband back. The thought made her wince. Still, Elaine was nothing if not practical. She decided to see what there was to see.

One Tuesday evening after Walter telephoned her at her office and told her he'd been held up at a meeting and not to hold dinner for him he'd have a sandwich sent in, Elaine decided to act. She left her office early, rode across town in a cab, and sat in the cab a half hour, parked on the block opposite the entrance to Walter's office. With the meter ticking the dimes away, she waited until 5:40. She was about to give up and go home when she saw her husband come out of the building and look for a taxi. Her heart pounded and she felt ridiculously like a woman in a daytime soap serial, as she waited while he got into his own cab. Then, leaning over to her driver, she remarked in what struck her as a too theatrical tone, "Follow that cab. But stay well behind it." The driver nodded and pushed his foot down on the pedal. He did not seem to think any of it scandalously melodramatic. He was simply following another cab. Of course, at one point on his way uptown, he half turned to her and asked matter-of-factly, "Say—you a policewoman?" Elaine thought it less embarrassing to nod.

Walter's cab came to a stop in front of Betsy's East Side apartment house. He got out, paid the driver, and hurried into the building. After he disappeared into the lobby, Elaine decided to get out of her own cab. She paid the driver and then walked into the lobby of an apartment building across the street. The doorman asked who she wanted to see and, fumbling for a name, she said she was waiting for a friend who was meeting her there, and then she would know where they were going. Since she looked highly respectable and smilingly pretty, he nodded and she sat down in the lobby. She settled herself in a position where she had a fine view of Betsy's building across the street. After she had been sitting for half an hour, the doorman became nervous and suggested she telephone her friend. She agreed she would do that. Instead, she walked to the corner and stood leaning, flattened as much as possible, against the side of the building. When the summer evening darkened, Elaine felt a wry gladness that Walter's alimony and child support permitted Betsy to live in an expensive neighborhood. Here, at least, she did not have to worry too much about drunks and junkies.

The sky was dark—it was after nine—when Walter came out of the building, hailed a cab, and set off crosstown. Shortly afterward, Elaine caught another cab and gave the driver her address. When she walked into the apartment, as she expected,

Walter was already home and waiting for her. "Where have you been?" he asked petulantly. "I called you from the office, and Jack said you'd not come home. You'd telephoned Mrs. Murphy and told her to prepare dinner for the boys. Where have you been?"

Elaine did not answer immediately. She wanted to make sure the boys were in bed before she spoke. She knew their marriage was like a closed clam about to be split open by her discovery.

Never before in the history of the monogamous world have so few children had so many mothers and fathers. It is a measure of the spread of our economic polygamy. Nor, as we have seen, is economics the end of it. It has brought with it psychological polygamy. And after that—what? Unless we take precautions, some of us may one day find ourselves confronted, as Elaine Archer was, with full-blown sexual polygamy.

I for one am not sufficiently open-minded to argue the pros and cons of a sexually polygamous marital arrangement. I am too inclined by training and tradition to be against it. Nor do I think it is an immediate danger to the synergistic family, since sexual polygamy is far more difficult to support in an industrial society than in an agrarian one. Still, we are living in a new cultural form, and we cannot afford to take at face value either our own motives or those of our exes.

At any rate, if the likelihood for sexual polygamy is low, the same cannot be said of psychological polygamy. For the ambivalent pull of psychological polygamy, when both ex-husband and ex-wife use financial matters to manipulate each other's lives for what are often only purely emotional gains, can be regularly observed. It is something to be avoided as religiously as a bad credit rating. It poses a real threat to the stability of the synergistic family by setting up rivalries that can only cause heartache. In the light of this reality, I would like to make a few suggestions.

Preventive Ploys—Avoidance Practices for Ex-Wives and Ex-Husbands

1. *Recognize that the secondary incestuous impulses between you and your ex may still be alive and well.* Once remarried, it is the better part of wisdom to keep your social distance and perhaps, like the Eastern Bantus, inconspicuously cross the street before you meet.

2. *Your friends will have to choose up sides.* Contrary to sophisticated conceit, it is not a jolly good idea to see the same people socially, to patronize the same parties, spas, or bars at the same time as your ex.

3. *Leave the diplomacy to your current spouse. Your ex and you cannot be chums.* If your current and your ex-spouse can handle it, there is something to be said for encouraging a peace treaty negotiated by your current spouse. Lunches, drinks, taking the children out together, getting to know each other—all this may make life easier in the synergistic family.

4. *It's détente between you and your ex.* If either you or your ex-spouse is constantly playing war games and making warlike noises, one or both of you should go talk to a psychiatrist. It means that secondary incestuous impulses are having a heyday.

5. *Don't play Machiavelli with money.* It makes no difference. If you're on the giving or the receiving side, don't use money to manipulate your ex-spouse. It will only lead to grief on grief. One synergistic family, where the ex-husband and ex-wife were at constant sword's point, skirted the hazard of money machinations by having the current wife, a cool-headed accountant, write the alimony and child support checks. When a question arose of a need for more money for the ex, all three spouses, current and ex, as well as the child, sat down and talked it over; the current ex, a sensible woman, acted as moderator. Eventually, everyone was on speaking, not screaming terms. Eventually, the ex-wife so recovered from her feud with her ex-husband that she decided to remarry, and that ended the alimony payments. Indicating the value of having at least one moderate in the group.

9

Gothic Tales of Our Times

PREPARING for this book I read quite a few other books on the subject of the family. Some I applauded, some I disagreed with, some struck me as nonsense. I also talked to a great number of poly- and bio-parents in synergistic families with whom I more often than not deeply sympathized. Out of the interviews came personal stories that I believe could prove useful and fair warning to you. Usually, we learn best by our own perspiring experiences. But lacking firsthand, you-are-there participation, other people's experiences will do.

To give you this close-up "experience" of what happens in a family when there is no recognition that incestuous impulses—real or displaced—are prowling, I would like to share with you a few of the "gothic tales" I was told. On behalf of the tellers, I've changed names and locales and sometimes professions. But that's interior decoration. What remains untrifled with is the architecture of the house that Oedipus, Electra, and Phaedra built. Once inside, you can step into the minds of the people living the events and, gazing through their eyes, allow their perspectives to become your own. When the tale is ended, perhaps by "experiencing" their passions gone awry, you will be persuaded not to make the same mistake yourself. For, as our first kiss, job, or marriage should have advised us, experience is still the best teacher.

There is no room in this book to do all the variations of love-hate themes I encountered that might be useful to you in thinking about your own family interactions. So I chose those with the broadest themes: the ambivalent relationship between a father and son, a mother and daughter, a mother and son. If these tales do not precisely echo your own family structure, you can substitute a son for a daughter, a mother for a father, and so on, and it may then have a more familiar ring.

You will find, too, as you read these tales that they revolve around the hostile behavior of children in their teens. This is in keeping with reality. For it is far easier for an older child to directly express his or her feelings, for or against a bio- or poly-parent, than it is for younger ones. Of course, if you have younger children in your synergistic family, you may wonder what these tales have to tell you now. They can tell you a great deal. For though the extreme behavior reported—the Oedipus and Electra complexes carried to their logical conclusion—occurred in the teen years of these children, each disaster had its origins in the earlier childhood experience of the pre-divorce and remarriage behavior of the parents.

For you will see as you read that the children in these "gothic tales" did not start out life as extremes, nor did they grow up under bizarre circumstances. They were raised in homes as "normal" as most. With all the standard frailties that "normal" homes are prey to. There was no alcoholism. No drug addiction. Or financial irresponsibility. Little sadism. Little overt seductiveness toward the children. No rape. Instead, there was only the ordinary, everyday ambivalence between husband and wife, parents and children. Barring divorce and remarriage, these children would probably have grown up to lead similar "normal" lives. But divorce and remarriage triggered the previously repressed, hostile emotions. What went wrong with these children had its source in the blindness of the bio-parents originally, and the poly-parents later, to the strength of the innate, incestuous fantasies of the young. Only one poly-mother recognized and took deliberate advantage of the situation. Otherwise, what happened happened, as it were, by premeditated accident. With a resulting failure of both self- and family respect.

At the end of each tale, I will identify the interpersonal blunders made that turned these families into statistical losses. From these blunders I have, as I said I would earlier, derived preventative ploys. These ploys are intended as roadblocks, to stop you from running smack into the same fool's paradise.

The first case-fiction is Phaedra, the name borrowed from the great Greek dramatist Euripides. Phaedra is the story of the young, beautiful second wife of King Theseus who falls in love with the king's son, Hippolytus.

In the classic Greek play, Phaedra was a stepmother. In our current "gothic tale," Hermine, her parallel, is a poly-mother. But, as a commentator on the Greek play has remarked, "It is not necessary to debate whether to the fifth century B.C. Greek, sexual relations between stepmother and stepson would be technically incestuous or not. It is enough that we can be sure that they involved an extreme violation of the trust and affection between father and son, and something worse than that, even if the evil cannot be exactly charted."

Every word that holds true for a stepmother holds even truer for a poly-mother. And "the evil that cannot be charted" is implicitly the destruction of the family organism.

Phaedra

Chuck Gitney was lounging in his room at prep school, getting ready to pour another beer when Western Union called. Chuck listened with quiet attention, then hung up and telephoned Elizabeth.

"Father is going to marry that French woman he met in Vegas."

At the other end of the telephone, Elizabeth's face grew somber. She had the clear, unsentimental eyes that under other circumstances could have counted the house. "How do you know?"

"Western Union just called. He said something gooey like, 'At my age I feel as young as you. I'm in love. Hermine and I are getting married tomorrow. Love, Dad.'"

"Did you think he would ask your permission?"

Chuck felt as though someone had hit him in the stomach. "Why don't we meet earlier tonight?"

"Okay. Do you have any idea what she's like?"

"He never mentioned her before."

"You just said she was French. And he met her in Vegas."

"That's right. I guess he did mention her before. I forgot about Vegas."

"You mean you blocked it out."

"Oh, can the psychoanalysis."

"He is actually marrying someone he met in Las Vegas?" She tried not to sound snobbish. "Do you think she's a stripper? Or a Mafiosa?" Elizabeth started to giggle.

"Don't be dopey."

"Actually, I think it's a growth industry—the Mafia, I mean. I'll see you on the steps of the library."

Phil Gitney was not as young as he used to be but he wasn't that old either. He was a lean, bony, gray-haired man, with features that were rough, even ugly, but his smile clicked on a kind of energy field, and his movements suggested its force. Phil had led an irreproachable life for twenty years, dedicated entirely to business achievements and his family, which consisted of his wife, Roberta, and their two children, Chuck and Del. By the time he was forty-five, he had amassed both a substantial amount of money and a substantial amount of fantasy life. He was, when he paused to think of it, and somewhat to his own embarrassment, envious of his maturing son, Chuck. With less embarrassment and more forthright resentment, he was also envious of his divorced bachelor friends. He viewed them with the typical naiveté of the respectably married man, imagining their lives as filled with voluptuous corruption. During the night, while his wife was asleep, snoring slightly with a mask on her eyes, he would read pornographic novels or picture to himself the sensuality of orgies that would have done justice to ancient Rome.

Being at heart essentially a man of action, not a passive dreamer, he set himself to the attainment of these goals. When the children were old enough and he was rich enough, he decided he would ask Roberta for a divorce. It is a tribute to his business genius that his children's ages coincided nicely with the growth of his fortune. When Chuck was fifteen and Del fourteen, his personal worth reached seven figures. Having met his own projections, he asked Roberta for a divorce.

At first she was shocked. Then she was relieved. The older she had grown, the cooler she had become sexually and the less she felt the need for a man in her world, except as an escort when an escort was necessary. It was not that she did not like men. She simply preferred her own company or the company of other women. Women were more companionable. They both understood more and required less.

Phil was, in fact, mildly chagrined at how readily she acquiesced to the divorce. Since her alimony and child support payments were considerable, the entire divorce proceeding was conducted on an enviably civilized plane.

In the first two years after his divorce, Phil enjoyed himself immensely. He was a child turned loose in a candy store. He lived in a deluxe apartment on the East Side of New York and squired a succession of models, actresses, heiresses, and other amiable, youngish, young, and even younger ladies around the city. He even managed to be present at a number of planned and unplanned orgies. Some that were catered with canapes and champagne. Some that were grubby with cheap pot. On the occasional weekends that his daughter, Del, spent with him, he made no dates, took her to museums and movies, and was continuously moody and uncomfortable. Counting the time till she left. Chuck was much more fun. When the boy occasionally came in from prep school for a visit, Phil would relish getting him a young date. He felt more like his older brother than his father. He talked to him man to man. It was all a great life. Until it palled.

On his way to a business meeting in Los Angeles, Phil stopped at Las Vegas for a weekend, in an effort to alleviate the boredom. More and more these days he had the impression he should be boisterously happy. But he wasn't. He had the feeling he was missing out on some important event. But he couldn't decide what it might be. Never having been in love, it did not occur to him that he longed to fall in love. He was a man who had always given a considerate, businesslike affection to his family. And that was what he had expected in return. More would have been excessively and foolishly sentimental. But he was feeling foolish and sentimental.

Not being in the mood for the gaming tables or for watching the newest, nudest, most expensive floor show, he ended up eventually wandering into a dim bar in his hotel lobby and ordering a double bourbon from a girl in a costume that left little to be guessed at. He was on his second double bourbon and feeling slightly tight when he noticed a youngish woman playing the machines in the lobby beyond the bar. She drifted along, seeming not to care if she won or lost. But she won often enough and her purse grew heavier with coins. As she leaned forward abstractedly to place a coin in a machine, he watched with fascination her full breasts jiggle without control of a brassiere. In unexpected contrast to her upper torso, her narrow hips and slender legs outlined against the clingy material of her dress gave her a tomboyish air, a curious androgynous appeal.

After three straight wins, she scooped up her last take and dropped the coins into her purse. Straightening up, she scanned the lobby for signs of life. Finding nothing of interest, she turned toward the bar; and Phil's heart quickened as he saw a face of fierce sensuousness, the look of a sun-tanned fawn. The girl stared speculatively around the room and then, with an almost invisible shrug of impatience, walked toward the bar. Once inside, she scanned the tables with resignation. They were either empty or else filled with couples. She started to purse her lips gloomily when she noticed Phil sitting alone at a wall table. He held his breath, wondering if he knew her. Slowly she crossed the room to stand in front of his table, her eyes retaining an odd half-mischievous, half-knowing look.

"I like you," she said.

He watched her without moving in his chair.

"Are you alone?"

"Yes," he said, still neglecting to breathe.

She sank down in the chair opposite him, her soft shoulders relaxing, her tanned bare arms resting on the table. They sat in silence for a few moments, and then she said half playfully, "Can I buy you a drink?"

Phil started to laugh with embarrassment. "I'm sorry. I wasn't thinking. What would you like?" He signaled the waitress.

"Scotch and sympathy." After the waitress left with the order, Phil adopted the self-conscious attitude of a man prepared to listen. He watched the fawn-woman attentively, expecting to hear the statistical facts of her life that strangers often tell in the first five minutes of meeting. But she only smiled and said, "You don't look a bit like a sex maniac. I hear there's one loose in Las Vegas."

It was not until early next morning, looking over from her pillow, that she remarked that on the Richter scale of sex mania he rated about eight. She also told him her name was Hermine.

"I wish you'd stay longer," murmured Hermine to Elizabeth

while she savored the bluefish. "It's so pleasant getting to know Chuck's friends. A week is hardly any time at all. And it's so lovely here. I've seen a lot of the world, and I don't know how I missed a place as beautiful as East Hampton in the summer."

It was a warm Sunday afternoon. They were lunching beside the pool while all around them stretched the wide green lawns that ended in a row of privet hedges. Elizabeth Allan listened politely to whatever Hermine said, but something in her manner intimated that she thought very little of Hermine's opinions.

"I'm lucky I could come for a week. Someone has to stay with the boys when my parents go to Scotland," Elizabeth answered virtuously. "And Martha's Vineyard is pleasant too in the summer."

"Oh, I'm sure it is," agreed Hermine. "Somehow I've missed going there, too. I seem to go more often to France, Spain, the Caribbean—places like that."

"Oh yes, I can see how you'd miss the Vineyard. There really isn't much hotel business there. It's mostly families who've lived there forever, summer after summer," Elizabeth explained with a nice mixture of girlish frankness and conscious snobbery. "Of course, it can be very dull. You'd be bored silly, probably."

"I manage never to be bored for long," remarked Hermine, sipping her white wine and smiling at Phil, who watched her with blatant joy. Elizabeth too watched her, but with a feeling uncomfortably akin to hate. She objected heatedly to everything about the woman. Her large breasts, her long legs, her mouth. Though Hermine was thirty-eight and actually looked thirty-eight, she made it seem as though thirty-eight was the best age to be. Alongside of her Elizabeth felt clumsy, colorless, and too waspish.

"Well, perhaps you can come back at the end of summer and visit us again," Hermine suggested. "When your parents return. Chuck and you could come at the same time." She smiled appealingly at Chuck, who managed to flush and swallow a rather large bite of tomato.

Driving to the station, where Elizabeth would pick up the 7:15 to New York, Chuck's face had a sealed, stamped look. What Elizabeth felt she didn't bother to hide. She gave him a quiet stare that forced him to face her.

"Well, she does look like a Hermine."

"What does a Hermine look like?" he asked, puzzled.

They drove in silence for a while and then Chuck said, "You don't like her, do you?"

"No, I don't. I'm sorry it showed." She really was sorry, being a well brought up young woman.

"I can read you like a book. Why don't you like her? She's good-looking, a good sport, and good for Dad. I like her."

"I can see that. She gives me the creeps."

"Why?" Chuck glided the car into the station as the train whistled in.

"It's my ESP. I don't know. She does." She picked up her bag. Chuck grabbed it and they ran for the train that was rolling to a three-minute stop. When they found her a seat, Chuck tossed her bag up on the luggage rack. "I'll call you," he said, looking down at her. She made a small moaning noise and lifted her face to his. He bent forward, putting his mouth on hers, and her arms went around his neck. Then she relaxed. She turned her face toward the window. "You'd better get off, the train's moving." He turned too, saw the station slipping by, and ran for the train door. "I'll telephone you when I get home," she called, following him to the door. But he didn't hear her as he leapt for the platform.

That night Phil took Hermine in his arms and talked to her of his love for her, his pleasure in their marriage, and his worries about Chuck. The boy had been turned down by Yale. He couldn't understand why. Hermine half listened, half didn't, snuggling against him and drawing him into lovemaking, slowly, patiently. Phil made love, though not every time, as though he were thirty. He had told Hermine solemnly that at his age "a man cannot be a sexual athlete every night"—and every night he wasn't. Still, he was a good lover; she drew him to her, caressing him wisely.

Hermine woke in the middle of the night with a start, as though a cat had jumped on her legs. She stared into the dark, remembering the dream that had wakened her. It was Chuck—she and Chuck clasped together like the hands of the clock at midnight. She could feel desire flowing through her body.

The idea that she could be aroused by Phil's seventeen-year-old son both titillated and embarrassed her. She was not without a sense of the proprieties. Of course, long after she herself was out of her teens, she had continued to enjoy an occasional encounter with a teen-ager—a delivery boy, a boat boy, a gas station attendant. She regarded these talented young men as a natural resource. Shortly before she met Phil Gitney, she had passed one of the most inspiring nights of her life with a seventeen-year-old Puerto Rican pool boy who actually managed to have seven orgasms within five hours.

Hermine had been married at eighteen to a wealthy industrialist of fifty, and after fifteen years of a marriage of musical beds they amiably agreed to call it quits. After her divorce, having considerable alimony, no children, and no interest in anything except enjoying herself, she had wandered from party to party, country to country, resort to resort. Hermine had no minor vices—not drugs, not liquor, not even cigarettes. Her essential interest was sex. And it was at resorts that she rediscovered the sexual superiority of the aroused teen-age boy. But Hermine was not without honor. Recognizing the niceties, she declared her own social circle off limits, never permitting her appetites to extend to the sons of friends.

Still, with the best will in the world, it became more and more difficult to ignore Chuck's constant presence. During the first two weeks of his vacation visit (he spent one month with his father and one with his mother), she had become aware of her growing interest in the boy. She had always been a sensible and reasonable woman—thanks to her practical French mother—and though now she was interested, she continued to be reasonable and sensible about her interest. She had entered his life by accident, but from here on what happened she knew must not be accidental. Every step of the way had to be planned, calculated. Constraint and common sense were the watchwords. Still, as time went along she had more and more difficulty practicing either.

After three weeks of soul searching, finally Hermine had rationalized her lust satisfactorily: 1) She had married a man who was kind and sexual and rich, but who was fifteen years older than she, and she was now, at thirty-eight, at the height of her capacity for sexual enjoyment. At least so said all the medical reports. The years were coming when she would feel relatively cool. That's why she'd made provision for them with Phil. 2) She had been a good and faithful wife through the past ten months of their marriage, during which she had had—if she had chosen to exercise it—ample opportunity to be unfaithful, with Phil's business partner, golf partners, bridge buddies, to say nothing of random members of the country club. Honor bound by her own pragmatic code, she had prudently refrained from needless indulgence. She had even gone so far as to snub the tennis pro, who was the idol of three quarters of the women in the club. 3) She was a woman not only at the height of her sexual powers but also with a higher degree of sensuality than most women—which, in fact, was why Phil married her in the first place. She knew she gave off the aroma of sexuality—it was not simply a matter of her physical makeup, it was psychological and spiritual, too. 4) It would be unhealthy for her to thwart herself. She had much to offer a young man such as Chuck and much to enjoy from his gratitude; if he could be persuaded to see the experience in the proper light, they would both be immeasurably enriched from their experience of each other. 5) He was not by the remotest stretch of the imagination any relative of hers. If they had met by chance at the beach, neither of them would have had a moment's qualm about meshing their mutual needs. 6) And of course her life would not be affected by this experience, and her marriage to Phil would be the better for it—she promised herself she would make it up to him a thousand times over. 7) Chuck himself would benefit from the relationship and be able to give more to whatever girl he finally chose. All as a result of having intimately known an older, sexually sophisticated woman.

Once Hermine had analyzed the situation to her own satisfaction, she felt infinitely more at ease. After all, Tuesday, Wednesday, and Thursday Chuck and she occupied the house alone, since Phil was in New York City at work. All in all, it had been rapidly becoming impossible to subdue her rampant fantasy life. After all, she was not made of steel. She was constantly bumping into Chuck in the early morning hours padding around barefoot in his shorts. Or at night when she couldn't sleep and wandered the house in a filmy negligee, sometimes she would find him stretched out on the couch, half naked, reading a book. Under the circumstances, it was better for her to know exactly where she stood.

Now at the country club, rather than lounging by the pool and enjoying the yearning looks of other women's husbands, Hermine allowed herself to sit beside the tennis courts in her scantiest bikini—almost bare at the breasts and cut high on the thighs—hypnotized not by the spin of Chuck's backhand or the smash of his service, but by the toss of his sun-bleached golden head when his service hit the net. Whenever Chuck gave Hermine a lesson, which she managed to arrange at least twice a week, she would wear no panties and no bra under her cotton shorts and top. Then she watched with secret triumph as the dripping perspiration made everything cling to her body, revealing her nipples, suggesting her pubic hair, and making Chuck miss occasionally even the simplest returns, blurring his timing, scattering his concentration. When she looked at him she no longer tried to conceal the longing in her eyes.

One Thursday, in the last week of Chuck's stay, they played tennis through the long, warm afternoon, and in the evening Hermine told Amy, the housekeeper-cook, that she could leave early. It was so hot. Chuck and she would have a light snack by the pool; there was cold chicken and ham in the refrigerator, remnants of previous meals.

Left to themselves, Hermine and Chuck swam until twilight filled the sky. Then Hermine mixed herself a martini while Chuck slowly sipped a beer. Watching her in the gathering twilight, he was conscious of what went on between them. His dominant emotions were excitement, perplexity, and fear. He knew quite well how he was supposed to think of her, and he had gradually realized that what he thought of her was something else entirely. Not as his father's wife—his mistress perhaps, but not his wife. Having had some experience with women since the age of fourteen, and recognizing how continually he and Hermine were alone together, he had done his best to stay out late at night, to stay out of her way as much as possible. Alone with her this night, he knew he was asking for trouble.

They sat together by the pool in their half-nude state. Whatever conversation they were making was meaningless. What was going on loud and clear was the language of their bodies. Thinking of his father made Chuck feel like a thief. He wondered if the old man wasn't satisfying her. With a body like hers, she might need a lot of servicing. Now he understood why Elizabeth disliked her—Hermine's aroma of undiluted sex. She had felt it, too. There was an involuntary tension in his arms as though he were forcing them to be still. The inner recognition that what he was doing was stopping himself from taking her in his arms was so shocking it made him blush in the dark.

After an interval of silence, Hermine made a suggestion. "Why don't you have a martini? Have one, with me."

"I'll sip yours." He did that and made a face.

"You don't like it?" She laughed gently.

"I suppose you get used to it." There was another silence. Then he reached for her martini and swallowed it down, the entire contents. She sighed softly.

"I'll make us another." She lifted her face to him, and he gave her a look of guarded anger.

Seeing the look, she read his thinking and knew he was frozen with uncertainty and fear. "But suppose we'd met as strangers?" she asked, moving her face closer to his.

"But we didn't." He was dogged and honest and miserable.

"You're not really my son," she said. "We're not even related. If we'd met at the beach . . . or on a tennis court."

In spite of himself, Chuck was breathing heavily. "I know. But we didn't. And my father loves you." He choked the words out, biting his nails restlessly, without knowing what he was doing.

"Don't bite your nails," she said quietly, and obediently, like a small boy, he took his hand from his mouth. "This has nothing to do with your father and me. Or you and Elizabeth," Hermine continued. "This is something special. Something between us—for me, for you, for nobody else. It will hurt nobody else. Everyone will benefit."

By now Chuck was struggling wildly with himself. Between her appeal and his inability to agree, he felt as though he were being crushed.

"My dear," she said softly and moved very close to him. Hesitantly, she put her hand on his hair and her face on his chest. That did it. He pulled her down to the side of the pool.

The next morning, when Hermine woke, she went looking for Chuck. Amy, already in the kitchen, said that Mr. Chuck had come down early, with his suitcase, and driven back to the city. He said he wanted to get an early start. He had left a note for Hermine.

She opened it and read, "Thanks—for everything. Tell Dad I'll talk to him tonight when I get to Elizabeth's. It's okay."

That evening when Phil Gitney talked to Chuck, he said the boy sounded quite strange. When Hermine asked, "How strange?" Phil said he didn't quite know. "Distant" was the word maybe. He looked at Hermine. "Did you two have a fight?"

She shook her lovely dark head in wonder. "A fight? What would we fight about?"

HINDSIGHT

It took Phil Gitney fifteen months to find out why Chuck almost continuously refused to visit him and Hermine. When he did find out, he was beside himself with rage. He might have forgiven her if he had discovered that her infidelity involved one of his business associates. Or one of their social friends. That kind of a casual thing he understood. It was the way things were now. But his own son! His shame knew no bounds. And there was nothing to be done. Chuck and he, once, long ago, the best of friends, now could hardly talk. The young man's remorse and guilt, and Phil's shame and jealousy, permanently impaired their relationship. Phil's divorce from Hermine did little to heal the breach between them. The fabric of the father-son relationship was irrevocably shredded.

PREVENTIVE PLOYS

Never Forget—Between Divorce and Remarriage Falls the Shadow

1. *The happy home complex.* Debunk with finesse or suffer the consequences. Chuck Gitney believed he lived in a happy home. When word came, by mail, that his parents were divorcing, it felt like a blow to the stomach. When his breath returned, he wrote to his father, asking if the divorce were

necessary. Phil's note left something to be desired. Writing man to man, not father to son, he explained that Chuck's mother was wonderful but Phil had a lot of living to do, and living with Roberta would be a crime against the natural man. Chuck wrote no more letters on the subject, but the answer bugged him. It turned shock into resentment. The resentment ricocheted around his unconscious and metamorphosed into something ugly. His admiration for his father entered a twilight zone.

2. *Remember, you will never be an ex-parent.* Phil's second blunder was another beaut. He decided he was too young for fatherhood. While accepting his financial responsibilities to his ex-family, he reneged on all his psychological obligations. He rarely invited his fifteen-year-old daughter, Del, for visits. She reminded him uncomfortably of the girls he now dated. And Chuck he over-invited. He relished introducing the boy to the young, young women who were now his dinner and bed companions. He hoped to impress Chuck. He was mistaken. Chuck came to see his father as a dumb, "dirty old man" fooling around with girls not much older than Del.

3. *In the mating season, keep your wits about you.* Hermine was an extreme example of improper mate choice. I told her story to show you how serious the wrong choice can be. But secondary incest can also show its menacing face in the presence of a perfectly decent young or not so young wife with high intentions but no sense of discretion. That story comes later. I call it Oedipus.

4. *In the same vein, think twice about child brides.* You're in the prime of life. Bully. You're not as good as you once were, but once you're better than you ever were. Great. Applause here. But if you want to remarry a young, young woman, and you've a past puberty son slopping around your house, you could use some serious second thoughts. Suppose when the house lights dim you find them eyeing each other? Do you need this anxiety? No. What's the answer? Right off, I recommend an unblushing chat with your heart's desire about your son; about this and that; about the implications of the Synergistic Imperative. Don't be shy. Spell it out. The do's and don'ts and doubts that you quite reasonably have, about life with you and she and he breaking bread and eating salt together. And then listen. If she's the solid citizen you think she is, she

won't be indignant, and you'll get your message through. If she's not that solid a citizen, you may have some hard lessons to learn after your wedding night. Should this prospect seem vaguely possible, I suggest you consider finding another child bride for remarriage.

5. *The same goes for child grooms.* If you are the bio-mother of a teenage daughter and you are contemplating marrying a much younger man, the question to ask yourself is: Why?

Getting Remarried Is Only Half the Hassle

1. *Remember, Little Boy Blue, barring sex changes, will eventually shave.* To a boy of eight or less, a mother is a mother is a mother. Your new wife will be a mother to him, even if she's just old enough to vote. But what he feels about you and his poly-mother, as he grows up, depends on the kind and quality of emotions, experiences, ideas, opinions that you share and pass around between each other. With a little luck and good judgment it can all go well. Meanwhile, keep the odds on your side. Make sure he has his own private sleeping quarters and you do not confuse him with an overexposure to your sex life.

2. *Remember, Little Girl Pink will one day wear a bra* (maybe). Little girls, like little boys, make affectionate, easy adjustments to a change of parents. But little girls have birthdays. If one day it becomes necessary to remind your husband of the danger to family stability of the magnetism of unchecked young female hormones, don't be offended, insulted, or embarrassed. Don't even bother to be jealous. It's too silly. Talk about it. Talk it out. It is neither a unique nor insoluble dilemma. It's the way it is, one of the hazards of remarriage.

Electra

Electra is the distaff side of the Oedipus complex, Electra being to girls what Oedipus is to boys. Here is the sorry story of a daughter's love for her father, Agamemnon, head of the house of Atreus, who is murdered by his wife, Clytemnestra, with the help of her lover Aegisthus. Weeping in rage, Electra says:

> What sort of days do you imagine
> I spend watching Aegisthus sitting
> on my father's throne, watching him wear
> my father's self-same robes, watching him
> at the hearth where he killed him, pouring libations?
> Watching the ultimate act of insult,
> my father's murderer in my father's bed
> with my wretched mother—if mother I should call her
> this woman that sleeps with him. . . .

All the Greek dramatists—Aeschylus, Sophocles, Euripedes—have dealt in their own way with this legendary family feud between the lustful mother—the queen, Clytemnestra—and her daughter—Electra, the virgin princess. In all the stories Electra in her fantasy longings for her father is jealous of her mother, resents her own virginity, and her one goal is revenge.

The horror of incestuous desire and consequent jealousies—fear of matricide and patricide, the theme of family hate-in-love—is even older than the legends of Electra, Phaedra, and Oedipus.

And with us still today. In our synergistic families, the most destructive elements of family competition and jealousy have irresponsibly been allowed to surface. Economic polygamy has led us backwards into a state of secondary incestuous polygamy that can, and often does, demolish our new families.

Take the story of Ellie Halston. Normally, a daughter's jealousy of her mother in relation to her father is well repressed, buried quietly in the unconscious and mediated by affectionate feelings of loyalty to the mother. With the coming of divorce, the hostile tendencies can be set free—particularly when a daughter becomes suspicious of a mother's own disloyalty to the father. This happened to Ellie Halston. Growing up, she saw too much and heard too much. In time she reacted too violently.

When the bell rang, Ellie, an agile five-year-old, flew down the stairs, jumping two at a time, and sprang to open the door. A man, tall, thin, angular, in a sport shirt and slacks, carrying a briefcase, stood there waiting.

"Andrew!" Ellie crowed and flung her arms around his legs, not being tall enough to reach his neck. "Andrew! I missed you!"

"I missed you, baby," he said, picking her up and hugging her.

"Come see my garden," she shrieked the instant he put her back on the floor. "Please." She grabbed the tweed of his pants and tugged at him wildly. He nodded obediently, dropping his briefcase on a foyer chair, and followed her through the long hall to the back of the house, which opened on a charming, if unmanicured flower garden. Ellie ran around to some plantings and then came dancing back to make sure he was following.

"Where's your mother?" asked Andrew, trailing after her submissively.

The garden was shut in by a high wall of surrounding apartment buildings.

"Here I am," said Claudia, coming to the door that opened on the garden. "You're back from your tour of duty." She was surprised to see him. Surprised and glad and shy.

"Look at the buds! The buds! Not at mother!" cried Ellie. "I planted everything myself."

"I am looking at the buds," laughed Andrew, following her around the garden.

"Ellie," said Claudia, "until Andrew arrived you were supposed to be getting ready for bed. It still is bedtime."

"No!" Ellie spit back, reckless as a puppy. "Daddy isn't home yet. And Andrew just got here. I must wait for Daddy and talk to Andrew."

"You must do what your mother says," said Andrew. "I'll be around now for a while."

"No, I mustn't do as mother says. Daddy isn't home yet. Give me a swing the way you used to."

"You look pretty heavy to lift."

"I'm forty-one pounds."

"You're one hundred and forty-one pounds," laughed Andrew.

"Give me a swing, up and down, up and down."

He bent over, put his hands under her armpits, and swung her high over his head, laughing low to himself while she shrieked with fear and pleasure. He did this three times. Then he brought her down and held her close while she clung to him with her arms around his neck.

"Ellie," said Claudia, in the soft, musical tone of a woman who is in love. "It's bedtime." She laughed as she tried to pry Ellie loose from Andrew. But Ellie only hung on tighter and laughed harder. It was a game. But she was no match for adult strength. Finally, she pleaded. "I'll go if Andrew puts me to bed."

"All right," said Andrew laughing. "But go now and get undressed."

"Why don't you help me undress. Untie my shoes," said Ellie, hugging the young man tightly.

Her mother looked at her thoughtfully. She was an engagingly ugly child, the way little girls are apt to be ugly who in later years may become unexpectedly stunning. The spark was there. She had a dazzling smile, and her hazel eyes were daring and full of a challenge she didn't yet understand herself. And she was growing too old for Andrew to undress.

Later she sat on Andrew's knee in her bedroom, eating a slice of apple with bites of fierce indignation. "I don't want to go to bed. I am not ready," she kept repeating. "I want to stay up with you."

"Kiss me good night," said Andrew, and he bent his cheek

forward. The incorrigible child raised her face to his, and then
gave his cheek a wide, sloppy lick with her wet, soft tongue.

Andrew and Claudia sat in the living room together, she sipping Scotch, he sipping sherry. "And how are you?" he asked,
his hands trembling a little.

"Exactly the same. It's heavenly to see you again."

He explained that he'd returned to town last night. He was
doing a book about the Berlin blockade. Ellen looked more like
Claudia than ever. And how was Robert? Claudia said he was
well.

Sitting there in the golden light of the lamp, they were engaged again in the long, half ironic, half serious dialogue that
had been going on since the day they met at work on their
hometown newspaper. The emotional content that filled the talk
came more out of their history than out of anything they said.
They'd fallen in love years ago, but then Andrew had been
married. Now he was divorced and Claudia was married. So it
goes.

But he dominated and attracted her still. He had a keen,
somewhat sardonic mind, idealistic but without illusions, an odd
mix of sentiment and cynicism. He accepted without reservations the world of infidelity, self-interest, personal ambition.
He had introduced Claudia to his best friend, Robert, a brilliant doctor, and when they decided to marry he agreed to be
best man. He knew that when his reputation as a journalist
reached a certain level, he and Claudia would resume their
affair. Which they did, interrupted only by his assignments
abroad.

"Will you stay for dinner tonight? Please." Claudia's voice
sounded faint and tipsy.

Andrew looked at the photo of Robert and Claudia on the
mantelpiece and shook his head.

"Well, if you can't come tonight, come to dinner Friday,"
Claudia said, following him into the foyer, as Andrew opened

the door to leave. "Ellie wants to see you, too." Claudia raised her voice against the roar of the outside traffic.

In her bedroom upstairs Ellie murmured, "Yes . . . come to dinner . . . come to dinner. . . ." And fell asleep.

When Ellie was twelve years old, Claudia and Robert decided to divorce. Claudia had told him that she and Andrew were in love, had been for years. Now time was passing. They felt they must do something. Robert couldn't help a grim smile as he thought of his absolute idiocy. The extraordinary thing was that he had not had the remotest idea that Claudia wasn't as happily married as he; that she really hated the house they lived in with its yards of beige carpeting; that she longed for moody, verbose Andrew with all his vague brilliances. The two people Robert loved best in the world had betrayed him. He and Claudia had been married thirteen years. He had been a loving husband. An excellent husband, he thought. Even a faithful husband. Certainly a good provider. Yet none of it seemed to matter. She no longer wanted to live under the same roof, sleep in the same bed. Coming to the decision to divorce had not been easy. They had not really slept for weeks thinking about it. Talking about it. Evaluating it. Did it make sense? Did it make nonsense? The only thing they did not do was fight over it. They were surprisingly calm. It was like pushing an egg up a mountain. The egg kept slipping and having to be gently caught. One day it slipped entirely out of control and rolled down the hill, hit a rock, and broke. That night they agreed to divorce.

That same evening Robert packed some things into a weekender—he would return on the weekend and really organize his belongings for moving out. Then they called Ellie from her room to tell her. Claudia opened the conversation.

"Darling, Daddy and I have decided that though we're very fond of each other, we don't make a very happy married couple." She stopped and swallowed, intimidated by the long, clinical look in Ellie's eyes. Then she gathered her courage. "Anyway, Daddy and I are going to get a divorce. And you mustn't be unhappy. The divorce has nothing to do with our loving you. We both love you very much."

"Hmmm," said Ellie.

"And it doesn't mean we won't be seeing each other, honey," said Robert. "I'll be seeing you almost as much as I do now."

Ellie was either unwilling or unable to say anything for a moment. She was bent on looking at the floor. Finally she asked, "Can I go to my room now?"

Imperceptibly, Robert flinched. "Well, don't you want to sit and talk with us awhile?" he pleaded.

"Must I?" She looked at him, her eyes filled with defiance, holding back tears. "I have homework to do."

"All right, honey," Robert nodded. "Do what you have to do."

Ellie left the room slowly, reflectively, pulling her hair. Robert watched her go, his heart in his mouth. "Well, I guess that's it," he said, getting up from the couch.

"How else could we tell her but by telling her? There's no easy way."

"I guess that's true." He picked up his suitcase and started for the door. Then came back. "I think I'll go up and say goodbye to her myself. I'll tell her I'll be back Saturday. Give her my private office number."

"You're being overdramatic. I'll tell her she'll see you Saturday."

"I'd rather do it myself." He started up the steps and Claudia almost tried to stop him. Then, realizing it was his right, she sat still, thinking about the way her world was going to change once he was out of the center of it.

Robert's frightened voice shocked her out of her reverie. "Claudia—where's Ellie? She's not in her room."

Claudia went rushing up the stairs. The child was not in her room. They started searching the house, calling her name. But there was no sign of Ellie anywhere. After about fifteen minutes of desperation, Robert said, "I'll call the police. Tell me, I can't remember—what was she wearing?"

In a little while the doorbell rang. A police sergeant and a plainclothesman were there. They took off their hats. "Now if you'll give me the facts again, Dr. Halston. We already have men looking for her in the neighborhood. You say she went up to her room about a half hour ago?" He checked all the data with Robert. "Now I don't want to frighten you unnecessarily, but would anyone want to kidnap the child? We must think of everything."

Claudia shook her head vehemently. "Why would someone do that? We're not rich. Or famous. Or anything." Robert put his hand gently on Claudia's forehead and ran it over her hair.

After the police had searched the house and grounds more thoroughly, they searched the neighborhood and rang doorbells. Then the police sent out a call with a description of Ellie and alerted all radio cars to be on the lookout for a twelve-year-old girl with pigtails dressed in beige-colored jeans.

"They'll find her. The police will find her, won't they?" Claudia asked Robert when they were left alone. "My God!" she added. "And when I think of the awful things I've said about the police."

A police car was still parked in front of the house when Robert went out to look. "I'm going to patrol the neighborhood again," the policeman told him. "Do you want to come along?" Robert agreed to go.

When he came back he found Claudia had been cleaning ashtrays.

"They'll find her," Robert said. "Or she'll find us. I know my girl."

"She ran away. I know it," wept Claudia. "She hates me."

Claudia and Robert spent the night in the living room drinking black coffee and Scotch. They were closer than they'd been in years, and Claudia sobbed a good deal, tears rolling down her cheeks, making her nose red. She kept saying, "I've been a good mother. Maybe I've been a lousy wife, but I know I've been a good mother. If anything happened to her I'll never forgive myself."

As time passed, Claudia decided that if anything happened to Ellie she'd never forgive Robert either. Robert did not say that the whole idea of divorce had been Claudia's, not his.

Eight o'clock in the morning the doorbell rang. Claudia sprang up to answer it, hoping it was news, and found Charles Sobel, one of Ellie's schoolmates, standing in the doorway. He stared at Claudia with the deadpan expression of a dedicated troublemaker.

"Mrs. Halston," he said. "My mother said to tell you she didn't think it was such a good idea for you to let Ellie sleep on the roof that way."

"Sleep on the roof?" Claudia rubbed her hand across her forehead, and her voice had a shrill edge.

"That's what she's doing Mrs. Halston. Sleeping on the roof."

Claudia stepped out of the door and onto the front lawn. She looked up at the roof of the house, and there indeed, back against the chimney, feet resting on the upward slope of the roof, was Ellie. She seemed to be fast asleep.

Naturally, Claudia and Robert were afraid to waken her. If they startled her, she might lose her balance and fall down on either side. Robert tiptoed back into the house and called the police and fire departments.

After the firemen stealthily circled the house with a net, Robert called gently, in a voice intended not to startle her.

"Honey, it's Daddy. Time for breakfast. We have pancakes."

Ellie turned her face sideways, wide awake, and said matter-of-factly, "Pancakes?"

"Yes. With maple syrup," said Robert. "Honey, this gentleman here," he nodded to the plainclothesman on his right, "is going to climb up a ladder and come on the roof and help you to come down and have pancakes."

"Oh," said Ellie. "What a bother. I'll just roll down and fall into those nets."

"Darling, don't!" screamed Claudia before Robert could stop her.

"Oh Mother, really. That's what the nets are there for."

"Shut up!" Robert whispered to Claudia. "Honey, roll if you want to. It's fun." He held his breath waiting for this maneuver.

"Mother will faint if I do," Ellie said with some contempt. She then gracefully stood up and carefully slid down the side of the roof to the ledge, kicked open the dormer window to the attic by which she had exited onto the roof originally, and climbed back into the house.

When Claudia reached her, she threw her arms around her in furious relief while Ellie remained aloof within the embrace. Claudia said, "You mustn't be unhappy darling. You know we love you. And I'll be marrying Andrew. You've known Andrew all your life." Ellie's eyes narrowed and for a moment Claudia had the feeling Ellie disliked her. This was an odd thought. It seemed unnatural. Of course she and Ellie had had their rows. But so did all mothers and daughters. Probably she'd blurted out everything too soon. But having started she couldn't stop. "Ellie, you know how much you like Andrew. It'll be like having a second father." Robert winced, while Claudia went on in that vein.

The night on the roof had taught Ellie a great deal. Adults, like kids, could not be trusted. She listened to her mother with the air of a person listening to an improbable lie. Then her father started to talk, and in spite of everything she felt sorry for him. Once he had bought her a doll and she had taken that doll to bed with her for a year, until by accident it got swept away by the waves on a beach. Then her mother had bought her a doll to replace it and Ellie had cut off its feet to make sure it would fit in the old doll's bed. After that, she took pretty good care of it.

Some months after the divorce, Claudia and Andrew were married. Robert felt an amused grimness at how well Claudia had managed first to separate Andrew and himself and then to appropriate Andrew for her own uses, now that he was a famous foreign correspondent. Claudia was an adroit woman.

It was nine-thirty on a Sunday morning in April, and Robert found Ellie standing waiting for him with the doorman in front of the new, very expensive apartment building where she now lived. "I knew you were coming!" She was shaking with excitement beneath the adulthood she had been trying to wear like her mother's dress. He took her in his arms, lifted her up, swung her around, and said, "I'm glad to see you, Cupcake."

They went back into the apartment foyer and sat down, whispering together happily so that the doorman wouldn't notice them. Ellie gave him her news. The dentist said that soon she'd be exchanging the harness she slept in to straighten her teeth for more ladylike braces. She didn't like her French teacher at the new private school she went to because he spoke French with a Haitian accent. She did like her music teacher. She thought she'd become a veterinarian when she grew up. Abruptly, she questioned her father. "You never really did love Mother, did you?"

Startled, Robert answered, "I did honey. Once."

"You always said you loved her. But I used to listen to her with Andrew before you came home at night. She didn't love you the way I do."

"I guess she didn't."

"She loves Andrew."

"That's good," Robert stammered. He wiped a smudge of dirt off Ellie's cheek. "We're better off apart." He sighed deeply, without sighing. How do you explain to a child what you don't understand yourself? "But that doesn't have anything to do with you and me. We'll always be together. Father and daughter. That's a permanent relationship."

"Andrew said I could call him 'father' or 'Andrew.' "

Robert wanted to ask her about Andrew, but he restrained himself. "He's your mother's husband now. But I'm your father. And you are my daughter. That does not end with divorce. That goes on forever."

"You can't divorce me?"

"I can't divorce you."

"I know. It's against the law. But you wouldn't if you could, would you?"

"No. Not if they paid me millions."

"And daughters can't divorce fathers."

"They'd better not try. Don't you want to be my daughter?" He was feeling stupidly insecure.

"Yes," she stated firmly and flatly. "I call Andrew, Andrew. And you, Father. Or Dad. You know." She threw her arms around his neck, half laughing, half crying. "I'll never divorce you!"

As they started out the building door to begin their Sunday excursion, she remarked softly, "It's too bad, though, that daughters can't divorce mothers."

The house was quiet and empty and there were only a few cars passing on the lane this Saturday noon. Andrew sat at his desk in his study and tried to persuade himself that he was working. He looked at his typewritten pages and then at his notes, then at his watch, and finally at the ceiling. An expression of resigned endurance came on his face. He got up from his seat at the desk and looked out the window. Then he stared blindly at the various photographs, taken by himself around the world and now framed and hung on the walls. In a state of self-irritation he walked out into the living room and found Ellie, still home, pacing the floor. He knew Claudia was at the hairdresser preparing for the party tonight. But what was Ellie doing home, not racing around with her friends?

"To what do I owe the pleasure of your being home at this hour?" he joked. "Weren't you going horseback riding with Tracy?"

"No, today's the day Dad is supposed to give me my fifth driving lesson."

"Oh, I forgot." He nodded in a businesslike way.

"He's going to call and tell me when he's coming."

Andrew nodded again and retreated stiffly into his study.

Ellie was tall for her sixteen years. Slender. Her hair was arranged simply about her long, pale, clean-cut features. The exaggeration of feature, of mouth, of eyes, of high forehead, that had made her ugly as a child had been transmuted by time and changing body chemistry into a spectacular face. The mobility of her face gave a continual impression of intense life. Watching her from the study, Andrew was aware of how mature and female she had become.

And how much she disliked him. Ever since he and Claudia had married, Ellie's manner toward him had subtly changed. She was polite. Agreeable. Remote. And the older she grew, the more polite, more agreeable, and more remote she became. It wearied him that this lovely girl, this proxy daughter whom he had loved as a baby, should have grown into a young woman who seemed to despise him. He was a kind and intensely good-natured man, who would have enjoyed showing her off to his friends, boasting about her, and doing things for her. It was impossible. Though he'd been prepared to do as much for her as her own father would, Ellie would not permit it; she kept her distance and her almost tangible distaste.

Ellie had not always disliked Andrew so much. Once, long ago, she remembered having deep, joyous feelings of affection for him. It was when she was too young to know better, she told herself now. When she was eight, she had drawn and pasted and colored for him a Valentine card. When she was nine, she had suggested that they be engaged. But that was before she saw how things really were: the deceit, the infidelity, the ugliness that he and her mother had practiced on her father, that they had destroyed her home with.

The telephone rang and Ellie reached for it.

Without waiting to find out who was at the other end of the phone, she screamed, "Daddy, where are you? You're late!"

Robert's voice, troubled, tender, came through the other end. "Honey, I can't make it today. I'm still in the city."

"Oh—" She listened with quiet apprehension.

"I forgot. Hallie and I have to take our blood test today."

"You mean Wasserman, Daddy?"

"Well, yes. And then we have to go look at the new apartment and take measurements. We have a room for you that's beautiful."

Silently Ellie thought about Hallie. Hallie who wasn't a real person to her. Hallie who was simply a result of everything else. None of which was Hallie's fault. How could you hate someone who didn't matter?

"Cupcake, are you there?" Robert's voice was worried.

"I'm here."

"Honey, you understand. It's my fault for forgetting about the blood test. I apologize." His tone begged her to forgive him.

"It's okay." There was a doggedness in her voice. "Well, sure, you have these things to do. You're getting married."

"But next Saturday. Next Saturday we'll be out for sure. I promise. Okay?"

She felt cold all over. "Sure. Okay."

"And you're coming to dinner tomorrow night at Hallie's?"

"I have to ask Mother." Her heart felt like lead.

"I thought you did."

"I forget too. I may not come back to the city till Tuesday."

"Well then, Tuesday night. Talk to your mother."

"I will, Daddy, I will. When she comes home. She's at the

hairdresser. All right, I will." But she felt hot with resentment.

Ellie put the telephone back in its cradle very carefully. Then she strolled over to the window and looked aimlessly up and down the street for a car that was not coming that day. Anguish, like dust, lay over the room.

Hearing the silence, Andrew walked out of the study. "What's the matter?" he asked, seeing Ellie slumped in the window.

"Nothing. Nothing. Daddy is stuck in the city today. He can't give me a driving lesson. He's going for his Wasserman with Hallie. And they have things to do."

"Oh, that's a shame," Andrew said impulsively, a nervous and unwilling witness to her pain. Then, feeling embarrassed, he added, "I mean it's a shame about your not getting a lesson. Not the Wasserman." He seemed always to be walking on thin ice with Ellie. He waited a moment uncomfortably, then started to return to the study.

"Andrew—" Ellie began and stopped. Her heart was beating strangely.

"What?" He hesitated, hopefully. The way she said his name sounded like a request for a favor, and he would like nothing better than to do this child a favor.

"Andrew—" She colored slightly and then continued with an appealing perversity. "Would you give me a lesson? You know how to drive?"

Andrew felt the relaxation that comes when pressure is lifted. "Of course. I'd be delighted to."

Ellie smiled, her eyes shining and triumphant. Later she would tell her father how Andrew had given her a lesson. Andrew, who knew how to drive racing cars. Let him have his precious Hallie. She had Andrew.

In the car Andrew allowed his professionalism to estimate Ellie's abilities. Unlike her father, he was a superb driver, and he saw immediately that Ellie had no sense of the machine or how to control it. She alternated a slow and fearful driving pace with sudden bursts of bravado speed as though she was embarrassed at her own fright and wanted to show off by passing every car on the road, changing lanes, and weaving in and out.

"Let's get off the highway," Andrew said sternly, having seen a police car in the rear-vision mirror.

"No. I can handle the highway. Daddy says I'm great."

"You may be great, but there's a police car behind us. So let's get off the highway." Andrew was smoking and his mouth was set. "Move slowly into the right lane and get off on the next exit."

Looking up into the mirror, Ellie saw the police car too, and her breath stuck in her throat. She swung sharply into the right lane to get off the highway, just missing a passing car by inches.

"Ellie, pull over to the side and let me drive," said Andrew firmly. "The police car may pass us."

"Don't talk to me like that," she said angrily. "You're not my father." Suddenly they saw a young boy on a bicycle coming toward them, riding on the unpaved shoulder of the highway. Somewhere behind them a siren started to blow. While Andrew was trying to decide whether or not to take the wheel forcibly from her, Ellie hit the accelerator and swerved to avoid hitting the boy. Andrew lurched against Ellie's arm. The sun blinded his eyes as they blinded hers. The last thing he remembered of that day was the splintering sound as a cluster of trees on the side of the road came up to meet them.

Andrew was at home, convalescing. He tried to write but he found he could not keep a sentence straight in his mind. He seemed to have forgotten how sentences worked. Claudia tried to help him by taking notes, but as soon as he started to dictate he forgot what he wanted to say. It was no use. He could see that she was tense with worry, her high forehead ridged with anxiety. She had great patience and love for him, but she was frightened.

"Ellie is coming to dinner," she said to Andrew one afternoon. A panic started to rise in him. He could not remember who Ellie was. But he did not want to appear that out of focus, so he said nothing. Then the panic subsided. It did not matter. He often forgot who he was. The doctor had said this phase would pass as he recovered. If he recovered, he sometimes thought.

"She seems to like living with Robert and Hallie," Claudia continued.

Andrew nodded. Bully for Robert and Hallie, whoever they were. For some unknown reason he realized he took satisfaction in the idea of Ellie and Hallie living together. What would she do to her?

HINDSIGHT

In a dim, nonverbal way, Ellie knew that Andrew's near-tragic accident was not entirely accidental. She herself suffered minor bruises, but after leaving the hospital seemed perfectly healthy. It took a few months before she went to pieces. It started with her wanting to walk everywhere—she said cars made her carsick. Still, when absolutely necessary she would accept a lift. Then that, too, became impossible. If she had to go somewhere by car, her hands would start to tremble, she'd have difficulty breathing. Finally, her fear of cars became so acute she would not leave the house, either to go to school or out with friends. It took two months to persuade her to go to a psychoanalyst.

In treatment, Ellie's attachment to Andrew became alarmingly clear. All through the years of her growing up, she had known about "my mother and Andrew," which was the way she described the affair to the doctor. Listening at doors, making telephone calls for her mother, hearing her mother lie to her father, Ellie received a cynical education in the dingy arrangements of adultery. In order to repress her anger at her mother, she pretended to herself that what was happening wasn't happening. The more urgent the affair became, the more in her own mind she insisted on the reality of her romance with Andrew.

The news of the divorce brought more pain than surprise. But it was Claudia's remarriage to Andrew that was the unforgivable indignity. Her mother had poached on Ellie's fantasies, run off, so to speak, with her "dream lover": the other most important man in her life. With Andrew now as her second father, he was no longer a safe object for sexual fantasies. In need of a more socially acceptable attitude, she elected to despise him.

Ellie's jealousy of her mother and resentment of Andrew grew as she grew older. The need to act out her hostile feelings became increasingly acute. It was not that Ellie lay awake nights planning to poison her mother or Andrew. She'd have been shocked at the idea. But a Rorschach test, or depth analysis sooner, would have turned up something akin to these Borgia tactics.

When Ellie sat down beside Andrew in the car that fateful afternoon, she had the mind set of a kamikaze pilot. In those few stark seconds, when she pressed her foot too heavily on the accelerator and turned the wheel too sharply to the right, she felt she was settling accounts with Andrew and her mother.

That Ellie came out alive and unharmed was to her a continuing source of guilt. In the years following the accident, only Ellie's father knew the truth. Privately Claudia never forgave Ellie, but consciously she chose to see the whole thing as a hideous accident. Andrew himself wearily intuited the truth. Even after he was able to resume a semi-normal life, he, Ellie, and Claudia were incapable of a real family intimacy. The unspoken strain between them was too great. What they had to make do with forever was civilized politeness.

PREVENTIVE PLOYS

Between Divorce and Remarriage

1. *Don't be unfaithful to your children.* Earlier in this section I did some narrow-minded sermonizing on the hazards of familiarizing your children with your pre-remarital sexual adventures. I meant it. And the same goes for extra-marital sexual exploits. I would like to write the words NOT FOR CHILDREN in bold, block, phosphorescent letters. At the risk of sounding like a maiden aunt, I feel it necessary to insist on the old-fashioned proprieties—when sin knew its place and its place was below stairs, in the broom closet preferably. Your infidelity is nobody's business but yours, and certainly not appropriate for the rabbit ears and saucer eyes of your children. They are having enough trouble slogging their way to adulthood. You and your spouse are their working models for maturity. Right? Right! Should you start flaunting your quirky passions and thrashing about almost in plain sight of everyone, what you are saying by such action is, "Go to it, kiddies—do your number." And believe me, they will. You've no idea the vanload of destructive, junk behavior your children can have unpacked and waiting for you once you are remarried. You see, they'll feel you're entitled.

2. *Take care, Electras and Lolitas are made, not born.* Mothers and daughters are bonded by opposites; they blow hot and cold at each other. Family ecology keeps their interaction neatly balanced. In fact, the psychological control mechanism is itself a quite remarkable one, admirably suited for coping with the competitive feelings of the various females who appear in most domestic dramas. When things are going well, affection regularly short-circuits jealousy. It's as natural as breathing. It is only when mother or daughter for some murky reason displays off-kilter reactions—too grabby (the daughter), too bossy (the mother), too openly sexual (either), or too something that the other cannot abide—that the balance goes askew, hostile responses are launched, and anything can happen. It was Claudia's shortchanging of her own moral authority that gave the justification to Ellie's buildup of hostility. This can happen between any bio-mother and daughter (or bio-father and son; i.e., Phil and Chuck) when a child gets a 3D view of mother's feet

of clay. It encourages competition. Of every imaginable description. A hard competitor will stop at nothing. She may
sashay in as Lolita, the incestuous seductress. Or, like Ellie
Halston, choose the "Fuck You!" Sublimation and come done
up as an avenging angel. Neither of these colorful figures will
contribute much to your domestic bliss. So why, if you're a
mom, be the inspiration for either?

Oedipus

The term "Oedipus complex" was originally made famous by
Freud. It derives its name from a legendary domestic tragedy
written by the Greek playwright Sophocles about 2400 years
ago. On the chance that you have only a nodding acquaintance
with Oedipus, let me fill you in briefly on this primal story of
family life.

As a young man, Oedipus leaves his native city of Corinth
because he believed that Polybus, the king, was his blood father, and Merope, the queen, was his blood mother. He leaves
to escape the horror of a prophecy that foretells he was:

> fated to lie with my mother
> and show to daylight an accursed breed
> which men would not endure, and I was doomed
> to be the murderer of the father that begot me.
> When I heard this I fled. . . .

In his wanderings away from Corinth. He came to a place
where there was a branching of crossroads, and there

> . . . I was encountered by
> a herald and a carriage with a man in it. . . .

Subsequently, there were harsh words, tempers were lost,
and a skirmish occurred over who had the right of way. Being
young, strong, and irritable, Oedipus ultimately killed the

herald and the man in the carriage. From the Greek standpoint, this kind of roadside ruckus was hardly worth gossip among beggars. It happened every day. So Oedipus simply picked himself up, dusted himself off, and continued on his way to Thebes, where he was going before he was interrupted.

Once arrived in Thebes, in a manner not explained by Sophocles, Oedipus meets Queen Jocasta. One thing leads to another; they marry and have children.

As Fate would have it—and in a Sophoclean play fate moves on swift footsteps to the doom that must be—the man that Oedipus so unceremoniously disposed of on the road from Thebes turns out to be in reality his biologic father, King Laius. And the woman he inauspiciously married, Laius's widow, is his real mother, Queen Jocasta.

Clearly, if you're Greek you have one devil of a time escaping those prophecies. With the best intentions in the world, Oedipus managed to sin against his society.

Aside from the fact that the story of Oedipus concerns kings and queens in ancient Greece, a parallel plot could be replayed in present-day Chicago, Los Angeles, or Keokuk, Iowa. And once replayed can cause as much emotional havoc as it did 2400 years ago in Thebes. Witness what happened when, to everyone's grief, we see Oedipus revisited in a New England university town, in the house of Professor Lawrence Wilson.

"Edward isn't home yet. He said something about stopping at the art shop to pick up some materials," said Rowena Wilson to the tall young man standing in the doorway. He looked almost young enough to be her son. "In the meantime you will have to put up with me." She smiled, nodding her head in the direction of the living room. "Come along. Edward's talked so much about you, I feel as if we're old friends."

"Edward is an excellent student. I think he has a future," said the young man. And then he felt like a fool or a school fund-raiser for making that kind of remark. He brushed a loose strand of long blond hair back from his brow and nervously followed Rowena into the living room. The woman had unsettled him. He had not expected Edward's mother to look so young. She was of medium height, slim, supple. Her face was flushed and animated, with only the merest trace of age lines. It's these American women, Hans thought with some impatience. They are raised on protein, dentistry, exercise, and mirrors.

Sitting in the golden brown living room, the walls lined with books and paintings, he had a self-conscious air of not knowing where he was. Yet he liked the room. It was one he could have lived in himself—spacious, quiet, with gleaming wooden floors covered by small Oriental rugs and deep chintz-covered chairs and sofas that looked as though they were used regularly. In the early spring twilight, the room seemed more luminous than the outside world.

"How do you like teaching at our university?" Rowena asked, arranging her long skirt so that she almost squatted on the couch, one leg tucked away under her like a teenager.

"I like it very much." He spoke English slowly, with a certain harsh accent. He was a man accustomed to being listened to, but now he was at a loss for words. Still, he would make the effort for her. So he said the winter had been colder than he expected. He said he missed his family back in Berlin. He had a wife and a baby daughter. This had been an interesting experience, but in June he would be glad to go home.

Rowena felt full of generosity, kindly toward his short, blunt fingers, compassionately for his homesickness. Ultimately she was seduced by his strong wrists.

When the doorbell rang she had been listening to his theories on functional self-expression. At the door were her son and husband, Edward and Lawrence Wilson. Edward was loaded with packages. They'd happened to meet at the walk to the house.

"You're late," she said, looking at her husband with mild irritation. "Edward, you found your supplies?" With her son she used a tone that would have made a chance listener feel he was eavesdropping.

"Yes. Did Etzel come?" His tone matched hers for intimacy.

"He's in the living room. I've been keeping him amused."

"I knew you would, Mother." From the height of his six feet Edward leaned down and kissed Rowena's cheek. Then he bounded away into the living room. Lawrence and Rowena continued to stand in the doorway, Lawrence's face quiet and expressionless.

"The bacteria detained you for drinks?" she teased him.

"A departmental meeting. It occurred spontaneously."

"Like some fires." She patted his cheek with her hand. "It's all right. What's a little lateness? The stew will keep."

Lawrence relaxed; and as he did he realized how tense he had been. For the last few months—perhaps even a year—Lawrence could never anticipate when Rowena would be in one of her moods: sarcastic, biting, cold. But why? Why? He could not understand any of it. Sometimes in the morning, walking to school, he would wonder about what she had said; that she wanted to get away from him, from living, as she said, "in his shadow." But what could he do? How could he cast a smaller shadow?

"We must see to our guest," he said practically. He was always aware of the amenities.

"Come, darling," she said, slipping her hand through his arm. "Yes, we must see to our guest."

The Wilson family lived in a New England university town, where Edward's father, Lawrence, was Schnitzler Professor of Microbiology, possibly in line for a Nobel Prize. The family was a curious mix of art and science. Jenny, Rowena's firstborn, was done in the mold of her father. Cool, patient, precise,

she was permanently skeptical, atheistic. Yet you could see by
the way she responded to Lawrence's every word at the dinner
table that to him she gave a deep, unquestioning allegiance.

Edward and his mother belonged to the same world of the
arts and imagination. From childhood, Edward's artistic bent—
and the museums, galleries, books, talks, and theories they
shared because of it—was Rowena's real source of pleasure.
The scientific social life of the university had long ago begun to
weary her. Listening to the confusing, interminable conversations about "a reagent for the detection of endotoxin from gram
negative bacteria" or "cell regulatory mechanisms" made her
yearn more and more for what she felt to be the simplified
experience of color, shape, texture. Lawrence's life seemed to
her an abstraction. It was not her life of touching and seeing
and feeling. But where was her life?

When Edward entered the university to study architecture,
he and his mother were closer than ever. In good weather, they
would go on drives around New England looking at old houses
and studying the evolution of the salt box, investigating various
land sites—wooded lands, fields, lands sloping to streams—and
explaining to each other the kind of houses that would be suitable for the site. By the end of the day, Edward's paper would
be full of pages of sketches.

Sometimes it was quite dark by the time they returned home,
and dinner had long ago been served. Lawrence would then
come out of his study to greet them. Their windblown faces, their
happy air of play would make him unconsciously envious,
make him think for the first time in his life of the long hours
spent studying cell membranes while they were gazing at skies
and contemplating hills and streams. Then an odd expression
would cross his face: a look compounded of doubt and a kind
of blood resentment, which Rowena recognized as jealousy.

But she knew how little Lawrence had to be jealous of. Edward would find his own group in school. Soon he would find a
particular girl. Her pride and intelligence warned her, that

though she loved Edward dearly, her days at the center of his universe were numbered. It was with Rowena in this mood of resignation that Edward first invited his instructor, Hans Etzel, to dine.

Hans Etzel was invited three more times. The third time was not quite the success of the previous visits. Lawrence did not, as he usually did, talk biology or politics, even when Jenny pressed him. Edward had nothing to say about architecture. Now only Hans and Rowena kept the conversation alive, talking about buildings with glass skins, post and beam construction, the Bauhaus school. Rowena had kept pace with Edward's developing interest, and Hans, now fascinated, found in the mother of his star pupil the source of the young man's talent.

But the dinner was not a success. All through the evening Rowena sat relaxed in her chair, her glance remaining on Hans, regarding everyone else with a kind of second-hand favor. Rowena was a woman who had always thought she was happiest being loyal to one man. The idea of infidelity and its shabbiness had no appeal. But life had tripped her up. She was at that state—for the first time in her marriage—when being wanted by a stranger could compel her to want. And Hans was inclined to let her see he desired her.

At the same time she was no fool. She did not possess the gift, so desirable in adultery, of being able to lie to herself. Her right hand knew exactly what her left hand was doing. So shamelessly, purposely, she took the initiative with Hans. But that does not tell it all. Their natures played upon each other. He merely waited for her to respond to his signal. It had to happen and it did.

They had been lovers for six weeks when the semester ended and Hans had to return to Germany. They had managed to see each other about a dozen times, their meetings both ardent and guilty because of their fear of discovery. They said their last good-byes in the same motel room, hopeless and insatiable. "Please don't cry," he whispered, holding her tightly against him. "Why not?" she asked, smiling. "Tears are another form of kisses."

The next day when Edward asked Rowena to go with him to take Hans to the airport she was startled. Was he asking her to come because he suspected—did he want to see how she would behave? "He's a very pleasant young man, but I was planning to see Mr. Seymour about re-upholstering the couch." She paused to breathe. "Are any of the other students going?"

"No," said Edward.

"Well, then, of course I'll come. Two's company, but at an airport a crowd is more fun."

After picking up Hans and his luggage, the presence of Edward made private conversation between the lovers impossible. Actually, Rowena was glad. There were many years and miles dividing them now. There was nothing more to say.

At the airport they all wished each other well, and Hans said to no one in particular except the blue sky, "I'll be back." But Rowena knew it wasn't true.

Hans was the last passenger to enter the plane, and once he boarded, the hatch door was closed and the stairway removed. It was a clear, beautiful June morning when the plane took off. So the affair was ended.

At Nantucket that summer, the Wilson family had some unsettling moments. It was like waiting for a storm, hearing the sound of far-off thunder.

One evening Edward decided to expound on architecture, all about simplicity, line, form, and the relation of art to nature. Lawrence, usually mild and accepting, lost his temper. "All right, Edward, enough of this. Let me tell you about nature in your own terms. There isn't an architectural entity in the world to compare with—in terms of function, shape, and efficient elegance—the incredibly simplified complexity achieved by the double helix. Son, learn something. Occasionally more is more."

Rowena was having difficulty letting Lawrence make love to her. She knew she was making too much of it. After all, women had been embracing men whom they didn't want since the world began. It was like birth and death and rape and divorce ever since the world began. She had a variety of excuses. "I have a headache." Or, "I'm about to get my period." Or, "I'm exhausted." Sometimes she had no excuses, and she pressed herself to him desperately. After one of those nights Lawrence suggested wryly that they needed a book about sex after forty. Something that told about what caresses to make and new places to kiss. Things like that. Always something of a technician, Lawrence missed the point.

The sad truth was, as the years had shown her, that Rowena preferred Lawrence the eminent scientist to Lawrence the husband and lover. Every morning of that summer when she sat up and got out of bed she thought without malice that she would never lie down beside Lawrence again. But every night she did.

Finally, when she had said a dull, "No, I don't want to make love" three times to Lawrence, he stopped even reaching for her hand.

"Do you want to talk about it?" he asked her once uncertainly. Beneath his bitterness and depression there was still a boundless trust of her, of her goodwill toward him.

But she could only shake her head. "Not yet, not yet."

Sometimes at dinner, she would notice Edward watching her, his eyes shining with childish sadness and reproach. Her life with her husband had loosened and fragmented; now her love for her son, too, was painful and veined with guilt—the guilt of somehow feeling she'd betrayed him, too. She felt sorry for him and avoided the long rambling walks they used to take together on the beach. She wanted no company now but her own thoughts.

Edward accepted her detachment with a mixture of self-pity and relief. At the moment he wanted no intimacy with his mother. But he had curiosity about what his father was thinking and feeling, something akin to what an entomologist might have for an unclassified specimen. He took to asking him to play tennis, to go sailing, to do things with him.

One twilight in the dimly lit garden behind the house, musing over a chessboard, he was on the point of asking how his father had liked Hans. But a sense of respect restrained him, and instead he said, "Mother's in a peculiar mood, isn't she?"

Lawrence Wilson looked up from a consideration of his next move with a speculative, troubled expression. "What are you suggesting?"

Edward flushed. "I don't know. She seems so withdrawn and solemn these days." Then with rancor he added, "All she does is watch for the mails." This was a lie, but Edward wanted to see how his father would react. He wanted to hurt him as he had been hurt by Rowena's disloyalty.

"That's nonsense!" Lawrence spit out the words. The quickness of his response indicated how much he understood. "What the devil are you implying, Edward?"

"Oh nothing. Forget it." His voice sounded thin and choked, but he relished the sensation that his dart had found its mark.

"Listen to me, Edward," his father said with controlled calm. "You and I have never been close. You are your mother's son more than mine. But you are my son, too. And I do not expect my son to make insinuations that are subtly offensive to me and insulting to his mother."

"I'm sorry, Father," Edward said in a low voice, unexpectedly feeling remorse, for he had damaged some core in the family order. "Check. I think I have you."

The next morning, after another stifling night, Lawrence decided to look for Rowena on the beach. He found her far down
by the dunes, staring at the page of a book she wasn't reading. Rowena, seeing his shadow falling across her legs, knew
by its size that Lawrence was standing before her.

"It's been a very cold summer, Rowena." He paused, and
as she said nothing he went on. "All right. In this broad daylight world, safe from my advances, can I ask you a question?"
His lips trembled with his voice.

She shrugged her shoulders helplessly. "Ask away," she said.

Lawrence dropped his eyes in an effort to frame the question. "Are you in love with Hans?"

It was the first time he had ever mentioned Hans's name,
and it occurred to Rowena that he had guessed everything. So
she felt no purpose in lying. "Yes, for a little while I was
in love with Hans. But only for a little while. What's happening is not because of Hans. It's because of me."

Lawrence took this in, full of stiff pride and hurt. Then he
said half jokingly, "Are you aware you talk in your sleep?"

They were quiet for a moment, staring into each other's
minds. Then Rowena rose and started to walk on the beach.
"No, I wasn't aware." She stood motionless in her shadow. "It
must be very educational," she said, smiling, and resumed her
walk.

Lawrence knew now that they could not pretend nothing
had changed when everything had changed. Rowena had left
him without actually leaving. The reasonable being in him
could not accept it. It was too ridiculous. But the ridiculous had
become reality. So in the fall, while they were shutting up the
house, Lawrence suggested divorce to Rowena. She agreed that
it was an excellent idea. The only idea. Jenny was heartsick.
Edward could not forgive either of them.

Rowena asked only for a minimum alimony, since she had a
modest independent income of her own. She decided to move to

New York, leaving the house to Lawrence, Edward, and Jenny. She thought she would like to go back to school and study interior design. Jenny thought everyone had gone crazy, and abruptly enrolled herself in a West Coast college. Edward did nothing. He had two more years at the university, then he would see. He was disgusted with his mother but far angrier with his father. Affairs occurred every day. Half the professors and half the wives—this was not the Dark Ages. What was the sense of a divorce? Why had he permitted it? He admitted to himself half wistfully that he had never understood his father. Their relations could be reduced to a family convention that they both shared. And now the thread had snapped.

About six months after Rowena got her degree and moved to New York, Lawrence announced he would remarry. Jenny was stunned. Edward's pulse raced. Who could replace their mother? Vivid. Intelligent. Sensitive. What insanity!

On a visit to New York, Edward told his mother about the coming marriage, and she showed surprising compassion for his father. "I suppose he's quite lonely," she said thoughtfully. This reaction was not what he'd expected, and it came to him with a shock that the next news he might have was that his mother was remarrying. He had to stop himself from saying, "Mother, you can't do that!"

The first time he met his father's fiancée was when, unexpectedly, Lawrence Wilson brought her home to dinner. Her name was Jane Quitney, and impulsively Edward blurted out, "You're too young to be my mother." But Jane only smiled as if he'd said, "Pass the salt, please."

All through the dinner Edward felt at sea. Unable to stop himself, he found himself staring at her extraordinary prettiness in bewildered admiration. She had straight blonde hair streaming to her shoulders, freckles on a clear skin. Her mouth, too, was a heartbreaking matter—not too full but full enough, and she wore no lipstick. In her crisp white blouse and expensive tweed skirt, she looked more like the queen of the senior class than the thirty-three-year-old microbiology instructor she actually was. Unfamiliar with her field, he had difficulty engaging her in conversation. She answered his questions about her work, which he did not understand since he'd never bothered to pay any attention to his father's work; and she answered his questions about her background—her father was a real estate agent, her mother was a math teacher—with a polite formality that he found totally disconcerting. Edward was a young man more accustomed to the ardent attentiveness of ladies than this detached, merely scientific interest.

It was irony indeed. He, who had often held center stage at family dinners, now found himself feeling like an outsider. He did not understand what Jane and his father were talking about. Worse, they didn't seem to notice. After coffee, Edward rose abruptly and went to his own room to work. He did not intend to sit around and watch them "make love," as he described it to himself.

Lawrence Wilson and Jane Quitney were married about a month later, and Edward was Lawrence's best man, which made him feel exceedingly foolish. Jenny was sick with flu at the time, so she managed to avoid coming East for the wedding and Edward had to bear it alone.

He had to bear living with them alone, too. It was, he discovered, a thoroughly unnerving experience. It had not occurred to Edward ever that his father might be considered an attractive man—certainly distinguished but not exactly attractive. And yet clearly Jane regarded him not only with respect but with something else—the look in her eyes was much like the look he'd seen in other young women's eyes when they glanced at him. Somehow it made Edward angry.

What made matters more tense was that he was continuously fighting with his favorite girl, Maria. They fought over everything, but particularly they fought over Jane. Late one evening, after a lot of beers and a particularly stormy session, Maria heatedly warned Edward that if he persisted in talking about his new mother in her presence she was prepared to do without his presence permanently.

"You sound like a raving maniac," she screamed. "What's the matter with you? Can't you think of anything but Jane?"

"I hate her. I hate the two of them. That's why I talk about it so much. To get it out of my system," Edward said in a thick voice.

"You don't hate her—I've seen her. She's very pretty. You've got a crush on her. You may even be in love with her! And I find the whole business stupid and sick. Sick! Sick!"

Edward looked at her just long enough to reply with horror, "I'm not in love with her. I'm not a maniac! You are!" And he slammed out of her room, dazed and furious.

When he arrived home that evening, he found the downstairs house dark and the night light on in the dining room. He had forgotten that his father had gone to a faculty meeting and would not be home till quite late. He could hear water running upstairs in the master bathroom, and he knew that Jane must be taking a shower.

Without daring to think about what he was doing, he climbed the stairs slowly and walked toward the master bedroom. He stood outside the door listening to the water running, unaware of everything but the sound. After a while the water stopped, and Edward, now standing in the bedroom, heard the softness of Jane humming as she dried herself. Then there was silence, one moment, two moments; he wondered what she was doing, he wondered what she looked like nude. Out of control, his mind locked on one blind purpose. Edward opened the door quietly. The young woman was standing in front of the long mirror nude, contemplating her body, her high breasts, her slender torso, her long, well-shaped legs.

"You bitch!" Edward whispered in a hissing tone.

Jane gasped with fear as she whirled to face him, wrapping the towel quickly around her nude body. "Edward! For God's sake!" She was panting and her face was full of alarm.

Edward stepped toward her, his eyes gleaming like some wild creature. "You bitch!" he repeated softly. "I hate you!"

Standing barefoot on the bathroom floor, she stared at him, terrified. "Edward—please." Her voice was half a sob, half pleading.

Edward's brown eyes flared at the tone of her voice. Suddenly he ripped the towel from her hands, gave her naked body a slow appraisal, and then struck her face with the open palm of his hand.

Jane's head rattled like a loose marionette head, and her breath came in choking gasps. "You bitch—mother!" Then he slapped the other side of her face with the open palm of his left hand.

"That's for marrying my father—mother!"

Terrified and thrown off balance, Jane staggered back against the wall, a confused, piteous look in her eyes. She moved her mouth convulsively and tried to call for help. But her voice was very weak. Still, her effort seemed to drive Edward mad. He slapped her again with his right hand. "That's for fucking Hans —mother!" Again with his left hand. "That's for fucking us all—mother!" He slapped her with his right hand. "That's for being my mother—mother!"

Jane made a horrid choking sound. Her left eye was closed and bruised, and blood was streaming from her nose and mouth as she sank to the floor, weeping uncontrollably.

Edward stared a moment blankly at the sobbing woman, her hair disheveled, the blood dripping over her naked body, and suddenly a look of agony came into his eyes. "Oh Jesus!" He raised his hands to his face.

Wild with shame and remorse, he dropped to his knees be-

side the wretched woman, wrapped the towel clumsily around
her shoulders and, sobbing as deeply as she, murmured, "I'm
sorry . . . I'm sorry . . . I'm sorry."

HINDSIGHT

That evening, Lawrence Wilson came home to a nightmare.
At first it was impossible for him to grasp what had happened
to Jane. Her bruised face, her swollen eyes, the black and blue
marks—none of it made sense. He couldn't get it through his
head that Edward was responsible. The world had gone crazy.
In a daze he walked into Edward's room and found the boy
stretched out on his bed staring up at the ceiling. A nerve
snapped. This gentle and reasonable man went berserk. He
began pounding Edward's body with his fists, hitting him sharp
blows, weeping, hitting him again and again until Edward was
as black and blue and bruised as Jane. Edward did nothing to
defend himself. It was only when Lawrence became aware of
Jane pulling at his arms and sobbing for him to stop that he fully
realized what he was doing. Sitting down on the bed beside
the stunned boy, he wept uncontrollably. Jane telephoned for
the doctor.

The next day, shaky on his feet from the beating, Edward
packed a few belongings into a flight bag and moved out of the
house. Lawrence and Edward did not speak again for a year.

Rowena heard of the episode first from Lawrence and later
in aching bits and pieces from Edward, who could forgive neither
himself nor his father. Listening to Edward, Rowena felt a sour
self-disgust. She made no excuses for herself. She recognized
that at bottom she was responsible for Edward's bizarre fugue.
But what could she say that would not make matters worse?
The look in Edward's eyes warned her away from the subject.

Lawrence and Jane Wilson's remarriage was salvaged. In
time it was happy enough: very full, very active, always

troubled. For Lawrence and Edward rarely met. And when they did, they had almost nothing to say.

The hang-ups bequeathed to Edward by his affection for his mother were many and thorny. In time he came to shy away from any but the most superficial intimacies with women. He felt women to be dangerous and deceitful. He lost, too, his knack for friendship with men, in the casual manner of male bonding. His father had beaten him, and he carried like a stigmata the private shame of having deserved the beating. But what caused him to wake at night, drenched in sweat, was the persistent anxiety that he might again do something unpredictable that warranted humiliating punishment. To cancel this possibility, Edward retreated. His life spiraled downward into smaller and smaller circles, all but empty of intimate contacts, his energies poured into work.

PREVENTIVE PLOYS

1. *Don't be Jane—be wary of an Oedipus complex transplant.* Along with your remarriage license may come a son with a dangerous Oedipus condition. How will you know? There are no EKG's to give you a reading. You have to do the scouting yourself, with purpose and compassion, prying into the past, speculating on the present personality of the children you beget by remarriage. Jane did not. She never stopped to think what Edward was like, what becoming a poly-mother might mean.

2. *Remember the "Fuck You!" Sublimation. It needs no invitation.* Unlike Hermine, the last thing in the world to occur to Jane would have been to invite Edward's attention. And Lawrence, unlike Phil Gitney, was not ambiguous about his role as father. He never treated Edward coarsely. It was not his nature. He regretted his son's aloofness, but he respected it. What he did expect from Edward was the normal respect of a son for a father. But Edward's psychology was not normal. Could this anguish have been averted? Probably not in this family. Edward was a son, and Lawrence, Rowena, and Jane's notion of a son had been invented under the tight security of

the monogamous family. A security that was no longer theirs. *Footnote:* Many remarriers bring with them children. Others who are childless remarry into ready-made families. This latter circumstance calls for a comment. Sometimes I think that childless poly-parents, such as Jane, such as Andrew, are a more endangered species. When it comes to confronting the secondary incestuous impulses or the unfriendly displacements of poly-children, they lack something in the way of stature. A full-fleged bio-parent has natural authority. A poly-parent without children may find it hard to come by the honors and dignities of mother- or fatherhood. In the eyes of their poly-children they are no more than strange adults who have moved in on their lives. I know. I write from experience. And if you, too, are childless, I suggest that it will not hurt you to keep your eyes open to every little thing. The press of life when you are fending for yourself in the synergistic family is no laughing matter. It is not a crying matter either if you keep your wits about you and a weather vane on the roof to tell you which way the wind's blowing.

Encapsulation

The Four Horsemen . . .

1. There is no "innate aversion" to incest; what there is, is an innate inclination to it.
2. There is no built-in blood ban against incest, nor does primary incest automatically spell biologic disaster (babies with horns), even in the monogamous family.
3. But if there were a built-in, biologic blood ban, a goodly percentage of the synergistic family are not biologically related anyway.
4. The synergistic family also does not have the cradle-to-grave recognition of each other that have acted to restrain the monogamous family from incest.

How to Avoid the Apocalypse—Preventive Ploys

1. *Pre-divorce*
    *   Do not snipe at, strafe, and shell your future ex with the children as observers. Also avoid trench warfare.
    *   Do not train your children to inform on your future ex.

> * Do not acquaint your children with the niceties of adultery.
> * Do not suddenly "spring" a divorce on your children. Prep them for it.

2. *Pre-remarriage*
   > * Do not be over-affectionate or under-affectionate to your children when you are lonely in and out of bed.
   > * Do create sexual barriers between yourself and your growing children of the opposite sex; i.e., nudity is out.
   > * Do not inflict your pre-remarital sexual adventures on your children. Imitation, in this case, is not the highest form of flattery.

3. *In the matter of mate choice if you or he/she have children . . .*
   > * THINK how your future mate might view your children if your future mate is beseiged by seductive or competitive urges.
   > * THINK how you would respond under similar circumstances.
   > * THINK if there is a potential Oedipus, Electra, and/or Lolita in your brood-to-be.
   > * Also, maturity is called for when considering a child bride. Ditto a child groom.

4. *Remarried—hoorah! The synergistic family*
   The particular Preventive Ploys listed here apply to all versions of synergistic family. Some were mentioned earlier but are worth repeating. Those that are new, please note.
   > * Within the environs of the synergistic family, those related to a "prohibited degree" include.
   >> bio- and poly-mothers, bio- and poly-fathers
   >> bio- and poly-brothers, bio- and poly-sisters
   >> any bio- or poly-relatives sharing the household expenses and/or comforts
   >> every one of your exes
   > * Living quarters: Older children—over six—should have their bedroom or rooms at a distance from yours, or your sex life will be hamstrung and theirs accelerated.
   > * Parental modesty: No nudity and such. If it is not a super idea to walk around nude, or only partially clothed, in front of older children in a monogamous family, it is an absolutely rotten idea in the synergistic family.
   > * Language: Things being what they are, in some homes these days, obscenities are merely the norm. Still, if yours

       is such a home, it isn't the best of all ideas to use such language in the presence of children.

*   Family affection: Hugging and kissing is lovely, but never be sensual or seductive in your expression of love to your child.
*   Practice what you preach: The standard of sexual morality maintained in a synergistic household by the adults is the one that the children will adopt.

In sum, I would like to refer you back to the disclaimer that preceded this section. As I stated, this section was not intended to instruct you on any of the points outlined in the disclaimer. What it is concerned with is the nature of the basic, primary emotional interaction between parents and children in the synergistic family. In other words, it is concerned with first causes, those deep, unconscious drives that affect:

how much, how little or how you discipline your offspring;
what you feel are your rights against their rights;
your willingness to communicate without hostility that it drives you crazy when they don't make their beds, overeat, refuse to study, and so on;
your effectiveness as a parent;
their responses to penis envy and sexual role models.

For all parent-child relationships in the synergistic family rest on the stability of the primary and secondary incest taboo.

PART IV

All About the New Manners, Modes, and Customs

10

And Margaret Mead Said: "Let There Be Etiquette. . . ."

GIVEN the relatively recent appearance of the synergistic family—it is only in the last twenty or thirty years that the Bureau of Census has noticed its existence—we ought to forgive ourselves our lack of a generally acceptable book of etiquette. After all, it is no simple matter for human beings to live together at all, to consider each other's comfort, rights, and safety as family life requires, even in the traditional circumstances of the monogamous family. How then can we, a new cultural form, expect to find among our wedding presents a lavishly bound, hallowed, and indexed *Emily Post for Remarriage?*

We have other excuses, too. Even in the bio-family, in whatever form it has appeared on earth, empathetic, compassionate, considerate behavior seems to be a fairly new custom in the evolutionary time scale. It is well within the memory of parents that, in certain hard-pressed societies, survival etiquette required that baby girls be disposed of routinely by drowning. It wasn't a crime. It was the way things were done.

The rich world, too, has had its standard family murders. In our wealthier, theoretically civilized Western society, our history is chock-full of instances of sons who considered it fitting and proper to knock off their fathers for kingdoms or estates or trade routes. The century-long War of the Roses almost put family life out of business, with brother attacking brother and father and son splitting heads, all in search of that less than Holy Grail, the crown of England. Our own Civil War also provided much family carnage. And even today, in our staid corporate suites, we find Genesco erupting into a father and son feud. It seems only the Mafia exercises restraint and devoutly respects the sanctity of the family. When they kill, they kill outsiders, neighbors, policemen, and other "families." But not their own close kin. Their etiquette forbids it. Except, of course, under extenuating circumstances.

Obviously, what is etiquette in one culture can be bad manners in another, and against the law or a religious breach in a third. This is because man's social behavior has always been inventive and innovative. It is like water that will take the shape of any vessel that will hold it. Think about it and you realize that there is not the simplest form of social behavior—for example, a man shaving his beard—that can be depended on to be inherited by his son. Unless the father, or other males who shave their beards, are around to teach the son to shave, the boy, left to his own devices, may choose to grow his beard and then shave his head and body.

But if etiquette is variable, it is also universal. In whatever form it takes, etiquette, along with the incest taboo and other religious safeguards, as well as the law itself, provides "rules which pertain to sex, property and safety . . . ," which keep under control "human inclinations, passions and instinctive drives."

Now, with the coming of the synergistic family into Western culture, we are again being called upon to show the range of our originality and adaptiveness. We must now evolve an etiquette to guide us in our social arrangements with each other, in the same way that the Synergistic Imperatives clue us in on the housekeeping of our unconscious familial sexual impulses and budget-making stabilizes our economic polygamy.

Of course, to arrive at a workable etiquette presents a formidable task. There are countless small details to be considered, ranging from what kind of table manners are expected in the family, to more weighty subjects such as when disciplinary action should be taken with children and what kind it should be, to what sort of reward system is the most effective and on what it should be based?

The difficulty, naturally, is that each family is so different, with such differing lifestyles, personalities, and pressure points, that specific rules are impossible to come by. What might be good manners in the Schmidt dining room could be considered offensive by the Cameron clan.

I have no idea how to outline an orderly etiquette for such a hodgepodge family form. Given the overlap of our authority figures, the contrariness of our lifestyles, the blurring of the formulas for right and wrong, how can we finalize norms of behavior for the incredibly convoluted and unexpected social situations that can and do arise each day? It seems to me that, at best, there are two principles that can be useful in helping us decide how to behave. One or the other usually, but not always, applies in most situations we encounter. Ironically, but perhaps appropriately, the principles are mutually contradictory. (But so is everything else in our lives.) One is the *practice of avoidance*. The other is a *commitment to cooperation*.

With respect to *avoidance,* the principle runs as follows: The less ex-spouses see of each other, talk to each other, or remark on each other to the children, the better for all concerned. Even in those cases where both sets of exes are happily remarried, the practice of avoidance should be religiously respected.

1. Ex-spouses should do their reasonable best to avoid each other socially.

2. Where money matters or child-rearing questions come up, there are other options open to exes than heart-to-heart talks that usually end up in open-heart surgery anyway. Where the personalities of the current and ex-spouse are reasonably compatible—I said reasonably, not ecstatically—the current spouse can act as an intermediary in the coffee klatches to decide what's what. Naturally, this tactic won't work if the personalities of the new spouse and the ex are mutually inflammatory, and rather than talk they'll be at each other's throats. Money questions are particularly touchy, and if you can employ a professional accountant to make the alimony and/or child support payments, as well as work out other financial questions, it can help keep your pulse steady. If the service of a professional is too costly, then the next best way of ducking ex-marital forensics is for both current husband and wife, together, to sit down with each other's spouse and quietly discuss whatever needs discussing. This comes under the heading of cooperation.

3. The final avoidance is conversation with the children. They know. They sense. They smell. And they manipulate. Alongside of an intuitive child, Machiavelli was a bumbler who came to a sticky end. It is a favorite childhood pastime to pit one ex-spouse against the other for fun and games. So, if you are the mother, watch your cool when your Little Jack Horner tells you that "Daddy was wonderful. He let me stay up till three o'clock and watch *The Late Late Show* with him." Or, if you are a father, hold your temper when the apple of your eye sings out: "Mom thinks your wife isn't giving me the proper food when I come to visit you."

In the matter of *cooperation,* the point is that whereas it may be wise for ex-spouses to avoid each other, it is not also required that they *despise each other*. Nor is it called upon for new spouses to feel constantly threatened. Rather, you should assume, until proven otherwise, that your ex wishes you well.

And if not you, certainly the children. Believe that peaceful coexistence is possible. And when confusing situations arise, as they will, if you can't avoid the situation by avoidance practice, then do your best to solve it by cooperation.

In the process of interviewing couples for this book, and looking at my own experiences, all kinds of questions of social behavior arose—questions that you may now or someday find yourself embroiled in. What follows is a smattering of these puzzlers confronting the synergistic family and the kinds of answers I suggested: voting for *avoidance* where that made sense and opting for *cooperation* when the music had to be faced.

THE SOCIAL GRACES: *It is impossible to be in two places at one time unless you are a Yaqui Indian named Don Juan in a book by Carlos Castaneda.*

Q: For the fifth consecutive year, my ex-wife, Louise, plans to have our daughter, Josie, stay with her for Thanksgiving dinner. She always has her father in for Thanksgiving dinner and he's crazy for Josie. That way, Louise thinks she makes up to him for getting a divorce. He's a very difficult old man, and when he heard about our divorce he said he'd cut Louise out of his will. I can understand her feelings about her father and the will, but I have my own needs. I want my daughter here once for Thanksgiving, along with Grace's boys and her parents. Then it will be a real family affair. Louise had one other idea, but I thought it was lousy. . . . J. Z.

"Louise, Josie hasn't had thanksgiving dinner with Grace and me since we married. In all fairness—"

"James, please! Dad is seventy-eight. How can you deprive an old man of the pleasure of seeing his granddaughter? He's such a sentimentalist. And you know he can't go on forever. It's a sad thought, but perhaps you can have Josie next year."

"Your father is in tip-top shape. He still rides a bike. I'd be willing to make book that he lives to ninety. That means we've at least another twelve years to go before Josie can have dinner with us. By then she may be married and living in Marakesh."

"He won't live to ninety."

"Your grandfather did."

"James, you're morbid. Listen—I have one other idea. Suppose Josie goes to your house at three o'clock? You could have dinner in the afternoon—many people do that. And she could have a little turkey and cranberry sauce with you, Grace, and the boys, and Grace's parents. Then she would come home by five and have her full meal with Dad and me. That might work out nicely."

"That's a lousy idea."

A: Personally, I agree. It's a lousy idea. The principle is you cannot saw a child in half and expect to come out with a whole human being. By the time Josie, now twelve, is voting age, if this practice were initiated, she'd want to throw up at the mere thought of Thanksgiving. A better idea might be for Louise to explore the possibility of Christmas dinner with her father and Josie. Or, if that's not feasible, James and Grace could plan a Christmas tree trimming and family dinner with the boys and Josie. After all, Thanksgiving is not the only family holiday in the year, and it's more important to keep the child intact than the ritual intact.

On the practical side of etiquette, this business of who sees the children when is a continual migraine for the synergistic family and requires strenuous *cooperation* from all hands. Having, as we do, a plethora of mothers, fathers, grandparents, aunts, uncles, and so on, both bio and poly, there is frequently a shortage of children to do the honors at holidays, to carry tokens of affection from one house to another and keep us all in symbiotic touch. Besides Thanksgiving, there is also Christmas, Easter, Halloween, other religious holidays, birthdays, anniversaries, and so on, designed to keep relatives watching the mailbox and listening for the telephone. It is also true that, though many people have taken to saying, "It's all become too commercial," when speaking of Mother's or Father's Day, there are still many other people thoroughly committed to these holidays. At such times the children can be spread pretty thin, with so many mothers and fathers to appreciate. The truth is, there's hardly a child that can afford the Mother's and Father's Day gift list of the synergistic family. Or the Christmas list, for that matter. It seems to me that there is no answer as to how to spread children more thickly. Quite likely it cannot be done. For a bio- or poly-parent or relative to avoid feeling slighted at some holiday simply may not be possible. Maybe this is one of the crosses we are forever destined to bear: a continuing, aching sense of offended dignity, of not being sufficiently valued. Well, it could be worse. We might have only ourselves to think about.

PARENT-CHILD MANNERS: "The Battle of Waterloo was won on the playing fields of Eton. . . ." *Wellington.*

Q: How often do I have to let him beat me so that he'll feel secure? And what about my insecurities? I'm a natural competitor, and I have to admit it gives me a charge that I can beat him at chess. You see, Vic's the school chess champ. I also beat him at squash. Though we have had some sticky moments, slow he's not. But my hand and eye coordination is more practiced. Naturally, I'm a better swimmer because I'm stronger. Once in a while he'll come close at something. Then I cream him at chess. I don't think I'd be any less competitive if he were my own flesh

and blood. I think I'd be worse. Nancy disagrees. . . .
Mr. M. McN.

"Marty, I want Victor to love and trust you. How can he love and trust you if you won't ever let him win? His father always lets him win."

"Nancy, his father is wrong. Letting him win is no way to get love and trust. That kid is as competitive as I am. And nothing gets by him. If I let him win he'd know it. Anyway, I don't have to 'let him win.' He'll get there without my help."

"But once in a while. You know how important chess is to him. And you beat him every game. He was up last night till three A.M. working on moves."

"I believe it. We've had some very close matches."

"Then let him win, once at least."

"Nancy, he's thirteen and I'm forty, and there's nothing he can beat me at now, and that's the way it should be. I'm teaching him how to lose gracefully and how to play the game. Because, believe me, I don't have a long time to teach him. Three or four years maybe, and then he'll beat me at half the things you're complaining about. And in ten years he'll beat me at everything. But for now he's learning how to play the game. And winning is only one part of the game. The other part is losing."

A: Marty McNeil is right. Love and trust between parent and child is not lost because a parent beats a child at a game. Marty put it exactly right. "Winning is only half the game." Children must learn to handle defeat. It is a special kind of discipline.

In the same vein, it is justifiable for a poly-parent to discipline a child in any area of behavior, if the reasons are legitimate within the framework of that family's etiquette. A poly-parent must not be afraid to take positions, to say, "In this house we wash our hands before sitting down at the dinner table." Or, "In this house we do not flood the bathroom when taking a shower."

This seems to me to be the only way of handling the reality that the children of synergistic families have to live cross culturally and, like world travelers, have to learn the mores of varying households. They realize early, "When in Rome. . . ." If the training is done with malice toward none, and goodwill toward the child, a boy or girl coming out of a diversified synergistic background will have an edge over one from a more conventional life. He or she may well grow up to be a true citizen of the world, able to observe with a less prejudiced, less fearful eye the customs of strangers and able to adapt more flexibly and cope more easily with the changing mores of our ever-changing world.

COURTESIES OF EVERYDAY LIVING: *Anyone for mixed doubles? Well, not exactly anyone. . . .*

Q: Sam and Joanna grew up together, and so everyone fainted when after ten years their marriage came apart. But it did. After I married Sam I could see that nice as she was, Joanna could be a drawback. She was so used to Sam that she acted as if they were still married and I was his live-in housekeeper. She was very friendly, too friendly I'd say. She'd have him doing errands for her, balancing her checkbook, and all kinds of maddening things. It took me a year to re-educate them both. Once she called and told me, "I want Sam to come to dinner Thursday. Dennis is having trouble with his math and Sam can help him after dinner." I told her okay, and then told Sam we were invited to dinner. I included myself into that dinner party. I remember the way Joanna looked at me in the doorway, sort of puzzled and not understanding. She said she didn't have enough stew for four, as if then I would disappear into the woodwork. I said, "That's all right. I love scrambled eggs." It was only mildly embarrassing for everyone, and by coffee she'd gotten the message. After that, when she invited Sam to dinner, she had enough food for all of us. Now something has come up. Something always does with Joanna. Sam and Joanna play a lot of tennis. And for the last five summers they've won the mixed doubles at the club. Now the tournament is on again and I know Sam wants to play with her. . . . Mrs. S. W.

"Why can't Hannah be your partner?"

"She's not a good doubles player. She's a singles player."

"How about Rhoda?"

"Terrible backhand."

"Oh, I knew there was someone—Mary Lou. She's super."

"I'd rather play with Joanna."

"I'd rather you didn't."

"You're being ridiculous."

"Okay, I'm being ridiculous. Mary Lou is just as good as Joanna."

"Jo's ground strokes are better."

"M.L. is faster."

"I know Jo's game by heart."

"And she knows yours."

"Yes. We're synchronized."

"Like husband and wife."

"No. Like two people who've been playing tennis together since they were kids."

"Well, now that you're thirty it's time you stopped being a kid."

"Oh Christ! All right, I'll ask Mary Lou."

"I already asked her. She said she'd love to play as your partner in the mixed doubles."

"Thanks for running my life, Irene."

"You hate it, don't you?"

"Hate is too strong a word. I want to win."

"Joanna will hate it, you think?"

"I don't know. I won't ask her."

"Well, you don't have to ask her. Mary Lou's brother Jim already did. You know he's played at Forest Hills. And she said she'd just love to play mixed doubles as his partner."

"You're a great little manager, aren't you?"

A: Under the circumstances, Irene did right. Sam and Joanna have no business playing mixed doubles together just because they've done it since they were tiny tots. One thing leads to another and another. And mixed doubles is the kind of "thing," full of shared high hopes, heartbeats, and sympathies, that can unexpectedly open locked doors and lead to other things; and who knows what. In such situations the way to win is to duck—avoid, avoid, avoid.

WEDDINGS, ENGAGEMENTS: *Here come the bride's children.*

Q: I plan to remarry in mid-June. It will be a small church wedding and my daughter, Mary, will be maid of honor. Daisy, the former wife of my future husband, and I went to school together. Actually, Daisy introduced Larry and me. Their divorce was quite amicable, and we've all known each other for years. But now, for no reason that I can fathom, Daisy has decided to throw a monkey wrench into the wedding plans. I would like Larry's sons to be ushers at the wedding. Daisy is objecting vehemently to letting the boys participate, even though she'll be a wedding guest herself. I think having the boys in the wedding procession will help integrate them into our new family lifestyle. What do you think? . . . Mrs. M. V.

"Daisy, I don't want to argue with you, it's all too foolish. But I think divorce and remarriage is hard enough on children. Having the boys in the wedding procession will help them get adjusted to the new state of our family life."

"They'll be adjusted soon enough. But they're my sons, not yours. And the idea of their being ushers at your wedding is bizarre."

"They're also Larry's sons. And their being ushers is a lovely way to consolidate the whole family. Mary is going to be my maid of honor."

"Well, I don't understand why your ex-husband permitted it. But that's his business. Anyway, you're Mary's mother. You can do as you please with her. But you are not the mother of my sons."

"That's absolutely true. I'm not their mother in the sense that you're their biological mother. But I will be their mother in a social sense, and it's important that they become accustomed to the idea. Look, I asked the boys about the wedding and they seemed delighted with the idea of being ushers."

"I don't care what they're delighted with. They're so shook up they'd say anything. At age twelve and fourteen they are not in a position to decide things of this kind for themselves. It's my decision that matters, and my decision is no!"

"Honestly, I thought you were pleased that Larry and I were getting married. You introduced us."

"I *am* pleased. But that doesn't mean I'm prepared to give you my sons, too."

"You're not giving me the boys. How can you think such a thing!"

"Louise, I've always liked you. That's why I introduced you to Larry. I knew he would remarry, he's the kind, and I wanted him to marry someone I could get along with too. I wanted us to be one big, happy family. I never expected to have this kind of hassle with you over my own sons. You're being very difficult."

"Daisy, where the devil did you ever get the idea that our kind of family life, with two mothers and two fathers for the

children, is not going to be difficult? Even with only one mother
and one father it's difficult. We're double that."

A: Yes, more is not always merrier. And what is showing in
       Daisy is jealousy, plus a certain amount of troublesome
       incestuous feelings for her sons. Which is undoubtedly a
       by-product of her own private feelings of being alone.
       Now that her ex-husband is actually remarrying, Daisy
       may be regretting her role of substitute marriage broker
       who facilitated her ex's remarriage, even though her orig-
       inal purpose in doing it was basically sound, pragmatic,
       and showed an unusual level of common sense. She should
       be pleased with herself at accomplishing her goal. Instead,
       she is feeling let down, alone, and rejected. Under the
       circumstances, she may act irrationally. It ought to pass.
          In the meantime, Louise should drop the idea of having
       the boys as ushers. It isn't a question of right or wrong,
       even though in this particular instance it seems to have
       been a good idea. The principle to be observed here is
       cooperation. Questions like these cannot be handled head
       on. They are exactly the kind of loaded emotional issues
       that, within a synergistic family, can cause tempers to rise,
       doors to slam, force children to take sides, and put every-
       one's nerves on edge. A decidedly unhealthy atmosphere
       for planning a wedding.
          Incidentally, while we're on the subject of casting the
       children to play bridesmaid, usher, maid of honor, etc., I
       would like to suggest caution before assigning these roles.
       It all depends on the nature of the divorce that preceded
       the remarriage, the personalities of the divorcees, as well
       as that of the new spouse, and the state of mind of the
       child or children to be cast in the nuptial playlet. This
       last is, of course, of prime importance. Adults should
       precisely examine their own motives for wanting their
       children to participate in their wedding ceremonies. Some

motives are questionable. It could be a desire to force the children's approval of the new marriage and so assuage guilt feelings about them in relation to the divorce. It could also be meant to compensate for some sense of public disapproval of divorce and remarriage. Or it might be to make a bravura public show of goodwill feelings between children, divorced spouses, and the new spouse. And if this latter reason is actually true, then why not? The main criteria for decision should be the genuine willingness of the children to participate and a surrounding atmosphere of reasonable goodwill. Otherwise your children should be spared these roles. Children can be quite embarrassed, in the wrong circumstances, at being included in what to them may be the heartbreaking ceremony of a parent's remarriage to a stranger. They will also become hostile if they sense they are being used to satisfy some parental insecurity that has little to do with love of them. All in all, before proposing your daughter as a flower girl or your son as an usher, think about it. And when in doubt—don't.

ANNOUNCEMENTS: *Hear ye! Hear ye! I do thee divorce!*

Q: For three years I have been receiving the Cornell alumnae mail intended for my husband's ex-wife, Edith. For some obscure reason she has refused to inform her alumnae association that her name is now Mrs. Edith Lerner, not Mrs. Frank Lerner. On occasion I have also received telephone calls from itinerant out-of-town friends passing through. Since our telephone number is in the book and hers is unlisted, they assume that she is still my husband's wife. Also, since we subscribe to some of the same magazines, when I was first married I frequently received her copy as well as my own. And of course I have on occasion been blessed with her junk mail. In all these matters, I have tried to stay cool. I have scrupulously forwarded all telephone calls, magazines, alumnae communications, and junk mail to their rightful owner. After a while the situation straightened out. More or less. Except for the alumnae mail and the midnight telephone calls. Once I wrote Edith an anguished note begging her that she inform the association of her marital status. To help my morale. She agreed to do something immediately. Maybe she did, maybe she didn't. That was a year ago. Yesterday I was invited to her twentieth class reunion. It made me so mad. I had a nasty idea. . . . Mrs. F. L.

"Frank, I have an idea."
"I don't like your tone."
"I think I'll go to that damn class reunion."
"You can't."
"Why not? I was invited."
"Edith was invited."
"They think I'm Edith."
"Yes, but I know and you know and Edith knows you're not Edith. You're Peggy. And when the class of '57 sees you, they'll also know you're not Edith."
"Twenty years have gone by. I could have changed."
"Not that much. Why don't you write to them and tell them they're sending their mail to the wrong Mrs. Lerner?"
"Why doesn't Edith? It's not my school."
"I don't know why Edith doesn't. I never knew why Edith did anything."
"What I'd really like to do is send out divorce announcements."
"Whose divorce?"
"Yours and hers."
"That's not a bad idea. Divorce announcements."
"But I don't have her mailing list."

A: It's little discourtesies like this, the calculated lack of cooperation, that can cause a lot of bad feeling in the synergistic family. Of course Peggy shouldn't go to the class reunion, and of course Edith shouldn't behave so provocatively by allowing her alumnae association to keep on sending her mail to the second Mrs. Lerner. To avoid these kinds of imbroglios, the sending out of divorce announcements is a genuinely practical idea. Once we accept that divorce, like marriage, is a fact of life, there is nothing more exotic about a divorce announcement than about a wedding announcement. A good format would be a simple printed card announcing the divorce and then giving the change of name and address: Mrs. Edith Lerner, 1250 Lake Shore Drive, Chicago, Illinois. (A divorcée usually takes her original last name and adds it to her former married last name.) It would go out to everyone, from the subscription department of magazines to the charge offices of stores to former camp bunkmates. In the same vein, another good idea is an informal, hand-written remarriage announcement, to go to friends.

INTRODUCTIONS AND GREETINGS: *Roses owe much to the International Rose Growers Association. By any other name they might smell.*

Q: Sometimes I could spit feathers. Tom and I have been married three years and he will still sometimes call me Tina. That's the name of his former wife. Then I see red. He'll apologize from here to Sunday, and there'll be no more nonsense for weeks. But then, clunk! Out of the clear blue he'll do it again. Or worse. I don't know what to do to teach him. . . . Mrs. T. H.

"Amy—"
"Coming."
"Amy—"
"Here I am."

"Amy, this is Dr. Edgar Warren. The man responsible for my going into physics."

"How do you do, Dr. Edgar Warren. I feel as if we were old friends. Tom has talked so much about you."

"He's talked about you too, Mrs. Hunter."

"Oh, Edgar, don't be so formal. She's very nice. Call her Tina."

"All right, Tom. Tina it is. Is that a nickname? Didn't you just call her Amy?"

"You have a superb memory, Edgar Warren. It must serve you well in your computer work."

"Ooooops! Edgar, old friend, I am sorry. It is Amy. And you will have to excuse Amy and me for a moment. We are about to have a private little set-to."

"I hope I didn't say the wrong thing, Tom?"

"No, Edgar, you did not say the wrong thing. I did."

As Tom followed me into the kitchen, I gave him what for. "How dare you forget my name, Tom Hunter! And in public! It's bad enough when you do it in private. We've been married three years and you still forget my name."

"I am sorry. Please, Amy—it was a slip. A mistake. The excitement of seeing Edgar."

"Why don't you try memorizing it? Or write it five hundred times."

"I don't have to write it. Please, Amy, darling. I don't know what came over me. Amy—A-M-Y. Please forgive me."

I forgave him. What else could I do? He did not call me Tina again that week or the week after, but about ten days later he came home full of smiles with a birthday present saying, "See, Judy, you thought I'd forgotten your birthday, but I didn't." Judy is his oldest daughter's name. It's all so exasperating. How do I train him? . . .

A: The confusion of past names with present names can create all kinds of ticklish, embarrassing agitations within the synergistic family. A wife with this problem might, one morning over coffee, absentmindedly call her husband by the name of her own ex. That ought to start a wheel turning. Lacking an ex, the name of any significant male in one's life before marriage can also cause a small trauma.

But the kind of slippage evidenced by Tom Hunter is only the beginning. The whole spectrum of introductions has to be relearned with remarriage. When introducing a poly-daughter, for example, you cannot say, "This is my stepdaughter, Judy" when Judy's bio-mother is alive and well. And to say, "This is my poly-daughter, Judy" is a bit new and startling. So take the line of least resistance. Say, "This is Judy, our daughter." Later in the conversation you can explain, should an opening present itself, that Judy became your daughter through marriage.

Of course if Judy is your bio-daughter, with her bio-father's last name, simply say, "This is our daughter, Judy Harris."

Conversely, when Judy introduces her poly-mother, she should not say, "This is my stepmother, Amy" when her bio-mother is alive. Even though she may think of her poly-mother not as her mother but as her father's wife, Judy should introduce her as, "This is my mother, Amy." In the course of conversation, it can come out more easily that Amy is a poly- not a bio-mother. Or, if Judy continues to address Amy by her first name, rather than by the designation Mother, it will soon become apparent to anyone listening what the relationship is.

The introduction of a poly-father is a little more complicated. When the son or daughter has a different last name than the poly-father, the correct introduction would be, "Pat, this is my father, Mr. Hunter."

What goes for poly-fathers with differing last names goes for poly-brothers, -sisters, and -grandparents. The boy or girl making the introduction of a poly-brother would say, "Pat, this is my brother, Lucas Hunter." The correct introduction for a grandmother would be, "Pat, this is my grandmother, Mrs. Hunter."

Aunts and uncles, cousins, and so on have always been treated in a willy-nilly, offhand manner by the monogamous family, with no distinction made as to the remoteness or closeness of the kinship. So I see no reason to be more formal in the synergistic family. Aunt Anna can be a bio- or poly-aunt. So can Uncle Ben. As can Cousin Harold or Cousin Elsie. It seems to me totally unnecessary in this case to draw any fine distinctions of relatedness.

ENTERTAINING: *Adam and Lillith and Eve and Noah and you and me.*

Q: When Lee and I were first married, I thought it was fun and very outré to meet one or the other of our exes at parties. Since we all know the same people, this inevitably happened. Now I am not so sure I like it at all. Every time we meet one of them we have a fight afterwards. I can't imagine why, but I'm jealous of Nora. And Lee, who is such a nice man, gets mean about my son, Allan. The two of us start acting like two other people. Is it impolite for me in the future to ask our host or hostess if they are inviting one or both of our exes? Can I? . . . Mrs. L. S.

"Who was that man I saw monopolizing you at the buffet table?"

"That was no man. Oh, come on, Lee—you know that was Robbie."

"Your ex?"

"None other."

"Christ! He's lost weight."

"Doesn't have me around to feed him anymore."

"Looks ten years younger."

"He does, doesn't he? Very handsome."

"He still has that shifty look. Never looks you straight in the eyes."

"He can't see anyway. He's terribly nearsighted. And he hates wearing glasses to parties."

"I don't like him."

"You don't have to like him."

"How could you marry such a peculiar character?"

"I was young and innocent, and he isn't peculiar."

"I worry about Allan taking after him."

"Now stop that this minute!"

"O.K., O.K., I'm sure he takes after you."

"After my father. A gentleman and a scholar."

"Yeah, your father."

"Incidentally, did you notice that Nora was wearing that Givenchy outfit?"

"No. Was she?"

"Yes, she was. Who do you suppose paid for it?"

"Well, not me, that's for sure."

"Lee, have you told me the truth about how much alimony you pay her?"

"No, Sylvie, I lie. I like to lie. Keeps you on your toes."

"Cut it out. But how could she afford to buy a Givenchy on what you give her?"

"How do you know it was a Givenchy?"

"Because I saw it in *Vogue*. It's $1,250."

"Wheeee! Undoubtedly she's met an Iranian."

"She was with Jerry Noyes. There's nothing Iranian about him."

"Sylvie, what do you want me to say? I slipped her an extra thou? Don't be crazy. Where would I get it? You see the checkbook."

"What about your Thursday poker games?"

"I'm up to my everloving in losses. I may be found dead in an alley one day."

"That's what you say."

"That's what I say. And what I also say is I have to go to sleep if I'm going to get up tomorrow and pay for your Bill Blass."

"You always want to go to sleep when I want to talk. You remind me of Robbie, with some improvement."

"You always want to talk when I want to go to sleep. You remind me of Nora, with some improvement."

A: The other evening at a large party I saw a man slumped in a chair, sipping a Scotch and glumly watching his ex-wife and her current beau do the Hustle. It made me mad and it made me sad and it made me think about the decline of manners in our permissive society and the rise of tastelessness. But perhaps our hostess thought she was showing her tolerance, liberality, and worldliness by inviting both the ex-husband and ex-wife to the festivities. On the guest list we are all just one big happy anonymous family.

I have the opposite view. As I indicated earlier, I think there should be something written into divorce agreements that precludes attendance at the same brunches, barbecues, cocktail or dinner parties. Even under the best of circumstances, a divorce is painful. Under the worst, it is worse. I think it shows a peculiar insensitivity on the part of hosts and hostesses, who very often themselves have been party to a divorce and have suffered this kind of callousness, to invite to the same celebration a man and woman who remember each other with pain.

This is not to say that one has to choose up sides and see only the husband or the wife. No! One is free to remain friends with both, as long as hospitality is extended only to one of them at a time.

From the standpoint of the invitee, if your social group includes your ex, and you happen to be on the receiving end of invitations that you know will include him or her, stand pat. Explain to your mutual friends that you would rather not toast the season or munch a canape with your ex standing by and that therefore you have a previous engagement, which you should endeavor to make as soon as possible. Explain that you don't mind which of the two of you they invite, but what you do mind is walking in and finding that he or she is going to be sharing the candlelight with you. Yes, you may miss some parties. But you'll also skip some bad dreams, too. Avoidance is the happiest policy.

MANNERS AWAY FROM THE HOME: *Render unto Mother that which is Mother's. . . . Which mother?*

Q: What can I do? It's an eerie situation. Strangers always think Joyce is my child. They say we look alike. And we do. At fourteen she has my nose, my eyes, and my dark hair. But none of my genes. Her mother, Betty, Henry's ex-wife, is a natural blonde, quite pretty, looks nothing like Joyce, and was hell on wheels for Henry. But Joyce adores her; Joyce wants to look like her, not me. Still, whenever we three parents meet at a school or camp function, someone invariably assumes that Plain Jane me is Joyce's unfortunate mother, displaced by Mrs. Pretty Blonde Jenkins, Henry's new wife. Like at the Junior Art Club showing. . . . Mrs. H. J.

"Mrs. Jenkins, I'm Ted Higgins, Joyce's art instructor. I want you to know I believe Joyce has an unusual gift for design. She's a true original."

"We think so too. We've discussed her taking extracurricular art lessons on Saturdays."

"Splendid. A talent like Joyce's should be carefully developed. I can suggest some teachers. Are you also artistic?"

"Me? No. I can't draw a straight line."

"How odd. I'd have sworn Joyce inherited her artistic bent from you. She takes after you in so many other ways—her facial structure, her movements. Being an artist, I notice such details."

"Do you? Well, Mr. Higgins, for the sake of artistic truth, let me introduce the lady Joyce does inherit her talent from—her mother. Mrs. Henry Jenkins the first. I'm the second."

A: That is definitely not the way to handle that kind of encounter. It embarrasses everybody. If this kind of bit occurs often enough to be a nuisance, it's up to Mrs. Jenkins the second to cue the speaker. The instant it became apparent that the relationship between Joyce and her parents was being misunderstood, then Mrs. Jenkins should have speedily and offhandedly interjected a remark about how much like her father or her mother Joyce seems. When Higgins said, "Are you also artistic?" that was her signal to reply, "No, but I believe Joyce's mother is." And not do the first Mrs. Jenkins number.

DECISION-MAKING ETIQUETTE: *Again, render unto which mother—and/or father . . . ?*

The confusion of outsiders in relation to synergistic family members is as nothing compared to the confusion of the family itself when matters of pith and moment must be decided and these matters do not relate to the etiquette of a particular household—like table manners or acceptable modes of dress, but are of a more general nature. Like deciding on schools. Or whether a child should wear contact lenses. The question then arises: who will call the shots? Who will take charge? Who will make the decision? Who? We have no orderly, well-defined hierarchy of blood kinship that automatically conveys lines of authority. I have personally found that the assignment of the decision-making process within the synergistic family is the hardest decision of all. You never know when you are stepping, rightfully or wrongfully, on someone else's foot. Let me recount one of my own harrowing experiences.

Since my poly-daughter, Sandy, and I first met, she's grown four inches, which makes her three inches taller than I am. As a result, since she turned sixteen I have found myself a very uncertain authority figure. It is not easy to issue dicta while you stare firmly UP into someone's blue eyes. In addition, when my young lady in blue jeans turned sixteen, she seemed to me to be sixteen going on thirty. Which on the one hand made her into a pseudo-girlfriend, chum, buddy. And on the other hand, like those extra inches she had on me, it was a pain in the neck.

Like, take our gynecological caper.

It all started innocently enough with one of our "girl talk" chats. You see, on weekends when Sandy wasn't with her mother, she stayed with us. And when she stayed with us, we often settled into a comfortable, cross-legged-on-the-floor chit-chat, while her father stretched out in the study to watch Jack Nicklaus swing on TV. Or Walt Fraser dribble and pass to the open man. On this particular Sunday, which I remember vividly all these Sundays later, Sandy and I settled into our usual discussion of things of note and worth. Like, do I think she should have her ears pierced for earrings? Or do I really believe she has a chance for the part of Alice in *Alice in Wonderland*? And what do I actually think of the pill versus the coil?

What pill? What coil?

"Oh! You know—the oral contraceptive pill. The intrauterine coil. The diaphragm—but that's old-fashioned."

"That's what I thought you said," I said, and I swallowed my Campari and soda and choked. Then I sipped my Campari, swallowed more carefully, and thought about a book I would write someday about how to avoid answering questions you don't want to answer, while Sandy calmly sipped her Coke and scientifically detailed for me the pros and cons of each type of contraception.

Now I know all about our American Puritan heritage and how guilty it makes us feel about sex. And I also know I'm above such narrow-minded prudishness. Today is not 1880. Queen Victoria, may she rest in peace in Westminster Abbey, is done for. And nobody wears a Scarlet Letter anymore. Today sex is wholesome. Friendly. Almost American. Today not only birds and bees do it. Today everybody does it. Even sixteen-year-olds. Sixteen! Sandy! Suddenly, I was somebody else. I, who believed in free love years ago, when it was supposed to cost money. I, who was always all for communes—if you want to share your bed or your toilet with eleven other people, that's your business. But here was Sandy telling me all about the pill. The coil. Suddenly, it wasn't me with my wide-open mind. It was me, Queen Victoria, in a turtleneck and corduroys.

My first reaction was to have a dizzy spell. Or lose a contact lens and spend the next hour looking for it. Or I could switch the conversation to movies. Or Joni Collins. Or was it Judy Mitchell? Or Joni Judy? I really was rattled. How do I sidestep this one? Or maybe I hadn't heard her correctly? After all—sixteen?

I myself was a progressive eighteen when. . . . Did I hear you correctly? Yes, you did. So there we sat, I sipping Campari, she sipping Coke, blithely kibitzing away about sex and contraception and so forth. Well, at least we were talking. And I knew that talking is the key. It shows openness. Trust. Relatedness. And we were relating like crazy. Facing the world together—she matter-of-fact and calm and forthright, I poised and mature and quaking. Anyway, I think to myself, better to be interested in boys than in drugs. Anyway, I think to myself, better contraception than someday an abortion. Anyway, I think to myself, there's plenty of time yet. She's still a kid. This is just talk. Curiosity. A learning experience. Which goes to show how smart and intuitive and aware I am not. For the gist of all this judicial discussion was that she wanted me to pick a gynecologist. Now. A gynecologist for her.

It's times like these that try a poly-mother's soul. It's times like these when a poly-mother could use a radiant tradition and a few poly-motherly songs like "Poly-Mother Macree" and other sentimental mementos like Poly-Mother's Day to bolster her own sense of purpose. And position. Because if I say, "Fine. Okay. Sure," well, is that the right thing to do? Am I sending this child down the primrose path? Into a life of sin? And for which her father will then divorce me. But if I say, "No, I'm flat out against it," will she hate me? Will I lose her trust? Her relatedness? Her friendship? Will she then run away? For which her father will also divorce me. As a matter of fact, what will her father say? What will her mother say? What is the etiquette? Where is the Emily Post I can turn to?

"What will your mother say?" I asked humbly.

"Oh—Mom," she remarked absently. "We won't tell her."

Splendid, I thought. Just what I need—a secret pact. Her mother will take me to court.

"Is that such a sensible idea?" I asked diplomatically.

"She'll scream. You know Mom. She thinks I'm still ten years old. She doesn't want me to grow up. That way she doesn't grow older."

I could understand that. But still— "Well, don't you think you are a little young for this kind of thing?" I suggested tactfully. "How about waiting till you're seventeen?"

"Peter won't wait," she answered firmly. "Would you rather I do it without protection?"

I breathed deeply. "Have you done 'it' already?" I asked crudely.

"No. But we're getting there."

Gertrude Stein should have heard her. There. There surely is a "there" there. "Hmmm. He's a nice boy, isn't he?" I politicked.

"Oh, he's a good kid."

"How old?"

"Seventeen."

"How do you know him?"

"He goes to the boys' school."

"He's clean and decent, isn't he?"

"You mean he takes baths?"

"No, no. I mean, I think, that you should know him pretty well. You do, don't you? What's he like?"

"He's good in math and lousy in languages."

"Well, what's his family like?"

"Oh, his father's a civil engineer and travels a lot. His mother has a boyfriend."

"How do you know that?"

"Peter told me."

"That doesn't sound like a very stable background."

"His parents get along perfectly when his father is in town."

"Even so."

"Honestly, this is your second marriage. As well as *Dad's*. Maybe they'll have to get a divorce someday. Anyway, I don't know yet what I think about fidelity."

What do you say to a non-child like that? "Okay. Okay. It's that I don't want you to get hurt emotionally."

"Everybody does if they stay alive. But I'm not ready yet for anything that important. This is sex, not love."

"Hmmm. Listen—" I decided to take a stand with my feet planted firmly in mid-air —"Nobody over seventeen. No older men."

"You mean like twenty?" She started to giggle.

"That's right. No twenty-year-olds or over. If you get into trouble, what will I tell your father?"

"I thought we were going to the doctor so I shouldn't get into trouble."

"I don't mean that kind of trouble. Not pregnancy. I mean emotionally. Or even physically. Suppose someone hurts you?"

"I am not going out with a sadist. I'm not that dumb."

What more was there to say? "Well, keep me posted."

"Do I have to?"

"I can't make you. But you should."

"You're so silly. Don't worry."

So, swallowing my stupefaction, and quite as though we were choosing records, I suggested a brand-new nice gynecologist whose name and number I'd just received from our family physician. Along with an optometrist to refit my contact lenses, which clouded up when I was upset. Like now. Sandy said fine, and then I said I would tell her when we would go. She preferred Friday, because on Friday she came home from school at two. And it dawned on me slowly that this great big mature sex-fiend of sixteen expected me to go with her. Wanted poly-Mama along. Wanted poly-Mama to make the appointment. And I thought back to my first gynecological visit at twenty-one. No one went with me. I wish they had. I never had the courage to even ask a girlfriend, let alone my mother. And I think to myself, she's still such a kid. Three inches taller, but such a kid. Good Lord—is this the right thing to do?

That evening after Sandy had gone into her room to watch television or talk to a girlfriend on the telephone or do her French lessons, I scrambled madly through a pile of old newspapers. There was an article in one of them, somewhere, on teen-agers and sex education that could save my life. But of course I couldn't find the article. And of course I hadn't clipped it. I, who clip out all sorts of articles on marine biology and American antiques and pasta and Ludwig the Money Man—why hadn't I thought to clip teen-agers and sex? Where was my sense of the future? Where? Nowhere. I couldn't find it. So, armed with lots of anxiety and good intentions, I went into the studio to tell my husband the hard facts of life. He paled.

"What'll we do?" His voice was gentle, controlled. The kind of voice he gets when he's under tons of work pressure.

"I'll take her to the doctor the way I said I would," I remarked calmly, like any other Rock of Gibraltar.

"But she's so young." Now his voice sounded young too. And so bewildered.

"It's the vitamins. These days growth is speeded up."

"She's so young."

"You already said that."

"Why did you agree? You never should have agreed." He sounded as if I'd betrayed him to the P.L.O. Or the Syrians. Or whoever you betray people to these days.

"She brought it up, and I couldn't duck. Listen," I said firmly, feeling rotten, "you saw that article the other day in the newspapers about sex education and teenagers. That wasn't me talking. Those were two professors—professors, that is, from Johns Hopkins—on the presidential commission. And these professors specifically recommended that contraceptive information be provided teenagers. I'll find you the article."

"Don't bother. I remember it."

"You even agreed with it."

"I don't remember agreeing."

"Yes, you did."

"But if you take her to a doctor, you're only encouraging her."

"You don't remember the article at all. It specifically said that if you don't give the kids contraceptive information, it won't prevent sex, it will just prevent responsible sex. They get pregnant." By now this Rock of Gibralter was close to tears. "What do I do? Say no and have her go ahead without protection?"

"Do you think I should talk to her about this?"

"Absolutely not. You're her father, and fathers do not get into advising their daughters on their sex life. This is woman's work. Also, you're my line of retreat if I need one. 'What will Daddy say if . . . ,' and so on. I need an authority figure behind me in case I need help. That's you."

"What about Helen? Why didn't she talk to Helen about it?"

"Because Helen will scream, she said."

"And maybe Helen is right."

"It's not morality. It's the aging process. Helen wants Sandy to remain ten years old forever. Then she can stay thirty."

"That's catty."

"Sandy said it first."

"God! She grew up fast. Remember when we were afraid she's never get interested in boys? That it would always be horses."

"I'd rather boys."

The next morning I took out my list of doctors and called the gynecologist on my list. The receptionist was very pleasant. I said, "Is this Dr. Paley's office? The gynecologist?"

"Yes it is," she said cordially.

"Well, Dr. Cyril Solomon recommended him."

"That's nice," she said. "But Dr. Paley has no free time till the fifteenth."

"Oh," I said. "But this is my daughter. It's her first time. She's anxious."

"Well, he'll be delighted to see her on the fifteenth. At three o'clock."

In an uneven voice I mentioned that she was sixteen and I hoped Dr. Paley was a gentle doctor and would be very careful examining her.

"Dr. Paley is a very careful doctor with all his patients," she said, quietly reprimanding me.

"Okay," I said, and made the appointment.

At three o'clock on the fifteenth, Sandy and I arrived at Dr. Paley's office. It was a typical outer office. The only thing to put me off a bit was a big, bronze Junoesque nude standing on the floor. But, after all, the doctor was a gynecologist. And after studying the nude for a moment, I realized she could have stood unembarrassed in a minister's living room. She was that respectable. That made me feel better about my choice of doctor. And, in fact, I liked the overall look of the office. It was so shabby and old-fashioned. None of that modern design stuff that tells you how much the doctor's wife was into the act. And worries you about the size of the doctor's bill to pay for all that modern design and art that his wife goes in for. On the other hand, there were two nurse-receptionists, which at least proved to me that, shabby or no, he did enough business to pay two girls' salaries. He must be a reasonably good doctor.

So Sandy sat down at one end of the comfortable, worn velvet couch and I went over to one of the nurse-receptionists and introduced myself. "I'm Mrs. Mayleas, and my daughter has an appointment with the doctor at three." The nurse smiled benignly and said, "Yes, that's right." And would my daughter mind filling out this medical information blank? I motioned to Sandy to join us, and when she did we both sat down on the first available chairs and she started to fill out the blank. First off, of course, she couldn't remember her birthday, which goes to show that under that calm, cool exterior beat a beating heart. I couldn't remember her birthday either, just vaguely that it was sometime in January. Or February? The nurse-receptionist looked at us both as if we were crazy. Then Sandy remembered her birthday and couldn't remember her home address. This time I rose to the occasion and gave our address, not hers. How would she explain to Mama a bill from a strange gynecologist? Finally she finished filling out the blank, and the nurse suggested that we two amnesiac ladies go over to the couch and sit down. The doctor was running a little late.

After we sat down I explained to Sandy that gynecological time was not like ordinary time—a short visit of a few minutes would undoubtedly turn out to be a short wait of an hour. Or two. Even more than with most doctors, when it comes to gynecologists, if you're not the first patient of the day you ought to bring reading matter. The magazines on the side tables are all always battered and dog-eared and out-of-date. You may also bring needlepoint. Or a few hems to put up, or take down. For you will wait. And wait. And wait. Which we did.

It was not as uncomfortable as it might have been if we weren't both so expert at putting each other at ease. As a poly-mother and -daughter, we both try harder. We talked amiably about movies and sex. About Joan Baez and sex. About Sandy's math problem, and if the first time she did "it" would "it" hurt. We both earnestly hoped not. Then she told me about her guitar teacher's broken wrist, and that she'd rather have the pill than the coil. And I told her I was sorry about her guitar teacher, but I wasn't for the pill because I'd read some alarming things. Well, she thought she might find a new guitar teacher, but she wasn't convinced about the pill. But she would be reasonable and she'd listen to the doctor. Not to be outdone in reasonableness, I said I'd discuss it with the doctor; then she could discuss it with the doctor herself, and he'd make the decision.

And after an hour of all this polite and sexual chitchat, we ran out of small talk and started looking around at the other patients in the room. It was only then that a curious fact emerged. All the ladies were gray-haired and older. Plumpish and older. Wearing comfortable shoes and proper dresses and no pants—dresses only. They were not the kind who are in their kicky forties or their jazzy fifties. These were dimmed-down, old-fashioned, grandmotherly ladies. If there is such a thing as menopause, which of course there isn't, it seemed, even to me, that all these women had gone through it.

Sandy couldn't understand how women that old could possibly need a gynecologist. How could they still be interested in sex? So I explained to her kindly that just because a woman is a bit older, it did not mean that she was automatically sex-less. It only meant she was older. Look at, say, Dietrich. Well, anyway, if Dietrich wasn't such a great idea, just take my word for it. Women can be sexy a long time. And probably these women were in for checkups or heaven knows what—whatever older women do. Then a very, very, very old man came out of the inner office, and both Sandy and I looked at each other, aghast. We both hoped that wasn't the doctor. Eighty was just too old. Even for the world's best gynecologist. Even a Nobel Prize winner. As it turned out, he was a patient. Because he made another appointment with the receptionist.

At this, Sandy and I stared at each other in awe. I probably in more awe than she. Because I'd seen men at gynecologists' offices before, but they were always young men. With pregnant wives. Or young men trying to have pregnant wives. But never a man this age. He must be something.

This got Sandy and me back to talking about sex and how probably it went on all your life, if you stayed healthy and handled yourself properly. Though probably this old man was a phenomenon. And we giggled.

Then a tall, well-dressed, well-built, handsome middle-aged black man with thick gray hair walked in the door and I said to myself, "That's Jackie Robinson." And I said to Sandy, "That's Jackie Robinson."

And she said to me, "Who's that?"

And I said to her, "That is as bad as my not knowing who Joni Judi was. He was once a big-time boxer."

And she said, "Do boxers have sex problems?"

And I said, "I don't know. Maybe he's having trouble getting his wife pregnant. Or his sperm is weak. Or. . . . I don't know."

But still, it was a bit of a startle. You don't think of athletes as having that kind of problem. . . . But why not? They're human.

By now I was uneasy enough to get up and go over to the receptionist and say, "Really, Miss, we've been waiting an hour and a half."

She smiled and said, "Yes, I'm sorry. But Dr. Paley will be with you any minute." Then she buzzed inside and talked to him sotto voce. I couldn't catch what she was saying, so I went over and sat down again next to Sandy. "Any minute," I said.

A few minutes later an extravagantly handsome movie-star type, in his early forties and a white doctor's coat, walked out of the inner office and stopped to talk to one of the nurses. Sandy and I stared at each other, stunned.

"Wow!" she whispered.

"I agree," I said, equally stunned.

"Oh, gee," she said.

"Well, you're the one that wanted a young doctor."

"Peter better not meet him."

"I see what you mean." And we continued to stare.

Then this incredibly handsome doctor walked over to Jackie Robinson and said, "Hello." After which he put some drops in Jackie's eyes. I must say that really impressed me. Obviously, there were all kinds of new techniques these days. Then the doctor came over to me and said, "How do you do, Mrs. Mayleas. Do you want to come into my office?"

"Yes," I said uncertainly. "I'd like to talk to you for a few minutes, before you examine my daughter."

"Of course," he said properly. "My nurse will send you in in a minute." And he turned on his heel and walked back into the sanctum sanctorum.

"You know, I always wondered why a doctor became a gynecologist," said Sandy.

"Well, now you know your reasoning was wrong."

"He doesn't look like a man with sex problems."

"The evidence seems against it."

"I wonder if he's married?"

"Sandy, I've known of girls getting a transference to their psychiatrists. That's part of the method. But you don't get a fix on your gynecologist. It's not done."

"I only wondered."

At which point of distress one of the nurses signaled to me, indicating I should go in to see the doctor. I rose promptly. "Think wholesome thoughts," I said to Sandy, and trotted primly off to the inner office.

The doctor's office was a big room with a mass of test tubes in a metal container and some machinery I didn't remember

seeing before but which was still familiar, and the doctor busy
at this desk scribbling away on a file card. Now my own prior
experience with gynecologists has been that they are fatherly,
plump, and slightly bald. And they wear glasses. They are not
sex objects. Often they are women. But this one wasn't bald
and he wasn't a woman and he was a sex object. And I felt
decidedly uncomfortable discussing sex at all with him. But I'm
one who does what she has to do, and since he came so well
recommended I knew he would never try to seduce my sixteen-
year-old. Providing, that is, that she didn't try to seduce him.
Anyway, I got down to cases.

"I don't know if she's too young or not for a checkup. . . ."

"Too young for a checkup? That's impossible." It did seem
to me he was leering. "What does she use now?"

"Well, nothing. I mean, she's a virgin. Or at least she says
she is." I really resented telling this obnoxiously handsome
potential seducer the facts of Sandy's sex life. But it was too
late to run. "You see, this is her first visit to a doctor. And the
reason I wanted to talk to you first is because I'm not her real
mother and her real mother would be against it. I'm her mother
by marriage, and I don't know if I'm doing the right thing. She's
only sixteen. Her father knows about it, but he doesn't really
care for the idea. But she doesn't know her father knows because I need a moral position to retreat to, in case she wants to
do something I think is awful. I need someone to discipline her
—that's Daddy." I knew I was talking too fast, but I couldn't
help myself. "Do you think we're doing the right thing? You're
a doctor. You must have an opinion. And she wants the pill,
not a diaphragm. Or coil." I spit it out.

The doctor looked at me for a long minute and then burst
out laughing. Frankly, I felt that was no way to behave, and he
was clearly a drunken libertine.

"I don't feel this is a bit funny," I said impatiently, getting
ready to collect myself and go.

"My dear," he said, almost choking with laughter, "you've

come to the right church. But not the right priest. Sixteen is not that young. But I'm not a gynecologist."

"You're not?"

"No."

"Oh," I said.

"It took me a minute to get the drift of your conversation." He choked again. "Then I realized you had the wrong doctor. I'm an ophthalmologist. I'd be glad to give her glasses. Or contact lenses. Hard or soft. But I can't give her the pill. Or the diaphragm. Or the coil."

I blushed and flushed, and smothered with embarrassment. "But your receptionist said—"

"Which receptionist? When did you make the appointment?"

"About two weeks ago."

"Oh my . . . ," he sighed. "She was a temporary. One of my regular girls was sick. The other was on vacation. We've had a number of aggravating experiences since. At least this one is funny."

"Not to me. You were on Dr. Solomon's list. He said you were a gynecologist."

"Do you have the list with you?"

I fumbled in my purse and pulled it out. He studied it carefully and nodded. "You must have asked him for an ophthalmologist. As well as a gynecologist. I'm the ophthalmologist. This one's the gynecologist—Hassid. My two daughters go to him. He's very good."

"You have daughters?"

"Oh yes. The oldest is nineteen. The other seventeen." He sighed. "I know how your husband feels."

Somehow he didn't look so sexy to me anymore. He looked fatherly. And concerned. "I'm so sorry," I said, flustered.

"Nothing to be sorry about. It wasn't your mistake. And do quiet down. It will work out. And it is better having her protected."

"But she's so young. It's such a responsibility."

"The good thing is she talks to you. My second girl was young too. They're all younger these days."

"It's the vitamins," I said weakly. And looking around the office, I realized that all the equipment that looked familiar but unfamiliar was really eye-doctor equipment.

And then we got into a cozy conversation about the nature of sex today, and of sex in "our generation" and how times have changed and we must be realistic and Sandy's mother was not realistic, and it was better to have Sandy under medical supervision than not, and I asked him if that was Jackie Robinson the boxer outside, and he said no, that it was Jackie Robinson—the baseball player. Sugar Ray Robinson was the boxer. I said I was glad *Mr.* Robinson wasn't having sex problems, and this time we both laughed. Then we shook hands and he told me to call Dr. Hassid, and somehow I felt better about it.

When I walked out of his office, Sandy jumped up from the couch to go into his office, and I shook my head vehemently. She looked bewildered, but being fast on the mind-reading, she plopped on the couch again. Just so it wouldn't be a total waste, I made an appointment for my husband and myself to have eye checkups. Then I walked over to Sandy, told her to put on her coat, and said we were going. She looked startled but did as she was told, and I put on my coat. As we were leaving the office, the doctor came out and put some more drops into Jackie Robinson's eyes.

Outside in the street I said to myself, "Now what do I tell Sandy? Should I say the doctor had no time? Should I say he was against sixteen-year-olds and sex? Should I tell her I thought he was a dirty-older-than-he-looked man who believed in Swedish sex experiences between gynecologist and patient?" No, I would be mature. Admit the muddle. The truth is, I may not have given his "temporary" the proper information. The truth is, I may have been asking for an eye doctor appointment. You know what Freud says. So I decided to tell her the truth.

Once the bewilderment cleared from her face, she started screaming with laughter. When she finished laughing, she sighed with relief.

"You know, I'm glad."

"So am I."

"He was too good-looking."

"If you realize he has a daughter of nineteen, he wouldn't seem that good-looking to you. He's over your age limit."

"I know. But I'm glad. I hope the next one is fat."

Then she was hungry and wanted a hamburger. I said it was a nervous reaction, we'd just had lunch. She said, yes, it was a nervous reaction. So we went off, looking for Stark's on Madison Avenue where the hamburgers aren't bad. But we walked south instead of north and ended up at Hamburger Heaven instead. It was that kind of day.

When we finally did find Dr. Hassid, who was in fact a gynecologist, he was rumpled, harassed, and, if not fat, he was short. He comforted me like a father and squirmed in his chair, oozing sympathy, empathy, concern.

He himself had a fifteen-year-old, and now he knew he was marking time. It would be her turn soon. And so Sandy, he said, was not too young. It all depended on the girl. Times are changing. He promised to talk to her about VD. And he said if she really were a virgin, she'd have to have the pill. The coil would probably not stay in. And she'd never put the diaphragm in in time. Kids don't stop to think or think ahead.

As I watched Sandy walk into the doctor's office, I felt I would weep. There went our child. Maybe not mine by blood, but certainly by feeling. Now she would never be a child again. Now she would be privy to all the "ills that flesh is heir to," all the joys and confusions of being a woman. The game was beginning. Wise as she is, she had no idea of the Pandora's box she was opening. But so it has to be. And so I sat there and waited.

After it was over, she ambled out of the office and sat down next to me, a little pale, a little shaken. She smiled at me weakly.

"It wasn't half bad. Not at all as bad as I expected." I had a sudden frightening glimpse of her own unspoken fears, and I swallowed hard. Seeing my face, she smiled more brightly. "I can see when I have a baby you're the one who will have morning sickness."

As we put on our coats, she told me that the doctor had said that for her the first time might not be difficult. Her athletic life helped. Then she gave me the pill prescription to have filled.

Wearily, I went to the receptionist and picked up the doctor's bill. Without the pill prescription, the bill came to forty-one dollars. I shrugged my shoulders. Everything costs money these days. Especially maturity. But at least it was less than orthodonture bills. Or allergist bills. Or scalp treatments.

There was no etiquette than, there are no guidelines now, for meeting these kinds of predicaments. To this day I do not know if what I did was right or wrong. I feared I was being too permissive. Might I not be encouraging Sandy toward a life of lax morality? Or, as troubling, could a bad early experience with a boy turn her against men forever? I feared her mother's indignation. I worried about social diseases. I fretted about pregnancies, heartbreak—you name it, I feared—and nothing happened.

When Sandy's mother ultimately found out about our caper, she did not like it. But she did not swoon away and require smelling salts. She accepted it quietly, I might add philosophically, as, "Well, that's the way things are these days."

And now at nineteen, the experience does not seem to have caused Sandy either any psychological or physical damage. She has not become pregnant. Nor contracted a social disease. Moved into a commune. Or picked up lesbianism, although that is more fashionable than it used to be. Neither has she been swept away by a grand passion for a younger or older man that could well have bolixed up her studies and turned her into a dropout. Her grades are good enough. She is now in college. And though she is heterosexual, she is hardly orgiastic. On balance, she seems to have made it to maturity.

But I am still not sure if it was good sense or good luck that pulled us through. There are no final answers for the synergistic family. What works like a charm in one home may play like *King Lear* at another address.

And therein lies the rub, we now know all too well. Ours is a conventional relationship without the support of conventions. Although it rests on an effort to uphold family ties, its very existence is proof of the fragility of those ties. Though mine is not a unique situation, though it is one that grows more common every day, the rules of social conduct remain by and large uncertain. With the best will in the world on the part of the parties of both parts, the most seemingly simple human situation can become as complicated as the twelve-tone scale. Still, we cannot excuse ourselves from our debts—we must do the best we can. Even if sometimes the best we can do is only avoid confrontations, scenes, manipulations. Or, conversely, hold our opinions, our egos, our exasperations in check, and cooperate with all our might.

11

Coda

WHEN, at the age of five, I stopped playing with dolls, I lost interest in motherhood. As the years passed, and I went from five to fifteen to forgetting about birthdays, I did not develop a "natural" drive toward having offspring, as is common to most of my sex. The reasons may be buried in some secret attic of my childhood, but it is an attic I have no need to rummage around in. Of course, rather than having Freudian roots, it may be, as some research has implied, that the so-called mothering instinct is no instinct at all. But, like eating with a knife and fork, simply a matter of social training. And, for whatever reason, I was never trained.

In fact, by the time I came to my thirties, having remained carefully childless throughout an unsuccessful marriage, I was firmly convinced that the status of motherhood was not all that peachy-keen. Indeed, as the cost of child-rearing rose, as the population explosion exploded and the designation Ms. was added to Miss and Mrs., my attitude, if not that of the non-silent majority, was now no longer an example of female eccentricity.

Given this state of the culture, I thought I would never have to take a course in motherhood, especially since the man I wanted to marry was not interested in the Little League, in being a Scout leader, in founding a dynasty. Of course, what I obstinately overlooked was that he came pre-packaged with an eight-year-old daughter and an ex-wife. He told me about it the first time we went out together. He said, "I have an eight-year-old daughter, Sandy. And an ex-wife, Helen." I did not hear him. By the end of the second week, I knew all about his daughter's teeth and his ex-wife's temper. But I still didn't listen. After a month, I learned that his daughter, Sandy, liked to ride horses and sing, that his ex-wife, Helen, was generous to a fault as long as they were her own faults. Also she was an Olympic-type skier.

Without doubt I knew quite clearly, with my usually competent IQ, that somewhere in the world was a Sandy and a Helen. But the glandular, muscular, sympathetic nervous system in me had another opinion. There was no Sandy. There was no Helen.

I clung to this self-deception even though I put in breathless lunch hours sleuthing to find Sandy exactly the right flowered canvas travel bag and a suede skirt because she got an A in French. There was no Helen even though I was frequently in his apartment when she would telephone collect from Washington so that they could discuss at length what camp Sandy could go to while the New York Telephone Company grew rich. It made no difference. It really never occurred to me that my husband to be had a daughter named Sandy and an ex-wife named Helen. They did not exist.

Then lightning struck. My swain broke a date to host a dinner party I'd planned because Sandy was unexpectedly in town to have her allergies checked. Afterward he took her to dinner at *our* favorite restaurant, while I hosted my dinner party alone. Later Sandy stayed overnight at his apartment, while I went to bed alone in mine. By this time my sympathetic nervous system was very nervous. The next day he and Sandy and I had lunch. I was convinced. There most definitely was a Sandy.

There was also a Helen. I met Helen for the first time early in the first year of our marriage. When my husband first told me about her, among the facts he chose to share, like her temper, her skiing, her penchant for fault-finding, was also that she looked like Ava Gardner. That is, the Ava Gardner of our childhood. Since ex-husbands tend to romanticize their previous mates, or despise them, I took this in my stride as poppycock. Then came the evening I met Helen. She did look like Ava Gardner. I disliked her on sight. The feeling was mutual. I comforted myself by remembering that looking like Ava Gardner could be a curse; the trouble was she also behaved like Ava Gardner. This won't play if you are not Ava Gardner. I also decided that, given such proclivities, she was hardly a fitting mother for Sandy. I was far superior.

So began my experience with poly-motherhood. And the joke was on me and continues to be. I, who never wanted to be a mother, have had to learn on the run the confusing, ambivalent role of poly-motherhood. I, who like W. C. Fields felt that anyone who disliked dogs and children couldn't be all that bad, have come to discover how important somebody else's child can be to me.

There have been other seismic shifts too. I, who was an only child, who never had a sister or brother with whom to compete, who had absolutely no training in not being sine qua non, suddenly was confronted with a sibling of sorts—Helen. I am embarrassed to admit that in the early years of our poly-kinship I experienced a virulent but sort of delayed sibling rivalry. When Helen would telephone my husband for one reason or another, I tended to go into orbit and see blazing green spots in front of my eyes. When she would lose her temper for one reason or another, so that I could hear her voice zinging through the telephone, I tended to subside into shivers of pleasure. The worse she behaved the better I felt. I was given to thinking up little diversionary tidbits to pass along via Sandy to provoke her. I was hardly a strawberry delish.

But with the passage of time and unwilling contact, a reluctant sanity dawned. I decided that if she looked like Ava Gardner, it was a more mature Ava Gardner than the lady in *The Barefoot Contessa*. And I also decided that she was not a monster but a woman like myself with dilemmas. She was not even that bad a mother for Sandy. I would have been a different kind of mother. But maybe not better. Just different.

It's been a moment-to-moment, year-by-year learning experience.

You, unlike myself, may already have a commitment to parenthood. In which case, should you become a member of a synergestic family, you will come more prepared than I did with the emotional know-how and muscle tone for handling your poly-children. Of course, if your abilities derive from practice with your own brood, chances are you will then have your own private quandary to muddle through. It's labeled *divided loyalties,* and has to do with which child comes first and when.

I've also noticed that my own "delayed sibling rivalry" syndrome extends to husbands, wives, and ex-spouses who I would have thought knew better. These are people who grew up in families awash with brothers and sisters. I would have thought them more habituated to taking into account other people's needs. It was a naive notion. When it comes to interaction between current husband, wife, and exs, the level of irrationality and modified paranoia is as high as it is in international politics.

I suppose it all takes time. We are only now at the beginning of learning how to handle the arrangements of the synergistic family. And we only learn by doing. Those who don't learn from doing go on to their next divorce.

I have tried in this book to set forth some basic principles. But beyond the principles, you will have to wing it. In the last analysis, life in the synergistic family will always be an art, not a science. In science there can be decisive answers, such as the capacity to deal effectively with polio. It is settled. Done with. Except for the Synergistic Imperatives, there are no such final answers for the synergistic family that will tell us exactly what to do when. Each family must work out the ethics of its own economic polygamy, must resolve the pros and cons of its own social behavior. My husband says it's like baseball. "You will win some, you will lose some, but the trick is staying with the game—don't get rained out."

BIBLIOGRAPHY

Chapter 1

Glick, Paul C. "Living Arrangements of Children and Young Adults." A revision of a paper presented at the annual meeting of the Population Association of America in Seattle, Washington, April 17–19, 1975.

Landis, Judson T. and Landis, Mary G. *Personal Adjustment: Marriage and Family Living.* Englewood Cliffs, N.J.: Prentice Hall, 1975.

Laughlin, W. *Laughlin's Fact Finder: People, Places, Things, and Events.* Los Angeles: Parker Publishing Co., Inc., 1969.

"Marital Status and Living Arrangements." *Population Report.* Prepared by Arthur J. Norton. Washington: Bureau of the Census, January 1977.

Mead, Margaret. *Male and Female.* New York: William Morrow & Co., 1949.

"Monthly Vital Statistics Report, Advance Report." *Final Divorce Statistics.* Vol. 26, No. 1 Supplement. Washington, D.C.: HEW, 1975.

"Monthly Vital Statistics Report, Advance Report." *Final Marriage Statistics, 1975.* Vol. 26, No. 2 Supplement. Washington, D.C.: HEW, 1975.

Norton, Arthur J. and Glick, Paul C. "Special Issue—Divorce and Separation: Marital Instability—Past, Present, and Future." *Journal of Social Issues,* Vol. 32, No. 1, 1976.

United Nations Demographic Yearbook, 1973. New York: United Nations, 1974.

Chapter 2

Bibby, Geoffrey. *Looking for Dilmun.* New York: Horizon Press, 1969.

Chiera, Edward. *They Wrote on Clay: The Babylonian Tablets Speak Today.* Edited by George C. Cameron. Chicago: University of Chicago Press, Phoenix Books, 1938.

Du Bos, Renee. *So Human an Animal.* New York: Charles Scribner and Sons, 1968.

"Group and Multilateral Marriage: Definitional Notes." *Family Process,* Vol. 10, No. 2, June 1971.

Klein, Carol. *The Single Parent Experience*. New York: Avon, 1973.

La Barre, Weston. *The Human Animal*. Chicago: The University of Chicago Press, 1958.

Lanes, Selma G. "Communes: A Firsthand Report on a Controversial Lifestyle." *Parents*. Vol. 46, No. 10, October, 1971.

Malinowski, Bronislaw. *Sex and Repression in Savage Society*. New York: Harcourt, Brace and Co., 1927.

Mead Margaret. *Growing Up in Samoa*. New York: William Morrow and Company, 1928.

Murdock, George Peter. *Social Structure*. New York: Macmillan, 1949.

Nimroff, M. F. *Comparative Family Systems*. New York: Houghton Mifflin, 1965.

Otto, Herbert A., ed., "Marriage as a Non-Legal Voluntary 'Association'." In *The Family in Search of a Future: Alternate Models for Moderns*. New York: Appleton-Century-Crofts, 1970.

Pfeiffer, John. *The Emergence of Man*. New York: Harper & Row, 1969.

Stern, Bernard J. *The Family, Past and Present*. New York: Appleton-Century, 1935.

Sullivan, Harry Stack. *The Interpersonal Theory of Psychiatry*. New York: W. W. Norton and Co., 1953.

Tiger, Lionel and Fox, Robin. *The Imperial Animal*. New York: Dell, Delta Book, 1971.

Wilson, Edward O. *The Insect Society*. Cambridge, Mass.: Harvard University Press, Bellnap Press, 1971.

Chapter 3

Darlington, Cyril Dean. *The Evolution of Man and Society*. New York: Simon and Schuster, 1969.

Despert, Juliette Louise. *Children of Divorce*. New York: Doubleday, 1953.

Engels, Frederick. *Origin of the Family: Private Property and the State*. New York: Pathfinder Press, 1972.

Fremon, Suzanne Strait. *Children and Their Parents*. New York: Harper & Row, 1968.

Heilbroner, Robert. *The Worldly Philosophers*. New York: Simon and Schuster, 1961.

Jones, Ernest. *Hamlet and Oedipus*. New York: Doubleday, 1954.

Laslett, P. and Wall, R. *Household and Family in Past Time*. Cambridge: Cambridge University Press, 1972.

Lowe, Patricia Tracy. *The Cruel Stepmother*. Englewood Cliffs, New Jersey: Prentice Hall, 1970.

Maddox, Brenda. *The Half Parent*. New York: M. Evans, 1975.

Nimkoff, M. F. *Comparative Family Systems*. Boston: Houghton Mifflin, 1965.

Nimkoff, M. F. and Middleton, Russell. "Types of Family and Types of Economy." *American Journal of Sociology*, Vol. 66, No. 3.

Rank, Otto. *The Myth of the Birth of a Hero, and Other Essays*. Edited by Philip Freund. New York: Vintage Books, 1959.

Stephens, William. *The Oedipus Complex*. New York: Free Press, 1962.

Thompson, Stith, ed. *Motif-Index of Folk Literature*. Bloomington, Indiana: Indiana University Press, 1955–58.

Chapter 4

American Collectors' Association, 1976 Report. Minneapolis/St. Paul, Minnesota: American Collectors' Association, 1976.

Blodgett, Richard E. *New York Times Book of Money*. New York: Quadrangle, 1975.

Finance Facts Yearbook, 1975. Washington, D.C.: National Consumer Finance Association, 1975.

Installment Credit Survey, 1976. Washington, D.C.: American Bankers' Association, 1976.

The National Delinquency Survey. Prepared by the Economics and Research Department of the Mortgage Bank Association, Washington, D.C., 1975.

Panel Study of Income Dynamics, 5,000 Families, 1968–1973, Vol. IV. Ann Arbor, Michigan: Institute of Social Research, University of Michigan, 1973.

"The Value and Cost of Children." *Population Bulletin* (Population Reference Bureau), Vol. 32, No. 1, April 1977.

Chapters 6 and 7

Barten, Harvey H. *Children and Their Parents in Brief Therapy*. New York: Behavioral Publications, 1933.

Bernard, Jessie Shirley. *Remarriage: A Study of Marriage*. New York: Russell & Russell, 1971.

Cross-Cultural Approaches: Readings in Comparative Research. Compiled by Clellan S. Ford. New Haven, Conn.: HRAF Press, 1967.

Durkheim, Emil and Ellis, A. *Incest: The Nature and Origin of the Taboo*. Trans. and Introduction by Edward Saragin. New York: Lyle Stuart, 1963.

Ellis, Havelock. *Psychology of Sex*. Buchanan, N.Y.: Emerson Books, 1938.

Fenichel, Hanna and Rapaport, Daniel. *The Collected Papers of Otto Fenichel*. New York: Norton, 1953.

Ford, Clellan S. and Beach, Frank A. *Patterns of Sexual Behavior*. New York: Harper & Brothers, 1951.

Freud, Sigmund. *Totem and Taboo*. New York: W. W. Norton & Co., 1952.

Goldstein, Joseph, Freud, Anna, and Solnit, Albert J. *Beyond the Best Interests of the Child*. New York: Free Press, 1971.

Laing, Ronald David. *Self and Others*. San Francisco, California: Pantheon Books, 1969.

Lerner, Michael. *Heredity, Evolution, and Society*. San Francisco: W. H. Freeman and Co., 1958.

Lévi-Strauss, Claude. *Totemism*. Boston: Beacon Press, 1963.

Maisch, Herbert. *Incest*. Trans. by Colin Bearne. New York: Stein and Day, 1972.

Masters and Johnson. "Incest: The Ultimate Taboo." *Redbook*, April 1976.

Personalities and Cultures: Reading for Psychological Anthropology. Edited by Robert Hunt. Garden City, N.Y.: The Natural History Press, 1967.

Plumb, J. H. "A Epoch That Started 10,000 Years Ago is Ending." *Horizon*, Vol. XIV, No. 3, 1972.

Schull, William J. and Neel, James V. *A Tale of Two Cities: The Effect of Inbreeding in Hiroshima and Wagasaki on Japanese Children*. New York: Harper & Row, 1965.

von Hagan, Victor Wolfgang. *The Ancient Kingdoms of the Sun*. Cleveland and New York: World Publishing Co., 1957.

Westermark, Edward. *The History of Human Marriage*. New York: Macmillan, 1922.

INDEX

Compatibility (continued)
knowledge of income and net
worth for, 51–52; lack of, 65–
111; psychological attitudes
toward money and, 62–64,
68; types of marital arrangements and, 65–68
Confusion of names, 230–32
Consumer Credit Counseling
Service, 51–57
Contraception, 6, 27–28, 238–
54
Cooperation with ex-spouses,
218–19
Children: costs of raising, 81;
custody of, 133–36; living
quarters for, 210; mate choice
and, 131–41; rights of, 211;
in weddings, 225–28
Claudius Tiberius, 21
Custody arrangements, 133–36

Debts, 50, 51, 57
Decision-making, 237–54
Declaration of Independence, 5,
6
Depth analysis, 190
Dilmun, 20
Dinesen, Izak, 44
Discipline, 211, 222–23
Division of labor, sexual, 17
Divorce announcements, 228–30
Divorce rate, 4, 5
Don Carlos, 37–38
Douglas, William O., 21

Eastern Bantu tribe, 146

Economic polygamy, 46, 48–49,
58–62; lifestyle expectations
and, 66; psychological polygamy and, 145, 155; secondary
incest resulting from, 174
Electra complex, 116, 117, 158,
173
Elizabeth of Valois, 37
Elizabeth Tudor, 26
Ellis, Havelock, 119
Etiquette: decision-making, 237–
54; for holidays, 219–21; for
introductions, 224–25; for social gatherings, 233–36; for
weddings, 225–28
Etzel, Hans, 193–94, 197–98,
200–01
Euripides, 159, 174
Expenses, 53, 56
Ex-spouses: avoidance of, 217–
18, 223–25, 233–36; cooperation with, 218–19; sexual implications of hostility between,
147–48, 156
Extramarital sex, 191, 210

Family: anthropological studies
of, 19–25; evolution of, 14–
19; see also Monogamous
family; Synergistic family
Family budget, 52–58
Fields, W. C., 257
Financial compatibility, 47–51;
costs of child-rearing and, 81;
economic polygamy and, 59–
62; family budget for, 52–58;
knowledge of income and net
worth for, 51–52